"Wow! A primer for the church on civil law pertaining to pastoral care and biblical counseling. The writers blend biblical truth, legal expertise, and case wisdom to help us 'honor the God-ordained authority of government while . . . remaining faithful to our call' to minister. They provide invaluable analysis and keen counsel for numerous common counseling scenarios."

Robert D. Jones, Biblical counseling professor, The Southern Baptist Theological Seminary; author of *Pursuing Peace* and *The Gospel for Disordered Lives*

"Dale Johnson is one of the most trusted voices in the biblical counseling movement, and his *Legal Issues in Biblical Counseling* is another helpful resource for ministers and churches alike. I highly recommend it."

Jason K. Allen, President, Midwestern Baptist Theological Seminary and Spurgeon College

"As a shepherd and one who counsels, I find this information very helpful and needed for churches. This book will help pastors and biblical counselors keep up with important legal matters in order to be 'wise as serpents and innocent as doves' in providing biblical counseling."

Nicolas Ellen, Senior Pastor of Community of Faith Bible Church; president of Expository Counseling Training Center; codirector of the MABC, Central Baptist Theological Seminary; Senior Professor of Biblical Counseling, College of Biblical Studies

"As a church administrator and biblical counselor, I have to be on top of the legal matters in order to help the church function efficiently and effectively in the area of biblical counseling. I find this book very useful in helping to understand and navigate the various issues one has to encounter in reference to legal matters in biblical counseling."

Venessa Ellen, President, Real Life Women's Ministry; church administrator, Community of Faith Bible Church; vice president, Expository Counseling Training Center

"This book raises questions your church *needs* to engage. The authors help churches understand both the biblical necessity and the current legal context of doing problem-centered discipleship, a.k.a. biblical counseling. Whether or not you come to all the same conclusions, every church in the US needs to grapple with the legal issues addressed in this collection of thorough and highly practical essays!"

J. Alasdair Groves, Executive Director, CCEF; coauthor of *Untangling Emotions*

"Any church that is serious about the compassionate work of biblical counseling will eventually encounter the secular legal court system. The relationship between the counseling ministry of the church and the jurisdictional authority of state is complex and rapidly changing. As society changes, so does its laws. *Legal Issues in Biblical Counseling* will provide insightful and practical recommendations to help your church maintain a wise and low legal profile while actively pursuing its counseling ministry. I highly recommend it!"

John D. Street, Chair of the Graduate Department of Biblical Counseling, The Master's University and Seminary

"More and more, churches and counselors need trusted guides and wisdom for navigating the complex world of religious freedom and the church. I am thankful for the work of T. Dale Johnson Jr., Edward Charles Wilde, and the team they've assembled to write *Legal Issues in Biblical Counseling* to provide direction and help that evangelicals can trust."

Jason G. Duesing, Provost and Professor of Historical Theology, Midwestern Baptist Theological Seminary

"A wonderful combination of biblical wisdom and legal experience, this book is a must-read for anyone hoping to start a biblical counseling ministry or those of us already engaged in such work. The team of writers has served the church well by discussing practical challenges and questions with a focus on real solutions that give hope and confidence to those seeking to provide biblical counseling services to their church and greater community."

Steve Viars, Senior Pastor, Faith Church, Lafayette, IN

Legal Issues in Biblical Counseling

Direction and Help for Churches and Counselors

Edited by

T. Dale Johnson Jr.
and Edward Charles Wilde

New Growth Press
newgrowthpress.com

New Growth Press, Greensboro, NC 27401
newgrowthpress.com

Cover Design: Faceout Books, faceoutstudio.com
Interior Design and Typesetting: Gretchen Logterman

ISBN 978-1-64507-246-1 (Print)
ISBN 978-1-64507-295-9 (eBook)

Library of Congress Cataloging-in-Publication Data on file

Printed in the United States of America

29 28 27 26 25 24 23 22   1 2 3 4 5

Contents

Introduction

T. Dale Johnson Jr.

As a ministry leader, you may wonder, *Do I really need to concern myself with the law?* It is a fair question, but there are several reasons that familiarity with the law is advantageous. First, consider that you will need to understand the circumstances of counselees involved in legal disputes, divorces, or criminal proceedings in order to be most helpful.

It is also important to know the law because God has placed us in a society that is becoming more secular, with rapidly changing values. As culture changes, so does the law. Our society's views on sexuality, for example, have shifted drastically in the past few decades, creating a vast chasm between what the Bible teaches and what people outside the church believe. Laws now reflect those culture changes. The relatively cordial relationship that Christian ministry and Christian counseling once had with the culture and law is changing quickly and fundamentally. As Dr. Al Mohler put it, we are experiencing "A Moral Revolution at Warp Speed—Now, It's Wedding Cakes."[1] Unless you desire for your ministry and the ministry of others to be unnecessarily hindered by legal limitations, it is important that you concern yourself with these consequential legal issues because the moral revolution has been moving steadily through the legislatures and courts.

Another reason to know the law is that we are called to be salt and light (Matthew 5:13–14). Every generation of Christians has to work out what it means to be salt and light in the context which God has placed them. Our current cultural and legal landscape raises

1. R. Albert Mohler Jr., "A Moral Revolution at Warp Speed—Now, It's Wedding Cakes," *Albert Mohler* (blog), December 11, 2013, http://albertmohler.com/2013/12/11/a-moral-revolution-at-warp-speed-now-its-wedding-cakes.

several important questions, and as a ministry leader, it is likely that you are asking some of these same questions:

- Will pastors remain faithful in shepherding their flocks despite legal threats?
- Should pastors even be involved in counseling?
- What are the liabilities of counseling?
- Should my church have a counseling ministry?
- Are unlicensed biblical counselors subject to the same regulations as licensed therapists?
- Is the church accountable to state statutes regarding counseling codes of ethics?
- How should the church deal with such evils as domestic violence and sexual abuse that are both sinful and criminal?
- How should the church cooperate with law enforcement and other state authorities?

Now more than ever, church leaders are aware of the pressures presented by these and other questions. These are the types of questions I regularly receive from pastors—pastors who want to honor God by honoring their governing authorities while at the same time not dishonor God by neglecting the work of the ministry. This book was written for leaders in the church and unlicensed biblical counselors who are fearless in their desire to honor God at all costs but who also wish to avoid any *unnecessary* confrontations with civil authorities.

As we wade into this complicated subject, it's important to understand that the law is an expression of culture. If we turn back a few decades in our history, homosexual conduct was a crime in the United States. In *Bowers v. Hardwick*, 478 U.S. 186 (1986), the United States Supreme Court upheld the constitutionality of a law prohibiting sodomy. Yet less than twenty years later in *Lawrence v. Texas*, 539 U.S. 558 (2003), the court found such laws to be unconstitutional. Interestingly, the words of the Constitution did not change between 1986 and 2003, but the culture did change. Because the law is an expression of the culture, laws will change if the culture changes. We need to understand the intersection between our culture and where the law stands today so that we can be prepared for where the law will be tomorrow and how it will impact the church and her people.

Recent regulations and rulings have already begun to limit Christian influence in the counseling room. Given court decisions and legislation in the past ten years on issues of sexuality, marriage, and gender, these areas are particularly likely to give rise to legal problems for biblical counselors. We can expect to see more such decisions and laws in the future, as well as further regulation of counseling—even for those who are unlicensed by individual states.

As this book is being finalized, decisions in the federal courts and decisions in legislatures are finding that "erotic liberty" (to use Dr. Al Mohler's phrase) is of more social value than First Amendment rights to free speech or religion. Biblical counseling in general, as a theological enterprise, and Christian ministry in particular are on a collision course with secular regulations, which are increasingly excluding biblical moral positions.

There are well-known cases of Christian wedding photographers being coerced to participate in same-sex weddings. A wedding (as opposed to a bare marriage license) is a religious rite with serious theological consequences for a Christian. In the recent decision of *303 Creative, et al. v. Elenis, et al.*, No. 19-1413 (10th Cir. 2021), the appellate court found that the law prohibited a Christian wedding photographer from refusing to create a website for a same-sex wedding. The court labeled it a content-based restriction on speech and held that the photographer was limiting the free speech of the couple.

In the past, only in the most extraordinary circumstances have the courts permitted such laws to stand. Under the law, the most vile racist speech and pornography is protected. But in this decision, the Tenth Circuit Court held that erotic liberty of same-sex couples was of such remarkable importance that the state could compel the speech of a Christian to approve of the marriage: "We hold that CADA satisfies strict scrutiny, and thus permissibly compels Appellants' speech."

Think for a moment. We allow "conscientious objectors" to avoid war—which can affect the very existence of the nation—on the basis of a religious objection. We cannot compel a Nazi to speak well of Jews. But the government can compel someone to approve of same-sex marriage.

In addition, there are well-publicized instances of the state taking a child from a parent who wished to protect their child from "transition," or sexual orientation change efforts.

You may think, *Yes, but I am a biblical counselor in a church, not a photographer at a wedding. I'm not making a hiring decision. I'm not a parent who has lost her child to transition.* Consider this: There are state laws to prohibit licensed therapists from counseling minors against same-sex attraction and behavior. Even now ordinances are being proposed in the United States to ban nonlicensed counselors, including biblical counselors, from presenting biblical truth regarding sexual immorality to a consenting minor. Your scriptural counsel may be called hate speech. A similar law has already been passed in Canada.

One of my goals when I began as the executive director of the Association of Certified Biblical Counselors (ACBC) was to offer help to pastors regarding religious liberty and counseling. I wanted to begin by addressing the issue in one of our conferences. However, I did not get far into planning that conference before I realized that I was out of my league. Through a series of providential events, I met Ed Wilde. He practices law and also holds a master's degree in biblical counseling. Ed understood my questions, and better yet, he had biblical answers! In fact, he had been teaching on some of these concepts in a biblical counseling course offered at The Master's University. In the middle of our planning, I pitched an idea to Ed that we should transform the conference theme into a book to help pastors and church leaders navigate legal concerns in ministry. What follows is the result of our collaboration, along with input from other Christian attorneys.

There are many fine attorneys who have advocated on behalf of religious freedom. Some of those attorneys have contributed to this book. Each author of this volume aims to encourage the church to engage responsibly in the ministry of biblical counseling while seeking to comply with governmental requirements that are not at odds with Scripture. They also seek to dispel the confusion, hesitation, and ignorance that so often surround questions of religious liberty in counseling—so that counseling ministries may flourish.

In the first part of this book, we attempt to answer the question that so many pastors are asking: How do I protect a counseling ministry in the church? We provide wise biblical guidance for establishing preventive and protective measures for ministry. I begin the book with a biblical and theological examination of the institutions of church and state, focusing on the role each has and the relationship between them. The goal is for us to set our gaze upon the honor and glory of God as we obey him and the institutions he has given us.

In chapter 2, Ed helps us understand why the government has an interest in regulating counseling. His discussion leads us to consider how churches should present themselves in proper documents in order to distinguish their biblical counseling ministries from secular counseling enterprises.

Chapter 3 hones in on the language that counseling ministries should use in their documents to make clear that biblical counseling is entirely different from secular therapy. Clearly articulating this distinction is crucial for keeping church ministry outside the domain of state regulations. We are trying to help church leaders ask, answer, and properly document the appropriate questions in their church ministry context.

Since these legal issues do not fit a one-size-fits-all formula, attorney Todd Sorrell explains in chapter 4 the importance of involving legal counsel in making decisions and creating ministry documents. Todd offers different scenarios to demonstrate the variety of legal issues that can arise and the way biblical wisdom applies to each situation. Have you ever wondered whether your counseling ministry is covered under your church's liability insurance? How do you protect the assets of your church when the counseling ministry seems to make the church more vulnerable?

In chapter 5, Ed offers wisdom on these complex questions as he explains different types of business formation and insurance options to reduce a ministry's chances of litigation. He also discusses ways to reduce harm to the ministry should a lawsuit occur.

Chapter 6, the final chapter in the first part in the book, addresses the issues of termination and reporting. At first glance, many may wonder why we included a chapter like this in a book on counseling ministry and legal issues. However, the church has recently been on the wrong side of several scandals of cover-up, where excuses abounded regarding the confidentiality of pastors or staff who had been involved in questionable, immoral, and/or criminal behavior. In situations where it is necessary to terminate an employee, many churches have been confused about the legal requirements for confidentiality or their responsibility to inform other churches so that sinful or criminal behavior is not hidden or perpetuated. Issues related to church discipline, which is a part of the church's responsibility in soul care, are also considered in this chapter by Judge George Crawford.

Then, in part 2 of the book, we answer the question, How do I protect myself and my counselees? While biblical truth is always to be obeyed above any earthly power, we do not want to leave our counselees or ourselves vulnerable to unnecessary litigation. We are called to live in a manner that is wise and above reproach, and we try to wed those two qualities together in counseling ministry (Philippians 2:15–16).

In this second half of the book, the authors provide detailed and specific clarity for individual counselors and counselees. In chapter 7, Tim Pasma shares a pastoral perspective on our discussion, followed by Ed Wilde and Deborah Dewart, who explain in chapter 8 what to expect if a lawsuit is threatened or actually filed against you or your ministry. It is often fear of the unknown that is most debilitating, and the authors help to enlighten us by tracing the stages of a lawsuit.

While we can never fully guard against being sued, in chapter 9, Todd Sorrell exhorts us to counsel in a way that is above reproach. And as an ounce of prevention is worth a pound of cure, he shares a model Consent to Counsel form, providing helpful explanations of each part.

In chapter 10, Deborah Dewart discusses the broader question of religious liberty. She lays out contemporary threats to religious liberty as well as protections to it that are built into the legal system, giving those in counseling ministries guidance on how to navigate these complex issues. While we must be prudent, we must guard against simply approaching legal issues with a mind toward self-preservation.

In chapter 11, we consider what life is like for a counselee who is involved in the legal system. A couple involved in divorce hearings, a child abuse case, or any number of civil and criminal proceedings affect our counselee and will impact the biblical wisdom we offer and our responsibility to the counselee. Ed Wilde and Tonya Braun help us to consider ways that legal proceedings may impact our counselees.

Deborah Dewart closes out the book with a chapter focusing specifically on issues of gender and sexuality. She explains recent legal and societal developments in these areas and offers advice to protect church leaders and counselors who give biblical counsel on these culturally sensitive topics.

We know that God expects us to exercise wisdom. "The prudent sees danger and hides himself, but the simple go on and suffer for it" (Proverbs 22:3). This book is not meant to cause fear, but rather it is a call to exercise wisdom. We pray that the contents in the pages that follow may not only challenge your thinking but also encourage your service. May you grow in the fear of the Lord, grow in submission to God's authority, and faithfully lead the church. These are difficult days, but the Word gives wisdom for all of our strivings, no matter how modern the challenges.

Part 1

How Do I Protect a Counseling Ministry in the Church?

CHAPTER 1

The Stewardships of the Church and the State

T. Dale Johnson Jr.

> I believe the church today is in real danger. It is in for a rough day. We are facing present pressure and present and future manipulations which will be so overwhelming in the days to come that they will make the battles of the last forty years look like kindergarten child's play.
>
> —Francis Schaeffer,
> *The Church at the End of the 20th Century,* 1971

I share the sentiment of Francis Schaeffer, "I believe the church today is in real danger." That is not to say that the gates of hell will prevail against the true church of Jesus, which he purchased with his blood. Rather, the church is in grave danger of losing its saltiness. Varying levels of compromise in both doctrine and practice are rampant among us, and we seem to struggle to persevere, let alone shine brightly as light into the dark world.

We are in danger of acquiescing to cultural tides. We are in danger of abdicating our responsibility. We are in danger of abandoning Scripture. We are in danger of relinquishing the God-ordained authority given to the church. Our pragmatic and politically correct conscience is, to varying degrees, eroding the foundations of our faith while preferring a form of godliness without substance.

Adding to the pressure, religious liberties are under great strain in modern America.[1] Questions regarding the definition of

1. See T. Dale Johnson Jr., "A Case for Religious Liberty in Soul Care from a Historical Perspective," the *Journal of Biblical Soul Care* 1:1 (2017): 34–55. This chapter contains several similar elements to the article in the *Journal of Biblical Soul Care*. The article, however, adds additional historical perspective to the discussion.

marriage, the biblical morality of sexuality, contraceptive mandates, value of human life, and many other issues are flooding our society. The pressures are not simply reserved for business owners like Masterpiece Cakeshop or Hobby Lobby they are increasingly encroaching upon pastors and their flocks.

Fears are rampant among pastors and church leaders. Pastors typically recognize their decisions are consequential, but liabilities seem to be interwoven into every decision. Inconspicuous to many, but pertinent in this book, religious freedom in the area of counseling is becoming a primary focal point of social activists who are intent on eliminating traditional Christian values. Often the regulations of government intended to keep peace in society have the unintended consequence of limiting freedom of religious practice.

Admirably, pastors want to abstain from unnecessary controversy regarding proper governmental authority; however, pastors must not allow fear to paralyze the work of the church commanded by God in Scripture. Religious liberty in counseling is one area where there is much confusion, hesitation, and ignorance. If states, for example, limit counseling practices that attempt to address deeply moral, religious, and spiritual issues, such as sexual orientation and marriage, then a state is encroaching upon the boundaries of religious freedom and the church cannot remain passive.

I have talked with countless pastors who firmly believe in the sufficiency of Scripture for practical ministry, but who fear being liable to the government when engaging in counseling by the Scriptures. Respecting, honoring, and obeying the government is a healthy desire and one that God is pleased by. However, the lines are often blurred between the freedom of the church, the role and responsibility we have been given by God, and the authority granted to the government.

Why did you pick up this book? Perhaps it's because you want to start a counseling ministry in your church, but you are not sure of the legal requirements. Or maybe it's because you are already counseling folks at your church—you might be the pastor, a biblical counselor on staff, or a lay counselor. You want to make sure that you are doing everything you can to comply with any laws that affect your ministry. But you are not sure which laws apply and which laws don't apply.

In this book, the authors aim to encourage the church to engage responsibly in the ministry of soul care while wisely complying with governmental requirements that are not at odds with Scripture. We want to provide confidence and clarity for pastors and biblical counselors to practice religion freely as unto the Lord in the way he instructs in Scripture. At the same time, our desire is to be obedient to the governmental authority God has placed over us, with great caution and with the awareness that civil disobedience is necessary when the requirements of the state breach God's clear commands.[2]

There are times to strategize and times to stand up. Good strategies help us to stand strong, and we aim to strengthen pastors and church leaders to stand with conviction. Before we address the details of legal issues and biblical counseling, we need to outline the basic biblical framework for how God has ordained the church and state to work together and what their differing spheres of authority are. In this opening chapter, I will set forth a brief biblical and historical perspective on the different roles of the church and the state and the relationship between the two. This perspective will form a backdrop for the chapters that follow.

Biblical Spheres

An inherent part of ministry is caring for broken people. The reason people need any type of care is that they have been devastated by the effects of sin. Ministry is deeply rooted in messy lives, and we who are pastors and biblical counselors should never waver in our willingness to engage.[3] But given recent changes in the laws and our culture, we are faced with new concerns about how best to minister to others when their lives are in disarray.

2. John Calvin, *The Institutes of Christian Religion*, 4.20.32.
3. Scott Mehl, *Loving Messy People* (Wapwallopen, PA: Shepherd Press, 2020).

As we care for souls in particularly difficult cases, the legal system sometimes becomes involved, and that involvement creates the potential for conflict between the counselor's religious beliefs and the requirements of the state. How do we navigate the potential legal pitfalls inherent in our ministry? We want to remain above reproach as we seek to be wise as serpents but innocent as doves (Matthew 10:16). How do we honor the God-ordained authority of the government while at the same time remaining faithful to our call, not neglecting our care for broken people or our responsibility to stand strong upon God's Word?

Scripture indicates that church and government have distinct roles. Baptist ethicist Barrett Duke sums up their roles this way: "Civil government is the institution charged with maintaining civil order. According to Paul it is God's minister to reward good behavior and punish evil behavior (Romans 13:1–5). The church is God's spiritual institution. Its task is to provide a structure for Christian ministry and spiritual maturity."[4] The authority of both state and church comes from the sovereign God, and we must always remember that anyone who holds authority will one day give him an account for how they have used it.

I hope the discussion of the government's legitimate authority does not diminish your view of the church but invigorates it. The church is intended for God's ordained purposes and should fulfill the mission he gave us in his Word using the methods he gave us in order to be salt and light in the world. God has not appointed any other institution to accomplish the purposes he has given to the church. In other words, we cannot expect the government to assume the roles and responsibilities given to the church—nor should we accept its trying to do so. The next several sections of this chapter should help to demarcate the proper spheres of authority for the church and the government. When the proper separation is

4. Barrett Duke, "The Christian Doctrine of Religious Liberty," in *First Freedom: The Baptist Perspective on Religious Liberty*, eds. Thomas White, Jason G. Duesing, and Malcom B. Yarnell (Nashville, TN: B&H, 2007), 22.

maintained between these two spheres, people will flourish and the gospel of Jesus will thrive.

God Has Appointed the Government

Although throughout history there have been disagreements among Christians about the necessity or role of government, the Bible is clear that the government is a divinely appointed institution within the social fabric of God's world. Scripture presents civil authorities as stewards to whom God has given the responsibility of maintaining societal order by punishing the evil and protecting the peaceful. In short, as Jonathan Leeman states, "The Bible says the government's authority comes from God."[5]

The God of creation establishes kings and rulers. He brings about increase and decline and appoints boundaries and years—and rightfully so since he is the Sovereign. In exaltation of the God of heaven, Daniel proclaims, "Blessed be the name of God forever and ever, to whom belong wisdom and might. He changes times and seasons; he removes kings and sets up kings; he gives wisdom to the wise and knowledge to those who have understanding; he reveals deep and hidden things; he knows what is in the darkness, and the light dwells with him" (Daniel 2:20–22). Not only does God appoint the ruling authorities to uphold justice and peace, he also directs the king's heart: "The king's heart is a stream of water in the hand of the Lord; he turns it wherever he will" (Proverbs 21:1).

Paul's words in 1 Timothy 2:1–4 give us insight into how we as Christians are to relate to the earthly rulers and authorities God has appointed:

> First of all, then, I urge that supplications, prayers, intercessions, and thanksgivings be made for all people, for kings and all who are in high positions, that we may lead a peaceful and quiet life, godly and dignified in every way. This is

5. Jonathan Leeman, *How the Nations Rage* (Nashville, TN: Thomas Nelson, 2018), 104.

> good, and it is pleasing in the sight of God our Savior, who desires all people to be saved and to come to the knowledge of the truth.

First, the call to prayer reminds us that there is a higher authority who is sovereign over earthly rulers and that our obedience to earthly rulers is first a duty to our God.

The societal order established by God is critical for the progress of the gospel. This is another reason we pray for our earthly leaders. In 1 Timothy 2, Paul weds proper rule of kings to quiet, peaceful, and godly lives. God does not need government for that purpose, but he has ordained government as a means of achieving it. Further, God calls this established order good and pleasing because he "desires all people to be saved and come to the knowledge of the truth" (1 Timothy 2:3–4). The flow of Paul's ideas in these verses indicates that societal turmoil hinders the spread of the pure gospel and the knowledge of the truth. This makes sense because when peace is absent in a society, there are greater barriers to proclaiming the gospel. In contrast, the freedom and peace afforded by a just government allow the church to grow.

Reformed Dutch theologian Abraham Kuyper gives us a beautiful vision of how freedom fosters growth: "We demand nothing other than freedom. Freedom, because no organism flourishes unless it can spread its roots freely and unfurl its crown of leaves in the fresh air. Freedom, so that the organism of our church herself may show her nature, spell out for us her law of living, and form the life sphere needed for her blossoming."[6] In keeping with Paul's exhortation, then, let us honor God's established authorities and pray for them to keep the peace and enact justice so that the church is free to flourish in the power of the Spirit and the Word of truth. After all, governing authorities are "God's servant for [our] good" (Romans 13:4).

6. Abraham Kuyper, *Rooted & Grounded: The Church as Organism and Institution* (Grand Rapids, MI: Christian's Library Press, 2013), 27.

God Has Given the Government Power

Since God appoints earthly rulers, giving them authority and executing judgments through them, our default posture as Christians should be obedience. We are at liberty to disobey the government only when its commands oppose the commands of God.

The Bible teaches that the governing authorities are necessary in God's order and worthy of our submission. Paul states clearly in Romans 13:1–2, "Let every person be subject to the governing authorities. For there is no authority except from God, and those that exist have been instituted by God. Therefore whoever resists the authorities resists what God has appointed, and those who resist will incur judgment." This passage provides several key takeaways for us as we seek to obey God and those to whom he has delegated authority.

First, we learn that we are to be subject to the government or "governing authorities" (Romans 13:1). Peter agrees that we are to be submissive and goes so far as to say in 1 Peter 2:15 that "this is the will of God." While submitting is not always comfortable, especially when authorities are not God-fearing, Scripture leaves no doubt that it is our default position. Our submission extends to obeying laws, paying taxes, and conducting ourselves uprightly, both in times when those in authority are good and gentle and in times when we believe they are unreasonable (1 Peter 2:13–25).

Second, Paul makes clear the reason believers are to submit: the authority granted to earthly rulers is from God. This is a delegated authority, one that the officials steward and will give account for. If God commands us to submit to earthly authorities, then we must subject ourselves to them, not because of their worthiness but because of our allegiance to the sovereign God.

Third, to resist the earthly authority over us is to resist God. Given what Paul has said, it stands to reason that our disobedience to God's ordained rulers is disobedience to God himself. Such disobedience is sin against God in the same way that children's disobedience to their parents is sin. Again, this is not without caveat since earthly authorities are delegates of God and not exact representations of him. They can be sinful and misuse their authority. In the same way children are to obey their parents "in the Lord" (Ephesians 6:1), so, too, we are to obey the ruling authorities as long as they do not ask us to breach God's commands or bind our conscience before the Lord. Our only option in such cases is to defy earthly authority to obey God rather than mere humans (Acts 4).

Finally, Paul makes clear that our resistance to governing authorities will result in God's judgment. God will uphold his established rule. The government is his minister to execute judgment. All righteous judgments have their end in God—either they are rendered by the human institutions to which he has delegated authority, or they are rendered by the Sovereign himself on the Great Day of the Lord (Psalm 75:7). In all cases, the judgments the Lord executes are just and righteous. So with submissive and tender hearts toward God, imitating Christ in his submission, we must seek to obey God by obeying civil authorities.

Taken together, biblical principles give us a straightforward delineation between the spheres of authority for church and state. Difficulty arises, however, in real-life applications of these clear teachings of Scripture. It is much easier to delineate clear lines of authority in theory. Discerning the lines in reality requires wisdom that considers the context and the particulars of a situation. The principles from Scripture remain fixed, but their application may vary. The need for discernment is, in part, why the wisdom of 1 Peter 5:2 is critical—elders should "shepherd the flock of God that is among you."

The Church Is Free

Whereas the government has authority within the civil sphere, the church, as Barrett Duke noted, is a "spiritual institution" whose God-given sphere is "Christian ministry and spiritual maturity."[7] Its domain is separate from that of government, and it looks not to the

7. Duke, "The Christian Doctrine of Religious Liberty," 22.

government but to Christ, its head, for its mission (Ephesians 4:15). As Christians in a free society, we look to carry out our mission to preach and worship the one true God freely, in accordance with Scripture.

Because the government's authority is civil, it should not encroach on matters of religious conviction and practice. The apostles model such obedience in Acts. When Peter and John are commanded "not to speak or teach at all in the name of Jesus" (Acts 4:18), they respond, "Whether it is right in the sight of God to listen to you rather than to God, you must judge, for we cannot but speak of what we have seen and heard" (Acts 4:19–20). Another time, Peter and the apostles are arrested, thrown into public prison, and "strictly charged" to stop teaching in Jesus's name. They reply, "We must obey God rather than men. The God of our fathers raised Jesus, whom you killed by hanging him on a tree. God exalted him at his right hand as Leader and Savior, to give repentance to Israel and forgiveness of sins. And we are witnesses to these things, and so is the Holy Spirit, whom God has given to those who obey him" (Acts 5:28–32). If we are ever faced with a legal demand that contradicts God's law, we also "must obey God rather than men" (Acts 4:29).

We who have been redeemed by Christ are compelled to bear faithful witness to him. As we do so, we, like Paul, "take pains to have a clear conscience toward both God and man" (Acts 24:16). We submit to the rule of the state. However, if the state breaches the freedom of Christian conscience, we have an obligation to peacefully obey the one true Lawgiver rather than the laws created by humans—being willing to suffer the consequences as so many in the history of our faith have done before us.[8]

The Church Is Responsible

Not only is the church free from the intrusion of the state; it is also responsible to God for the stewardship of the unique duties and authority he has given it. The church, with Christ as its head,

8. James 4:12. Also see John M. Frame, *The Doctrine of the Christian Life* (Phillipsburg, NJ: P&R Publishing, 2008), 618, regarding peaceable civil disobedience.

has been granted sovereignty in the sphere of the human soul, and through the church, Christ carries out his work of redeeming, restoring, healing, cleansing, and maintaining purity.

As the head of the church, Jesus provides its marching orders. He does this clearly with the Great Commission in Matthew 28: "Go therefore and make disciples of all nations, baptizing them in the name of the Father and of the Son and of the Holy Spirit, teaching them to observe all that I have commanded you" (vv. 19–20). We hear echoes of Jesus's words in Colossians 1, where Paul articulates the mission of the church: "Him [Jesus] we proclaim, warning everyone and teaching everyone with all wisdom, that we may present everyone mature in Christ" (v. 28). Christ is the head of the church, and believers are obligated to proclaim him, to bear witness to his name, in all nations.

In the name of Jesus, salvation is found, sin is forgiven, hearts are made new, the wounded and broken are healed, and sinful people are changed into his image and made whole. He is the balm in Gilead to heal the wounded soul, and he is the true bread of heaven to sustain us. The work of the church is to care for souls in the power of his name and gospel. No mere human institution has the power or authority to accomplish this work that God requires his church to do, by his Word, through the power of the Holy Spirit and the proclamation of human testimony. Jesus's church cannot hide its light under a bushel; it is responsible to God for the care of souls.

Every aspect of the work of the church is intended to fulfill this mission of caring for souls. Preaching, shepherding, one-anothering, applying church discipline, proclaiming the gospel as a missionary, and living in obedience all are intended to strengthen the soul to live faithfully and peacefully in a war-torn and sin-cursed world. Jesus himself cared for others in these various ways, and we who are called to imitate and be conformed to him can do the same.

The writer of Hebrews gives us more insight into the responsibilities of the people in the church and church leaders. He writes, "Obey your leaders and submit to them, for they are keeping watch over your souls, as those who will have to give an account. Let them do this with joy and not groaning, for that would be of no advantage to you" (Hebrews 13:17).

Two points in this passage are critical to understanding the church's responsibility. First, leaders in the church have authority, and it is proper and right for believers to submit to them in accordance with God's Word (1 Timothy 3 and Titus 2). It is no coincidence that the first command in this verse is for believers in the church to submit because our sinful reflex is to resist when someone is in authority over us. Believers must recognize that although church leaders' authority is not absolute and is not to be abused or used outside of its proper sphere, it is to be respected as an authority delegated by God.

Second, leaders are responsible for keeping watch over the souls in the church, and they should feel the magnitude of this responsibility. Leaders are to do their work tirelessly, constantly being watchmen who care for those entrusted to them—the broken, the hurting, the gullible, the wandering, the weak, the oppressed, the disadvantaged. The weight of their authority is even greater because they will answer to God for the way they shepherd the flock. The writer of Hebrews makes it clear that they "will have to give an account" (13:17). If church leaders are ever tempted to shy away from their God-ordained responsibilities out of fear of an earthly judge, they must pause and realize that they will face a far more powerful judge on the Last Day.

Jurisdiction Doctrine

Let us consider a brief historical perspective that will give us categories for discussing the church—specifically the church's roles and responsibilities as they relate to state authority. Interestingly, not many systematic theologies address the relationship between church and state. If anything is mentioned, it is often a cursory explanation to notice a distinction.

Throughout the history of the church, writers have expressed myriad views on the relationship between the church and the state.

Some have argued that the government is a necessary evil. Others have described the church and the state in terms of two separate kingdoms, with two distinct operating influences. Still others see both true distinction and natural overlap between the authority of government and the authority of the church.

Abraham Kuyper attempted to articulate the reality that there is only one supreme Sovereign in the universe. God is the supreme Sovereign, yet he has delegated smaller spheres of sovereignty to human institutions. Each sphere has its own domain; the domain is to be subject to the proper delegated authority, which in turn is answerable to the Sovereign. He writes, "this exalted Sovereign delegated and does delegate His authority to human beings; so that on earth one does not meet God Himself in things visible, but that sovereign authority is always exercised through an office held by men."[9] The danger in a world ravaged by sin is that "one sphere may encroach upon the neighboring sphere; thus causing a wheel to jerk and to break cog upon cog, and interfering with the progress of the whole."[10]

The concern Kuyper raises of one sphere encroaching on another is one we need to bear in mind as we think about the appropriate spheres in which God-ordained earthly authority should operate. But discernment is difficult; in a fallen world the lines of jurisdiction are not as clear as we would want, and in any discussion of sphere sovereignty, we can fall into a ditch in one direction or the other.

In the first ditch, the state attempts to assume authority in areas where God has not given them any. One way the state does this is by creating laws that go against the morality established by the one true Lawgiver. Such laws reflect secular morality—which is not neutral—and may begin to impinge on the teaching and practice of Christian morality, including biblical teaching on marriage.

The state may also overstep its authority by seeking to regulate responsibilities that God has given to the church, such as the religious practices of discipleship and soul care, including biblical

9. Kuyper, *Rooted & Grounded*, 27.
10. Kuyper, 27.

counseling. But the state has no jurisdiction over the human soul. The physical sword it wields serves as a deterrent to evil, but it cannot change the human heart. Only the sword of the Spirit can do that.[11]

In the second ditch, the church takes on more authority than is granted by Scripture. This happens when church leaders become abusive toward their people. It also happens when church leaders seek to coerce the state's authority to serve their own ends. In the days of the Reformation, for example, the church punished "heretics" by use of the physical sword of civil magistrates. The church must wear the mantle of the authority entrusted to it yet not attempt to assume the burden of authority that God granted to the state.

It is a matter of understanding the necessity and the differences between the two swords in Scripture. The first sword is a physical sword that God intended to use as a rod—a scourge to punish evildoers and keep civility. The second sword is the Word of God entrusted to the church. It is not a sword intended to enact physical punishment, but one employed by the church to change the hearts of men. The physical sword can never change the hearts of men; only the sword of the Spirit, the Word of God, can change the hardened and darkened hearts of men. Only the Word of God can comfort the suffering and admonish the unruly. Only the Word can be a balm to the broken and bruised. So we allow God's design and distinction of the two swords to rule in their ordained spheres for the good of peace and the glory of God.[12]

Potential Threats

We have examined the church's freedom and its responsibility, but the question remains of how to apply this knowledge. In fact, the origin of this book lies in the numerous questions I have received regarding the application of scriptural principles to legal issues.

11. Balthasar Hubmaier, "On the Sword," in *Balthasar Hubmaier: Theologian of Anabaptism,* eds. H. Wayne Pipkin and John Howard Yoder (Scottdale, PA: Herald Press, 1989), 429–523

12. The language of the two swords was not without influence from the work of Balthasar Hubmaier.

The pressures on pastors are immense. Pastors ask questions that express the tensions between honoring the government and acting as proper authorities within the church. Pastors wrestle with fear of incurring legal liability and a fear of God that compels them to engage in messy and broken lives. Pastors want to shepherd their flocks. They want to provide soul care, but they are often uncertain about the legal ramifications for them personally, for their flocks, and for the wider church body.

Three broad threats, and several smaller ones, confront the church. The first is the threat to religious liberty. This may not have been an issue in the middle of the twentieth century, but it is now. We want to safeguard the freedom of religion guaranteed in our Constitution, but we need to remember that this freedom comes with the responsibility to remain faithful to Christ as supreme authority, no matter what the government in this country or any other may decree.

The pressures on the church are not simply judicial or legislative; they are also cultural. The tide of the culture is turning, resulting in a moral code that in some significant ways contradicts scriptural morality. In the middle of the twentieth century, there was a shift in the Western world toward a relativistic view of morality, which allowed for a different "truth" for each individual.

More recently, another shift has occurred, this time to a new cultural morality that demands conformity of everyone. Those who do not conform must pay in some way. The Bible, with its moral absolutes, is no longer viewed by the culture as one of several ways toward good, as it was during the period of relativism. Rather, the Bible and those who promote it by their lives or their teaching are looked on as opposing the cultural milieu. The conflict between the morality of the culture and biblical morality is giving rise to legal threats to the freedom of religion. We need to be aware of cultural and legal trends so that we do not lose the freedom to express our religion with a free conscience and in lives lived quietly and peacefully according to Scripture.

The second threat is to orthodoxy. There are two ways orthodoxy is threatened. It is threatened when we neglect the truths from Scripture in our doctrinal confessions. But orthodoxy is also threatened when the church fails to act upon the doctrinal truths it teaches. Revelation from God has a purpose that extends beyond mere understanding; God commands us to respond to the truth he has revealed by acting and living in accordance with his wisdom. If the church is paralyzed because of legal pressures or fears, then we will be in danger of losing our orthodoxy.

History has demonstrated that orthodoxy is always at risk when the church is under cultural pressures. We must remain vigilant, fearless, and grounded in the Word of God, obeying his clear commands regardless of the shifting shades of "wisdom" and "truth" presented by our culture. If those of us who are pastors, teachers, and counselors acquiesce to these very real pressures and do not present the clear teachings of Scripture, we are in danger of harming the sheep. The prophet Jeremiah denounces the shepherds of Israel for not feeding the sheep with God's Word: "They have healed the wound of my people lightly, saying, 'Peace, peace,' when there is no peace" (Jeremiah 6:14).

Finally, there is a threat to the proper authority God has granted to the church.[13] God established the offices of overseers and deacon within the church to govern it in a wise and orderly way. When these church leaders fail to execute their roles with integrity, the church is impotent.[14] All of us who are in a position of authority need to be alert to the danger of becoming like the leaders of Israel to whom God spoke through the prophet Jeremiah: "For from the least to the greatest of them, everyone is greedy for unjust gain; and from prophet to priest, everyone deals falsely" (Jeremiah 6:13). We must

13. One way the church loses its power is by becoming subjected to the state's political system—by trying to exercise its power as a mere political actor.

14. I have appreciated 9Marks's ecclesiological approach as they discuss the authoritative role of elders—see *Church Elders* by Jeramie Rinne (Wheaton, IL: Crossway, 2014).

bear the burden of leadership with both humility and strength as we seek to lead God's people with his faithful wisdom.[15]

Looking Ahead

How do we navigate wisely through the tumultuous cultural seas? Christians have been doing this very thing for centuries.

In the pages that follow we have attempted to compile the wisdom of several folks who have intelligent legal minds with hearts that burn for the glory of Christ and his church. Our goal is to help you as pastors and lay counselors understand many of the potential legal pitfalls surrounding biblical counseling and to provide you with practical ways to guard your counseling ministry against unnecessary legal controversy. The wisdom found in the pages that follow will help you think biblically through relevant issues as you faithfully shepherd the people in your care against the devices and schemes of the evil one.

We want to clearly state our desires in writing this book. First, we hope to express the Bible's teaching as it relates to church and state. Second, we never want to cause unnecessary discord between the two spheres. We want to encourage believers and church leaders to act according to the authority and commands given by God in his Word. Yet we also want to follow God's command to obey his established civil rulers. Third, we want to provide practical means to navigate legal issues that may confront us as we carry out our God-given responsibilities. For example, we believe that creating proper documents expresses a due diligence in caring for people well, but also demonstrates a heart of humility and obedience toward earthly rulers. We pray that you are able to receive the counsel we offer in the spirit in which it was intended. We do not set forth a legalistic

15. The point of this work is to address legal pitfalls confronting the church. The church and its leaders possess a legitimate authority granted by God. We are certainly not advocating any type of abuse of the authority granted to church leaders. Negligence of the pastor in his legitimate authority is sinful, as is his abuse of any authority in the name of Christ.

line of demands. Instead, we attempt to share wisdom that will aid church leaders and biblical counselors as they seek to honor legal authorities while caring for souls by the sufficient Word of God.

To-Do List

- ❒ Write a list of roles and responsibilities God has given to the church from the Bible.
- ❒ Write a list of roles and responsibilities God has given to the government from the Bible.
- ❒ Review your church's guiding documents (i.e. doctrinal statement, mission, constitution and bylaws, policies and procedures, etc.). It will be important to be familiar with these documents as you read the following chapters.

CHAPTER 2
Why Would the State Seek to Regulate Biblical Counseling?

Edward Charles Wilde

Sharks eat surfers—apparently because sharks mistake surfers for seals. Sharks eat seals. For a shark with questionable eyesight, a teenage boy lying facedown on his board, hands and feet dangling in the water, is close enough to a seal. So the shark takes a bite. After a mouthful of epoxy resin, the shark learns the board is not a seal and moves on.[1]

Just as a surfer looks like a seal, a pastor or ministry work who gives biblical counsel to a congregant looks like a cognitive behavioral psychologist with a client. He acts like a psychologist: he listens, he makes notes, and he gives instruction about behaviors and thoughts and emotions.[2] From the outside, then, it can be hard to distinguish unlicensed biblical counselors from therapists who are outside the church and required to get a marriage and family counseling license.

Governments license psychologists. If you want to give counsel, the state will want to license and regulate you. It is what governments do. It fits the old proverb that says to a hammer everything looks like a nail. The people in government who seek to regulate what is said between counselor and counselee believe they are doing

1. If someone with greater knowledge of shark behavior balks at my perhaps apocryphal story, please don't tell anyone because the image makes my point well enough. I would rather not lose a good story to the predations of science.

2. In chapter 3, we look at the ways in which the work of biblical soul care/biblical counseling differs from "psychotherapy" of all stripes. For the moment, you need merely understand that our work appears similar to the work of a psychotherapist *from one point of view.*

good and protecting the public. When we "refuse" (in the view of the government) to be licensed and regulated, when we set our own standards, we may look like we have no regard for the law.

From the Surfer's Viewpoint

When the surfer looks down into the water and sees the shark beginning to circle, the surfer does not think, *Poor shark; he's making a mistake.* The surfer thinks, *He's a man-eater, and he's trying to kill me!*

When we look at the state trying to regulate our ministerial work, we do not think, *Poor regulator; he's making a mistake.* We think, *Evil regulator; he hates Christians.* So the two sides often misunderstand one another. To the government regulators, the "unlicensed" counselor looks like a scofflaw. From our perspective, the government appears to be motivated by hatred of religion. But that perception of government isn't quite right. I'm not saying civil governments are favorable toward our religion as practiced, but we will get nowhere if we don't have a clear understanding of what is actually taking place.

Elsewhere in this book we are going to look at specific decisions and laws concerning religious freedom. But in this chapter, we are going to think about our conflict with the state by looking out of the airplane at the forest, rather than examining a particular tree.

Understanding Reasons for Government Regulation

Ever since the fall, we human beings have had a poor history. We don't work very well together. We have conflicts with one another. Sometimes we hurt other people's bodies, take things from each other, and lie to one another.

In his mercy, God has given us the power and ability to form and maintain governments. To be sure, governments are imperfect means of order. But imperfect order is far better than no order. And governments vary in their degree of good and bad order as God, in his wisdom and grace, gives more or less wisdom to the leaders and restraint to the people.

Nevertheless, the general goal of any government is some kind of order. The government makes rules, and every rule of the government is backed by threat of force. Even a judgment in a civil court (not a criminal court), which only requires the payment of money from one party to another, rests upon a threat of force. If you don't pay the judgment, a court order can require the money to be withheld from your paycheck.

The power to set the rules and use force to back them up is a fearful thing. Therefore, we must give due concern to what a government may require. And, as Christians, we have an additional duty to give proper deference to the government (Romans 13:1–7; 1 Peter 2:13–14).

What should—or may—a government forbid? What should—or may—a government require? The general goal of peace and order has led to a seemingly uncountable number of laws. There is a Twitter feed solely dedicated to an unending list of crazy federal laws. What makes for good order? When have we finally regulated "enough"? The impetus to regulate and provide for good order arises routinely in response to crimes: the public demands a law against this or that bad act.

You may feel the pinch of government as you go about your work of discipling people, teaching them to observe everything Christ has commanded (Matthew 28:19–20). However, you need to understand that the government is busy pinching everyone in its effort to maintain peace and good order. The government's efforts may be well-intentioned and poorly effectuated. At other times, the government's efforts may proceed from hostility toward the practice of religion in the public sphere (which is most evident in laws pertaining to human sexuality). Finally, we must realize that the "government" is an abstraction at one level because the governmental function is the result of many people with their own particular interests and aims.

You may think the government is simply power mad, and certainly many people in government are bad actors—they are human after all. But you also must understand that in this welter of laws and regulations, the people making the laws think they are doing something useful. Even when a government official has a personal aim of stopping the public practice of the Christian religion, that official thinks that he is doing good (John 16:2).

To rightly understand how to work within the systems put in place by government without violating the law, we need to clearly understand what the government is seeking to do. An understandable misunderstanding is the belief that the government simply wants to keep us from using the Bible as a source for counseling. In support of this, we can point to specific legal limitations on counsel regarding human sexuality. Below I will address that matter generally. Then we will address some specific concerns in chapter 12.

I want you to consider the matter generally. We take it as an axiom that the first issue to be addressed in any counseling is regeneration. Will or has the counselee confessed and believed Jesus is Lord? The state will not prohibit such counsel. What if we discuss the Trinity? That is not prohibited.

This is where we make a fundamental mistake when we think about biblical counseling and the state. We think the state has some antipathy toward religion, particularly Christianity. We think the state wants us to stop using the Bible, but that is simply not true in the way that most people seem to think. Yes, there will be individual actors who have a personal antipathy toward Christianity. However, the official position of the government is one of indifference. The rationale for laws that affect the practice of giving counsel is not antipathy toward Christianity but a desire for some public good.

We can see the basic indifference of the government toward the doctrines of religion by merely looking at the world around us. If you were a licensed psychologist who prayed, read the Bible, gave homework, and all the rest, the state would be unconcerned. Right here in Los Angeles, you can see any number of licensed Christian psychologists. There are Islamic psychologists and Buddhist therapists, all licensed by the state.

Now this "indifference" toward religious positions is not absolute. You can be an Islamic psychologist and use Islamic principles, but you may still be required to "affirm" the government's given position on sexuality. A Christian psychologist could still use the Bible but would also be prohibited from telling someone that sexual practices outside of a heterosexual marriage were "sinful." Admittedly, there is a level of incoherence in these positions (traditional Muslim and Christian morality prohibit homosexuality, for instance). But the government's limitation would not be because the counsel was "Christian" but because the government has established a particular moral position on a particular topic (such as human sexuality).

To gain insight into what concerns the government and what does not, let's look at a couple of surprising sources of authority some people have turned to as a basis for therapy. There is a tacit belief that the state's concern in licensing therapists lies with "science." There is a belief that the motivation to license therapists derives from a concern that the content of (and thus the authority for) the counsel be based upon "science." That would be a false belief.

One surprising source of "authority" is witchcraft and magic, which have been touted in *Psychology Today* as means of therapeutic power: "Positive psychology correlates happiness with resilience, and with having some sense of control over our circumstances. Witchcraft offers both. Contemporary witchcraft is about asserting our own agency whenever that agency is threatened—and it's about building the psychic strength to fight back against abuse and injustice."[3]

Witchcraft and magic are not merely unscientific, they are anti-scientific. Witchcraft and magic are generally considered—at

3. Ariel Gore, "Does Witchcraft Hold the Secret to Happiness?" Women and Happiness (blog), *Psychology Today*, October 15, 2019, https://www.psychologytoday.com/intl/blog/women-and-happiness/201910/does-witchcraft-hold-the-secret-happiness.

best—to be fundamentally defective understandings of the physical universe. There is no "magic" that draws iron filings into a pattern; there is a magnetic field.

Another unusual source of authority appears in a blog entry on *Scientific American* concerning the use of tarot cards and astrology as the basis for psychotherapy. The author plainly favors what he labels "evidence-based" therapies of the more traditional form, and yet he closes with the following observation:

> Research into the brain and mind, I have argued on this blog and elsewhere, has yet to produce truly persuasive theories of and treatments for mental illness. As a recent essay in a British psychiatric journal argues, "it is still not possible to cite a single neuroscience or genetic finding that has been of use to the practicing psychiatrist in managing [mental] illnesses despite attempts to suggest the contrary."
>
> This failure helps explain why people still turn to Freudian psychoanalysis, although it does not stand up to scientific scrutiny, and to an even older mind-therapy, Buddhism. And it explains why many people in distress turn to astrology, tarot cards and other pseudoscientific methods. May they find the solace they seek.[4]

I want to take a moment to note that the point of bringing up these extreme examples is not to dunk on our psychologist/psychiatrist friends. As an attorney, I have had the opportunity to spend professional and personal time with psychiatrists, whom I have found to be deeply concerned for human well-being. For instance, attorneys need to know whether a person has the mental capacity to form a contract, make a will, sign a trust, or convey property. To determine whether a person has that capacity, attorneys turn to trained psychologists or psychiatrists for evaluation of mental

4. John Horgan, "Astrology, Tarot Cards and Psychotherapy," *Scientific American Blog Network*, February 24, 2020, https://blogs.scientificamerican.com/cross-check/astrology-tarot-cards-and-psychotherapy/.

functioning. Or an attorney might work with a person who claims to have suffered emotional damage as the result of another's bad act. In such cases, a psychologist or psychiatrist evaluates the extent of the damage. The psychologists and psychiatrists I have dealt with on a professional basis are routinely thoughtful and careful and quite helpful in appropriate circumstances. Disease of the nervous system and brain is a horror, and at their best, psychiatrists can provide some relief for real disease. So we need to resist the temptation to parade such concessions as the one made in *Scientific American*. I'm not trying to attack anyone for being "anti-science."

The point of mentioning these unusual examples is to demonstrate what the state will permit under the heading of therapy. Astrology is scientific nonsense; the claim that Mercury's position in the sky "made me do it" is patent nonsense. We can test whether astrology is true or false, and astrology is undeniably false. And again, magic and witchcraft are outright anti-science. If the state were simply concerned with "science" versus "religion," it would outlaw magic and astrology as a basis for therapy.

If the mental health world and the state can tolerate rank nonsense on the ground that it makes people feel better, it will certainly tolerate religious claims. In fact, it does. The state is completely unconcerned with the fact that we use the Bible, call ourselves Christian, ask people to pray, or practice any similar aspect of our counsel. It does not care if you teach that Jesus died for your sins. The state only asks that you get a license if you want to provide *therapy*. (We will discuss the word *therapy* in chapter 3, where we provide a comparison and contrast between therapy and biblical counseling).

This leads us to the question, Why would the state regulate the profession at all if it permits astrology and tarot cards as a source of authority? First, in a world where hairdressers need official training and an occupational license, we should not be surprised that something as significant as dealing with the human heart requires some standard.

Secondly, the state seeks to impose certain manners of practice over everyone. Remember, the state is in the business of imposing order. Training individuals to do and act and speak in a particular way has serious connotations for order, health, and safety. For instance, the state may permit magic as a means of counseling while prohibiting grave robbing to use a corpse for a spell. The state may permit astrology, but it prohibits instructions for drinking bleach.

It is no surprise that the state would seek to regulate therapists—regardless of what they use as the basis for their therapy. So if a pastor wants to preach and pray and engage in rituals, he may. But—as the representative of the state will say—if that same man wants to start engaging in *therapy*, he should be regulated. He can engage in his religion without a license, but therapy is for the state to regulate.

There is something else going on here beyond just the state's concern with occupational licensing. The state actually does have an interest in religion but perhaps not in the way you may expect. However, to explain what is happening, we will first need to take a detour and think about the United States Constitution.

What About Freedom of Religion?

When we consider the question of freedom of religion, we must do some careful thinking. A religion entails a set of beliefs about oneself and the world. A religion also entails a manner of worship. There is some liturgy, some formalized practice performed as reverence and worship. There are also public entailments of a religion—dress, food, family structure, sexual morality, etc.

The United States Constitution guarantees the freedom of religion in the First Amendment to the Constitution. And while the Constitution only governs the federal government, the law has developed so that the First Amendment applies to each individual state. Moreover, the individual states provide for freedom of religion in their own constitutions.

Now let's consider the practical aspects of freedom of religion. The original colonies that formed the United States began with many people seeking religious toleration—at least for themselves. As the various colonies became a country, there was a variety of religious opinion and practice. Certainly, more diversity of religious practice was accepted in the United States than would be common in the rest of the world.

Yet, the most distinctive aspects of religious diversity took place on Sunday morning. Yes, there were small populations of Jews and scattered Muslims, but the vast majority culture was broadly Christian. The distinctions between the Christian groups showed themselves on Sunday when the doors were closed and everyone was in church. The Roman Catholic priest and the Methodist circuit rider performed rather different services on Sunday. But come Monday, the Presbyterian banker could meet with the Roman Catholic dentist and be indistinguishable in dress, language, manners, and morality. The differences in dress or family would owe more to the country of origin than to any religious distinctive. The practical aspects of their various religious beliefs, family, work, dress, and food would not come into serious conflict. A Baptist and a Congregationalist could work in the same dry goods store because the outward public entailments of their denominations did not conflict.

However, in the present day in many parts of the world, the public entailment of religion *does* lead to conflict. Some non-Christian religious practices demonstrate clearly how the conflict appears from the outside.

- Many devout Muslims believe that a woman must not expose her face in public. However, California requires that everyone who drives a car obtain an official identification card from the state, which includes a full-face photograph. A Muslim woman comes to the DMV, passes the necessary tests without trouble, and then comes to the final step. Her government requires her to expose her face. Her religion forbids her to do so. What should we do?

- A Muslim cab driver believes that to be in the company of a dog will defile him. He refuses to permit a blind man with a seeing eye dog into his cab because his religion forbids the action.
- Or a secular Western woman from Europe who is in Saudi Arabia wants to walk down the street without wearing a headscarf. In fact, the Western woman finds the practice offensive at a religious level because the practice is mandated by the Islamic authorities and would indicate her submission to such law.

Christians who previously engaged in public behaviors that corresponded with public morality now find ourselves in conflict with public culture. Our sexual morality and family structure are coming into sharp conflict with the accepted public morality. In fact, some of our ethical positions are considered gravely offensive or even illegal.

What then of freedom of religion?

Freedom and Order

The balance of religious freedom and order is a complex story that precedes the United States Constitution. In *A Secular Age*, philosopher Charles Taylor considers a number of strands of Western history, including the rise of what he calls "polite society."[5] "Polite society" created two different spaces, one public, one private. In the public space, one was permitted a sort of religious practice that conformed to the general tenor of polite society. In other words, you can

5. Charles Taylor, *A Secular Age* (Cambridge, MA: Belknap Press of Harvard University Press, 2007). The discussion of "polite society" in particular begins on page 234. However, the entire chapters entitled "Modern Social Imaginaries" and "Providential Deism" provide relevant explanation for the rise and existence of a public sphere where potentially contentious matter can be discussed without violence. Interestingly, the scope of that space seems to be rapidly decreasing in the West.

be religious, but your religion does not have the right to make public demands upon anyone else.

In the history of the United States, there has been what Francis Schaeffer called a "Christian consensus." The broad outlines of Christian morality and public practice more or less created the space for the "polite society." Schaeffer wrote, "The Christian consensus gave a basis and a framework for our society to have freedoms without those freedoms leading to chaos."[6]

So basic expectations of marriage and family life, public morality, and business conduct were all anchored in a generally Christian understanding of the world. Even in areas where public morality fell short, such as ethnic relationships, the Christian consensus provided the moral structure to make an argument that the public morality—even among professing Christians—was wrong.

To understand the power of this consensus, you simply need to consider the brutality, racism, and oppression that were fully expected and upheld in the pre-Christian world. Life may have felt quite free to a number of well-off men—and in some instances women—in the Roman Empire. But there was no public morality to prevent someone from keeping children as slaves for sexual abuse. You may not have liked what your neighbor did, but there was no shared basis upon which you could convince him that he was wrong for abusing children.

The question in our country has been whether the deviation from the public morality dictated by one's "private" religion would cause damage to society as a whole. Consider the 1878 Supreme Court case *Reynolds v. United States*. This case concerned the legality of polygamy, which was a proper practice under the then-current teaching of the Mormon church. Here is how the court thought through this issue:

---

6. Francis A. Schaeffer, *The Complete Works of Francis A. Schaeffer: A Christian Worldview*, vol. 5 (Westchester, IL: Crossway, 1982), 286.

> In our opinion, the statute immediately under consideration [a law prohibiting bigamy in the territories of the United States] is within the legislative power of Congress. It is constitutional and valid as prescribing a rule of action for all those residing in the Territories, and in places over which the United States have exclusive control. This being so, the only question which remains is, whether those who make polygamy a part of their religion are excepted from the operation of the statute. If they are, then those who do not make polygamy a part of their religious belief may be found guilty and punished, while those who do, must be acquitted and go free. This would be introducing a new element into criminal law. Laws are made for the government of actions, and while they cannot interfere with mere religious belief and opinions, they may with practices. Suppose one believed that human sacrifices were a necessary part of religious worship, would it be seriously contended that the civil government under which he lived could not interfere to prevent a sacrifice? Or if a wife religiously believed it was her duty to burn herself upon the funeral pile of her dead husband, would it be beyond the power of the civil government to prevent her carrying her belief into practice?[7]

Now consider a case with a far different outcome.

Those who go by the name Jehovah's Witness will not salute the American flag. A local school board required the flag salute of all students upon pain of expulsion. The Supreme Court rejected that law, explaining:

> The very purpose of a Bill of Rights was to withdraw certain subjects from the vicissitudes of political controversy, to place them beyond the reach of majorities and officials and to establish them as legal principles to be applied by

7. Reynolds v. United States, 98 U.S. 145, 166 (1878).

> the courts. One's right to life, liberty, and property, to free speech, a free press, freedom of worship and assembly, and other fundamental rights may not be submitted to vote; they depend on the outcome of no elections.[8]

Now you may begin to see the outlines of a conflict. Both statutes, polygamy and flag salute, imposed a penalty upon a citizen who did or did not do a certain thing. In both cases, a citizen claimed their religion required such conduct. Yet in these two cases the state reached apparently opposite conclusions.

Lawyers and judges have developed a very specialized vocabulary and a series of complex tests to sort out and balance state power and personal decision in these kinds of cases. What you should understand here is that all such tests are questions of freedom and order. In *Reynolds*, which involved polygamy, the justices considered the history of marriage laws and the importance of marriage to an ordered society. In the flag case, the court said that things such as flag saluting are "matters relatively trivial to the welfare of the nation."[9] This line of reasoning became an issue directly affecting the practice of religion when the United States Supreme Court took up the issue of homosexual marriage in the case *Obergefell v. Hodges*, 576 U.S. 644 (2015).

The law is not a static thing. When seeking to understand the law, we need to read various cases together. Sometimes this means we need to change our understanding of previous cases in light of new cases. Such is what we must do when we consider the effect of *Obergefell v. Hodges*. While the case directly affected homosexual marriage, the results of the case will change far more than marriage laws.

The decisions of the Supreme Court are never only about the particular parties before it. While the justices rule about a particular situation, they are making law over the entire country. When we consider this law for the entire country, we must consider not only

8. Board of Education v. Barnette, 319 U.S. 624, 638 (1943).
9. *Board of Education*, 319 U.S. at 638.

the final conclusion (this person wins and that person loses). We also must carefully consider the reasoning that the justices use. We need to consider the reasoning of one case together with the reasoning of other cases. By doing this, we can gain a better idea what a decision means. The reasoning of *Obergefell* will affect the way we do ministry in the future because it will affect what the state is permitted to do in regulating citizens for the purposes of protecting public "order."

Bearing in mind the court's reasoning in the two cases above, consider this statement: "this Court's cases and the Nation's traditions make clear that marriage is a keystone of our social order."[10] And "the States have contributed to the fundamental character of the marriage right by placing that institution at the center of so many facets of the legal and social order."[11]

When you read this, you may wonder how the court permitted a change in marriage, "a keystone of our social order," while it is the goal of the government to maintain social order. Now you are asking the right question. Keep reading: "There is no difference between same- and opposite-sex couples with respect to this principle."[12]

In rendering this decision, the court was endeavoring to protect the social order. Even though the moral reasoning of the court was seriously flawed, the *stated goal* of the court was the protection of social order. Thus, we can agree that social order is good, even though we must disagree with the means by which the court sought to promote that goal.

Now we begin to understand the nature of the conflict between religious liberty and state control. The state is seeking to maintain a particular vision of social order. When the state perceives a particular religious act as dangerous to social order and safety, there will be a conflict between religious freedom and state control.

With this background, we need to think carefully about how and why the state would argue that it has the power to regulate

10. Obergefell v. Hodges, 135 S. Ct. 2584, 2601 (2015).
11. *Obergefell*, 135 S. Ct. at 2601.
12. *Obergefell*, 135 S. Ct. at 2601.

the religious practice of one Christian providing biblical counsel to another Christian. Until we understand clearly why the state might claim an interest in biblical counseling, we will be unable to chart a course to avoid state regulation.

Sinful Oppression and Rhetoric

While the government has the rightful responsibility of maintaining order, the government is populated by sinful people. The result of sinful people with power is abuse of that power. As Solomon says in Ecclesiastes 5:8, "If you see in a province the oppression of the poor and the violation of justice and righteousness, do not be amazed at the matter." The concern that the government is misusing its power is not false. Oppression and injustice are part of the world.

Our questions are (1) What does this actually look like? And (2) How do we respond?

At this point, we need to realize that oppression is not the state's stated goal in regulating counseling. Obviously, we will find individual legislators or regulators or judges who have a personal grudge against religion in general and Christianity in particular. But the rationale, the stated reason for the state's regulation of counseling, is public order and public good. We must agree that seeking the public good is not a bad thing.

We would also agree that the state's desire to regulate human sexual activity is an appropriate aspect of the use of state power to maintain public order. Laws against pedophilia are laws that regulate human sexuality upon a point which we agree is good. Not many people want to return to a world where rape was the prerogative of the powerful and children could be misused at will.

It is precisely here that trouble arises for the biblical counselor. As shown by the discussion of *Obergefell* above, the state's reasoning on what constitutes "good" public order on the question of human sexuality now conflicts with what the Bible dictates as the good of public social order. When you counsel someone to live in chastity, to refrain from same-sex behavior, to say that surgery and hormones cannot turn a woman into a man, you are providing counsel which the Bible requires and which the states find to be against public order.

Here we have a conflict between the content of our religion and the content of the state's rules for good public order. And it is here that Christians are finding difficulty. At present most of the active conflict involves Christian photographers (for instance) and not a pastor alone in a study giving biblical counsel to an individual. Yet that does not mean the law will not affect counselors.

There is a movement in the law that goes beyond individual cases. As the public and political environment change, the legislatures and judges change. The law progresses statute by statute and case by case, but there is an overarching movement of the law.

We see the movement of the law along three lines that will likely converge upon Christians giving biblical counsel. First, there is the movement in the law finding "erotic liberty" to be a constitutional right (see *Obergefell* above). Second, there is the movement in the law to regulate the content of counsel (generally) with prohibitions on discouragement of "erotic liberty." Third, there are the coercive laws under the guise of "public accommodation" that seek to force Christians to participate in and approve of things such as same-sex weddings (for a discussion of public accommodation laws, see chapter 10).

You would be correct if you were to ask, Don't we have freedom of religion? But you may not realize what a precarious protection that may prove to be. You need to understand that in the end the law is merely words.

While the law is backed up with a sword, the content of the law is words. When a judge makes a decision, the judge says something or writes something. When a lawyer presents a case, the lawyer talks. These words need to perform the work of justifying and convincing everyone that the decision of the court is fair and right. The words are used to make a moral case.

In the United States, the judge must consider the complication of words that explicitly limit the power of government: The government cannot abridge the freedom of religion. But as we saw above, that is not always true. The nineteenth-century Mormons were forbidden from engaging in polygamy.

To understand the difficulty of the problem facing the government today, consider examples that do not involve Christians: How do we balance Islamic rules concerning female dress with governmental interests in identification? May an Islamic taxicab driver refuse to transport a seeing eye dog or a man carrying a bottle of wine? What if a religion entails ritual prostitution? Human sacrifice? You see, the questions cannot be resolved as easily as answering "freedom of religion."

The government has a marked tendency to increase the scope of its power; its aim is always toward more control. The United States Constitution seeks to limit that move toward more control by various mechanisms, such as a division of power and the Bill of Rights.

Religion, in particular, has been a difficult matter for the courts to navigate and for the government to increase its control over. As we have seen, religion entails more than just a set of opinions that are kept around for special occasions. Religion also entails a manner of life. How then will the government be able to box religion into a set of opinions as opposed to a manner of life?

With this idea in mind, consider an incident in the book of Acts that demonstrates the connection between public and private religion. In Acts 18, we read of some Jews who come to Corinth and stir up trouble for Paul with the local officials. The accusation is, "This man is persuading people to worship God contrary to the law" (Acts 18:13). The proconsul refuses to consider the matter because it is only a private dispute among the Jews. The question does not concern "wrongdoing or vicious crime" (Acts 18:14).

The complaint of the Jews against Paul concerned a matter of private opinion. The Jews did not say that Paul was leading people to rebel against Rome or to attack the Roman army. Paul simply had an idea about God that led to a different manner of worship. Gallio didn't care about what Jews did or did not do on their own time. If Paul were committing a crime, then there was something to be concerned about, but Paul's decision to be an unorthodox Jew was not even interesting.

Compare that to Acts 19. The idol makers of Ephesus were furious that Christianity was cutting into their profits. The people rioted. The town clerk managed to calm the crowd and told them if they had a charge to bring it in the public courts. We don't know what would have happened in such a lawsuit because Paul left town.

The distinction between public and private religion goes back to Rome. But the United States' Constitution does not contain a distinction between public and private religion. In the flag case, the Supreme Court found that the public practice of the Jehovah's Witnesses was protected, so public religion is protected by the Constitution. However, sometimes a certain religious practice seems peculiarly dangerous to social order. Thus, in the polygamy case, the court found that the public practice of the Mormons was dangerous to social order because it overturned one the most basic elements of public and social life, marriage. Therefore, it could not be tolerated. On the other hand, the court recently found that the recognition of homosexual "marriage" was to be protected because it promoted social order. While the particular valuations change over time, the stated goal remains the same.

One solution would simply be to expand state power and regulate those behaviors that the state believes to be in the interest of public order. The government of China regulates the content of movies, the screen time of children, and the number of children a family may produce, all in the name of public order.

But those in the United States who wish to expand state power run into a difficulty when the behavior regulated also entails religious practice because religion under the Constitution is protected.

The word *religion* is a limitation on government power. In *Reynolds v. United States*, the Supreme Court did not prohibit the practice of the Mormon religion, only polygamy. How then does the government get around that word *religion*? It is quite a problem.

One method for solving the issue has been to change the language—a subtle shift from the constitutional phrase "freedom of religion" to the new phrase "freedom of worship." In prior years, the two terms were often used as equivalent, interchangeable phrases. But beginning during the Obama administration, there was a deliberate effort to argue for the freedom of worship rather than the freedom of religion.

An article in *First Things* from 2010 explains the reason for the linguistic shift to speak only of freedom of worship, rather than freedom of religion: worship is what you do on Sunday morning with the door closed, while religion is what you do on Monday morning at work. The article states,

> Any person of faith knows that religious exercise is about a lot more than freedom of worship. It's about the right to dress according to one's religious dictates, to preach openly, to evangelize, to engage in the public square. Everyone knows that religious Jews keep kosher, religious Quakers don't go to war, and religious Muslim women wear headscarves yet "freedom of worship" would protect none of these acts of faith.
>
> Those who would limit religious practice to the cathedral and the home are the very same people who would strip the public square of any religious presence.[13]

Thus, when the state seeks to regulate the pastor's counsel, the state is not interfering with "freedom of worship." The pastor may

13. Ashley E. Samelson, "Why 'Freedom of Worship' Is Not Enough," *First Things* (blog), February 22, 2010, https://www.firstthings.com/web-exclusives/2010/02/why-ldquofreedom-of-worshiprdquo-is-not-enough.

continue to organize worship however those in that church see fit. But when it comes to public conduct, the state will intervene.[14]

The problem is made worse when one Christian sits with another Christian, listens to problems, and then gives counsel on how to think or act. That counselor looks and acts and talks exactly like a licensed therapist—except for the "licensed" part. In such a case, we may ask, Should the state give the pastor a pass because he does the counseling in a church?

Where Does That Leave Us?

Like in any social or political process, the reasons for the state seeking to regulate what we do in ministry are complex, and any discussion of the reasons will of necessity leave out certain elements. I am purposefully leaving out elements relevant to this discussion because I do not wish to worry nor overly complicate a chapter meant to provide practical guidance.

At this point we can see two elements of the state's desire to regulate. First, there is the rightful expression of state power to maintain order in the world. Second, there is the natural tendency in human beings to gain power over others.

We looked at one aspect of the rhetorical war taking place—the rhetoric of freedom of religion versus freedom of worship. We will focus in on that element of "religion" versus "worship" because it provides us with a good strategy for protecting the space necessary to provide biblical counsel, as opposed to politically acceptable counsel that may reference the Bible.

14. The nature of legal landscape was well summarized in a blog post from July 2020: "Modern American law is effectively just a balancing act of how large or how small that private exercise space is allowed to be. When the balance does not seem appropriate to the public, religious exercise claims can be seen as frustrating technicalities used to justify unjust discrimination, restrict rights and illegitimately influence legal decisions." Gregory Caridi, "Bostock's Hidden Trap," *Ius & Iustitium* (blog), July 5, 2020, https://iusetiustitium.com/bostocks-hidden-trap/amp/.

The state regulates "therapy," but the state may not regulate "religion." Thus, to avoid state control over our counsel, we need to do two things:

1. Clearly demarcate the difference between our biblical counsel and therapy.
2. Be clear that the counsel we provide is unmistakably a demand of our religion.

In short, *we must be clear that we are engaged in the religious practice of discipleship rather than the secular practice of therapy.*

To return to our original image of a surfer and shark, we need to make it clear that we are not seals. Yes, sharks are aggressive and will attack almost anything. But sharks more often attack seals than random boards made of epoxy resin. We need to be that resin instead of a seal.

What that means and how we will do that will be addressed in the next chapter.

To-Do List

- ❒ We do have freedom of religion, in both worship and practice. Do not squander this remarkable gift from God that has been recognized in our law. Exercise your freedom to live as a Christian, and give thanks.
- ❒ Be supportive of legal and political organizations that act to protect our religious liberty. A list of such organizations appears in chapter 10.
- ❒ As we begin to recognize limitations on our freedom of religion, do not forget those around the world who do not possess our legal protections. "Remember those who are in prison, as though in prison with them, and those who are mistreated, since you also are in the body" (Hebrews 13:3).

CHAPTER 3

Truth in Advertising: Communicating About Your Counseling Ministry with Clarity

Edward Charles Wilde

As we saw at the end of the previous chapter, we face two tasks of great importance: We must plainly distinguish our work as biblical counselors from the seemingly related work of the licensed therapist, and we must demonstrate that it is an essential part of our religious practice.

This distinction between biblical counseling and therapy matters in two areas. First, it is important in the counselor-counselee relationship. In chapter 9, Todd Sorrell will examine this relationship and explain how the use of proper intake forms will set expectations and protect the parties. Second, there is also state regulation of the content of our counsel. This chapter will examine the nature of that relationship and provide some practical instruction on how to protect the counselor from state intrusion.

We need to make a clear distinction between what we do as biblical counselors and what is done in general therapy. To make this distinction will provide us with the strongest possible argument that we should not be licensed and regulated by the state.[1] We hold

1. There are significant legal and moral arguments that Christians who engage more plainly in what would be called "psychotherapy" should be given protection when they provide counsel in an explicitly Christian manner, and that the state should not regulate the content of that counsel in such a way as to contradict Christian belief and

on to our unregulated status because the state's interest in licensing and regulating therapists extends beyond merely confirming that we have some minimal training. As is becoming increasingly clear day by day, the state also requires certain ethical and intellectual commitments that are incompatible with biblical Christianity. The commitments we must fulfill if we are to remain faithful to Scripture will necessarily put us in conflict with the basic commitments required by state and public affiliations that license and regulate psychotherapy.

How then do we make this important distinction? We cannot distinguish ourselves merely by saying we use the Bible. As we have seen, the state is unconcerned with our source of authority: a therapist can use Adler or Jung, Maslow, or tarot cards and astrology. However, the state also requires and excludes certain assertions as beyond the limits of acceptable discourse. The ethical rules that govern a psychotherapist require that the client—not the therapist—determine the scope and goals of therapy.

Moreover, the therapist may not "impose" values:

> Counselors are aware of—and avoid imposing—their own values, attitudes, beliefs, and behaviors. Counselors respect the diversity of clients, trainees, and research participants and seek training in areas in which they are at risk of imposing their values onto clients, especially when the counselor's values are inconsistent with the client's goals or are discriminatory in nature.[2]

---

practice. Nothing in this book should be read in such a manner as to imply or concede that the state's legitimate interest in licensing therapists should extend to prohibiting a Christian counselor from discouraging sinful behavior.

2. American Counseling Association, 2014 Code of Ethics, Section A.4.b. Personal Values. However, we must realize that our own subjectively held beliefs may be utterly false when measured against the objective truth of Scripture: "Heart, soul, mind and might, the sinful man 'feels' his lies to be true. Crucial beliefs and opinions are deep-seated. What we 'really believe' is not casually discarded or exchanged. Lies and distortions are stubborn, plausible, deceitful, ingrained. We are usually persuaded that our 'feel that's' are true," David Powlison, "What Do You Feel?" ed. Jay E. Adams, *Journal of Pastoral Practice* 10, no. 4 (1992): 57.

In contrast, the work of the biblical counselor is by definition the imposition of values—a call to the counselee to be transformed and conformed to the image of Jesus.

We, as orthodox Christians who are intent on communicating the historic norms and life of the Christian church, hold to positions that are viewed as injurious to the current state of public morality. This is particularly true as concerns the life of the family, the nature of the human body, and sexual behavior. Indeed, Romans 1 lays out a fairly clear picture of the manner in which we will differ in our counsel from current public morality.

For example, California law provides, "Any sexual orientation change efforts attempted on a patient under 18 years of age by a mental health provider shall be considered unprofessional conduct and shall subject a mental health provider to discipline by the licensing entity for that mental health provider."[3] While the public impetus for this law is to prohibit something commonly known as "conversion therapy" (a practice which is inconsistent with biblical counsel), the language of the statute would prohibit reading Leviticus 18:22 ("You shall not lie with a male as with a woman; it is an abomination") to a group of high school students, particularly if any of that group was tempted toward same-sex attraction.

Asserting that one's physical body determines one's sex and that there is no gender detachable from physiology is considered hate speech. For consistency with that guideline, Abigail Shrier's book *Irreversible Damage* and Ryan Anderson's book *When Harry Became Sally* have both been banned from being sold on various platforms. Even those who would have previously been considered on the "left," as "TERFs" (feminists who reject transgender "women" as women) have themselves been attacked and ridiculed for expressing such positions.

Therefore, while the state's explanation for licensing therapy is ostensibly a laudable goal, it is not a neutral position.[4] The space

3. Bus. & Prof. Code §865.2.

4. The entire concept of "neutral" positions is itself problematic. However, a discussion of that topic (as interesting as it might be), lies far beyond our present concern.

open to licensed counseling, while it does provide some latitude, also requires certain ideological commitments that we cannot make without compromising our witness.[5] Thus, we need a means by which we can engage in our work as biblical counselors without running afoul of the state's role of licensing and regulating therapists. And here we must think carefully. The most obvious way of making a distinction between biblical counseling and secular therapy is to highlight the content of each: What kind of counsel is given to the counselee, and on what authority is this counsel based? If we focus on content, we will not be successful. Let's look at the reason.

There are various ways to analyze a counseling psychology. And biblical counseling presents a distinctive counseling psychology. By this, I do not mean that biblical counseling is identical with any secular psychology.[6] As we know, there is no such thing as an intellectual monolith called "psychology" when it comes to counseling. The psychology of Jung and the psychology of Skinner are both "psychologies," yet they differ dramatically at certain points. As Robert Feldman writes, "There are about 400 varieties of psychotherapy. Although the methods are diverse, all psychological approaches have a common perspective: they seek to solve psychological problems

---

5. For example, the "Competencies for Addressing Spiritual and Religious Issues in Counseling," Item 7, provides, "The professional counselor uses spiritual and/or religious concepts that are consistent with the client's spiritual and/or religious perspectives and are acceptable to the client." Accessed September 7, 2020, available at https://www.counseling.org/docs/default-source/competencies/competencies-for-addressing-spiritual-and-religious-issues-in-counseling.pdf?sfvrsn=8. This proposition would not be consistent with, for instance, Isaiah 42:8 or Acts 17:30.

6. As David Powlison wrote: "Christian faith *is* a psychology. A coherent, comprehensive understanding of how people work is intrinsic to thinking Christianly. The revelation of Jesus Christ offers a distinctive interpretation of the 'thoughts and intentions of the heart,' those schemata and motivations that structure and animate behavior. Scripture offers a distinctive interpretation of 'nature' (i.e., constraints and potential of the body) and of 'nurture' (i.e., enculturing voices and interpersonal experience). God reveals a distinct image of human flourishing toward which counseling aspires, and a distinctive change process by which we move toward that ideal. A Christian understanding systematically differs from how other psychologies explain the same phenomena. Christian ministry *is* a psychotherapy. Eric L. Johnson and David G. Myers, eds., *Psychology and Christianity: Five Views*, 2nd ed. (Downers Grove, IL: IVP Academic, 2010), 249.

by modifying people's behavior and helping them obtain a better understanding of themselves and their past, present and future."[7]

One way to evaluate a given psychological approach is by looking at the anthropology (what is a human being), the teleology (what is the purpose of a human being), and the methodology (how does a human being change) of a system (ATM).[8] On each of these points, biblical counseling advocates an understanding distinct from that of any secular psychology.

It is precisely on these points that biblical counseling will run into conflict with the positions the state advocates. When it comes to the question of anthropology (what is a human being), biblical counseling contends that human beings have physical bodies, which are a necessary element of their being, and that one's sex cannot exist independently of a "gender." The sex of the body is the sex of the human being.

To argue that a human being possesses a subjective gender that is independent of the body, and thus a biological man can be a woman, is a fundamental contradiction of the biblical anthropology. Yet this is precisely what the state has come to consider a matter of unquestioned truth. Indeed, to contravene this position, according to the state, is to be the worst sort of hateful bigot.

The conflict between biblical counseling and state regulation extends to more than just anthropology (what is, and what does it mean to be a human being in a body). It also extends the meaning and purpose of being a human being. The language of the Declaration

---

7. Robert S. Feldman, *Essentials of Understanding Psychology*, 11th ed. (New York, NY: McGraw-Hill Education, 2014), 489.

8. In private conversation, Dr. Gifford of The Master's University has clarified that epistemology is a necessary element of a properly developed counseling psychology. I completely agree with him. If we were constructing a complete theology of biblical counseling, it would be necessary to consider the matter of epistemology. I raise this issue here to make clear that I am not presenting a comprehensive theology of biblical counseling, but rather addressing the practical outworking of three areas that clearly distinguish biblical counseling from psychotherapy. An epistemology would underlie and inform each of these elements (ATM). So epistemology is a necessary element of a complete theology of biblical counseling, but as a matter of practically distinguishing our work from that of therapists, it can be held aside until a fuller treatment of these matters.

of Independence, our inalienable right to "pursue happiness," has transformed and become, in effect, a religious dogma where "happiness" is being "authentic," and "authentic" means whatever I may happen to feel. Our "telos," our end and purpose, is wholly subjective. As applied to counseling, as will be shown below, the counselee alone can define what telos should be.[9]

It is quite different for the Christian. Our telos is objective and grounded in the revelation of God.

The Scripture contends that a human being's highest purpose, our "chief end," as the Westminster Shorter Catechism puts it, "is to glorify God and enjoy him forever."[10] Our chief end is something beyond us, and thus immediate human ease or even present happiness is not our primary end. While we believe that we have a basis for "joy unspeakable and full of glory," we also acknowledge that alleviating suffering is not always the most important goal.[11] This belief runs

9. This points to a fundamental distinction between "therapy" and Christian discipleship. If there is a common element to the various types of modern psychological therapy, it seems to be the belief that there is an "authentic self" and a "public self" that exist in tension. When that tension becomes too great (such as a conflict between Freud's Id and Superego), there is a resulting breakdown that manifests as anger, depression, anxiety, or some other malady. The key to this way of thinking is the belief that the "authentic self"—that bundle of desires, thoughts, affections, expectations, etc. one would experience without much conscious control—is the "real you" which must be privileged, protected, and integrated into the public self. The Scripture has a very different view of things and seeks the transformation of the mind (Romans 12:1–2). The goal is not helping one to feel good about their sinful desires, but rather to "put to death" such rebellious inclinations. (See, e.g., Colossians 3:5.) A further discussion of this point lies beyond the scope of the present book.

10. Westminster Shorter Catechism, Question 1. "What is the chief end of man? A. The chief end of man is to glorify God and enjoy him forever."

11. The question of suffering and counseling goes well beyond the scope of this short chapter. However, we can acknowledge that avoiding suffering is not an end in and of itself. We may be called to suffer. Paul even calls it a gift of God: "For to you it has been granted [to] . . . suffer for his sake" (Philippians 1:29). God brings great good out of suffering. If Jesus avoided suffering as an end itself, there would have been no salvation for any human being. If the apostles had avoided suffering, there would have been no proclamation of the gospel. God uses suffering to teach us. "Although he was a son, he learned obedience through what he suffered" (Hebrews 5:8). If the Son learned through suffering, then how much more should we. As the Puritan Richard Sibbes wrote, "Nay, after conversion we need bruising, that (1) reeds may know themselves to be reeds, and not oaks; even reeds need bruising, by reason of the remainder of pride in our nature, and to let us see that we live by mercy." Richard Sibbes, *The Complete Works*

contrary to the ends of "therapy." As Philip Rieff writes, "Religious man was born to be saved; psychological man is born to be pleased."[12]

The state's goal is to permit each person to be the one who determines what is right for oneself. Meanwhile, our goal as biblical counselors lies in the opposite direction. We must not be "conformed to this world" (Romans 12:2). Our work is to see Christ "formed in" others (Galatians 4:19).

Thus, it is precisely at our most distinctive points that we come into conflict with the state's—and the general culture's—norms and expectations. If our attempt to distinguish ourselves rested upon these points (which are the places wherein we primarily define what is critical to biblical counseling), we end up putting ourselves into direct conflict with the state.

As biblical counselors, we have distinguished ourselves based upon the content of our counseling. We have contended that we are not doing "therapy" or "psychology" because we are giving counsel from the Bible. The trouble is that such an explanation is insufficient to provide protection for our work as counselors. From the perspective of people within the broader culture, we are not protected because we get our psychology from the Bible. In fact, they may see our using the Bible as an affectation or an error; it certainly will not give us any special rights.

We have considered the conflict between presuppositions and the goals of biblical counseling and the state. Having seen the theoretical nature of this conflict, we will turn our attention to the actual practice of counseling and the methodological conflict.

The Analogy of Our Methodology

We need to consider what biblical counseling looks like in terms of method. To do this, we will widen our lens to consider two broad

of Richard Sibbes, ed. Alexander Balloch Grosart, vol. 1 (Edinburgh; London; Dublin: James Nichol; James Nisbet and Co.; W. Robertson, 1862), 44. We could go to a book or two on this subject. But for now, know that avoiding suffering—which is the goal of therapy—cannot be the ultimate goal of Christian discipleship.

12. Philip Rieff, *The Triumph of the Therapeutic: Uses of Faith After Freud*, 40th ed. (Wilmington, DE: ISI Books, 2006), 19.

categories of relationships in society. First, we will look at the professional relationship, which the state legitimately regulates because, as discussed in chapter 2, the practice of biblical counseling looks like the practice of licensed psychotherapy. Our methodology looks like the conduct regulated by the state.

The law often works in terms of analogies. And if the analogy of the licensed therapist were our only analogy, distinguishing our work from that of licensed therapists might be difficult. But there is a second analogy which will help us more clearly define what we do as biblical counselors and provide us with a model of counseling that the state does not regulate. We will consider the personal relationship, the relationship between friends, which the state does not regulate. By examining these two different analogies, we will be able to see a path forward.

The Professional Relationship

By trade, I am an attorney. As such, I hold myself out to the public as possessing a certain education and level of skill. To become an attorney, I attended college, then attended law school, and then passed a painful examination that requires much study. After successfully completing all these requirements, I find myself under constant scrutiny by the State Bar.

I must complete certain continuing education requirements. My work is overseen by judges, who have the authority to report me to the bar for serious failure in work or ethics. My clients all have the ability to report me to the bar for review based upon a lapse of skill or ethics. I also must maintain a degree of a public reputation because continued work depends upon public reputation. Most clients come from referrals of previous clients (and sometimes from opposing parties).

The rationale for this public scrutiny makes sense. I hold myself out to the public and seek work from the public. While I provide a service, my work is, in some respects, no different from that of someone who sells a product. When I purchase a car, I have reason to expect a certain level of quality. Furthermore, the state requires that the automobile itself be tested for safety. It also inspects food producers and regulates medicines.

These public regulations are necessary because the provision of goods and services takes place between relative strangers. When I go into a supermarket, I may not have any personal knowledge of any employee. When I purchase food from a restaurant along the interstate highway, I am interacting with perfect strangers and yet can complete the transaction to mutual benefit because there are mechanisms which establish public trust.

When a member of the public comes into my office, that person has reason to know that I have not violated certain ethical norms (I have not been found to have stolen client money), and that I have certain minimal expertise (I went to law school and passed the bar examination).

The state's interest in regulating the professional relationship is critical: in a society where fundamentally important transactions take place between strangers, both sides need an institution trusted by all that can affirm the minimal competencies necessary to make the relationship possible. If there were no food or medicine inspections, I wouldn't know if I could safely purchase food or medicine while on vacation in a distant city. Not knowing the reputation of a local pharmacist, I would be taking a great risk when I sought medicine to heal my body.

It makes sense that the state would license and regulate psychotherapists. Therapists hold themselves out to the public as possessing the requisite skill to provide help. The people who come to the therapist are peculiarly vulnerable. It is their vulnerability and need that bring them to seek the help of a stranger. When they come to this stranger, they will reveal information that often is unknown even by close friends.

In a relationship between relative strangers which touches upon the most sensitive areas of life, it is not surprising that the state would seek to provide regulation and protections to the public. If I go to see a licensed therapist, I have reason to believe that the therapist possesses certain education and training. I know that the license is subject to review by the state. I know that a current license means the therapist has not been found to have violated certain ethical norms. The state's regulation makes possible relatively safe interactions between strangers.

When we compare this to our work as biblical counselors, we can see how our work exhibits similarities, from the state's perspective, to the professional relationship between a therapist and a client. While we may counsel people we personally know, we also know that we will counsel people who are relative strangers. Since the number of certified biblical counselors is small relative to the need, all of us who are counselors with ACBC—I am a biblical counselor as well as an attorney—have received calls from people who found our name on the website or were referred from another church. We have counseled and will counsel people with whom we have no prior personal relationship.

When we consider the question more carefully, we see more similarities between our work and the work of the licensed therapist. The client or counselee comes to us with some difficulty and seeks counsel. We listen to the situation. We ask questions. We confirm facts. We consult with some authority (whereas we consult Scripture, a licensed therapist will consult the tenets of a psychological theory). We give advice. We give direction to do one thing and to avoid another. And while not all (probably not most) therapists will pray with a counselee, it is certainly not beyond the scope of expectation.

When you look at the structure or methodology of biblical counselors without consulting the content of our work (the anthropology and teleology), our work looks like the work of any number of licensed therapists who provide counsel in the context of professional relationships to persons who were previously strangers.

Accordingly, from that position, it looks to the regulating authority like we should be licensed.

Friendship

However, a biblical counselor is also similar to a friend. A friend listens to troubles. A friend asks questions. A friend gives advice. A friend says, "Think about this," and "Do not do that," and so on.

We may have quite pompous or skilled friends who give us their advice with a rather insistent air and claim great wisdom or skill in providing such advice. In fact, a friend may tell us more definitively what we must do than even the most "expert" therapist. However, the state does not regulate the friend relationship—even if you buy your friend dinner in exchange for giving the counsel. The state does not regulate the friend relationship irrespective of the content of the counsel or the "expertise" of the counsel.

It is not the content of the counsel that draws state scrutiny, but the nature of the relationship. If we provide biblical counsel to a friend, there is no conflict with the state. If we provide biblical counsel to a stranger in the format of a professional relationship, we run into potential conflict with the state.

The question thus becomes, Is there another category of relationship that distinguishes us from the licensed therapist or other public professional and yet is not as limited as the category of "friend?" Or, to phrase the question a bit differently, Is there a way that we can present ourselves to the public as possessing and offering a certain kind of counsel that the state will not see as necessary to regulate? The answer is yes.

Religion

The state does not regulate all relationships between strangers. Unregulated relationships are typically nonprofessional relationships, such as friendships. The state's interest in regulating relationships has in mind an element of the professional, commercial transaction.

If someone is going to pay for a service, they should get what they pay for.

The state has also, as a general rule, refused to concern itself with the content of explicitly religious instruction.[13] It is the line that has been drawn between state interest and religious instruction that will enable us to distinguish ourselves successfully from licensed therapists. Although the content of religious instruction has historically been a matter of profound political concern, in the United States it is now outside the scope of political inspection. (Indeed, it was Christianity that effectively created such a free space for religion.) Because the Constitution guarantees this freedom, if the state seeks to regulate religious practice, it cannot do so on the ground of explicitly religious or political concerns.

The way the state has, in practice, regulated religious practice has been to treat the potentially offending practice not as a trespass against politics or religion, but against public safety. The state has an express interest in regulating public health and safety. As Arkansas's attorney general explained (in a statement which could be affirmed by any American court):

> In Springfield v. City of Little Rock [citation omitted] we recognized the city's plenary duty to exercise its police power in the interest of the public health and safety of its inhabitants. [Citation omitted.] The police power of the state is founded in public necessity and this necessity must exist in order to justify its exercise. [Citation omitted.] It is always justified when it can be said to be in the interest of the public

13. This is not to say that various state officials have not sought to intervene into explicitly religious concerns. For instance, in 2014, "The city of Houston has issued subpoenas demanding a group of pastors turn over any sermons dealing with homosexuality, gender identity or Annise Parker, the city's first openly lesbian mayor. And those ministers who fail to comply could be held in contempt of court." Todd Starnes, "Houston City Government Demands Pastors Turn Over Sermons Referencing Homosexuality, Mayor," *Christian Post,* October 14, 2014, https://www.christianpost.com/news/houston-city-government-demands-pastors-turn-over-sermons-referencing-homosexuality-mayor.html.

> health, public safety, public comfort, and when it is, private rights must yield to public security, under reasonable laws.[14]

That "police power" is the basis upon which a government regulates the licensing of psychologists or general contractors. But the state's police power does not extend to the content of a religion. The state may regulate certain practices or prohibit certain actions. For instance, no one would be offended if the state forbade the sacrifice of children to Molech. Yet, the state would not proscribe the belief that the idol Molech was a "real god."[15] As the Supreme Court wrote:

> But the "exercise of religion" often involves not only belief and profession but the performance of (or abstention from) physical acts: assembling with others for a worship service, participating in sacramental use of bread and wine, proselytizing, abstaining from certain foods or certain modes of transportation. It would be true, we think (though no case of ours has involved the point), that a State would be "prohibiting the free exercise [of religion]" if it sought to ban such acts or abstentions only when they are engaged in for religious reasons, or only because of the religious belief that they display. It would doubtless be unconstitutional, for example, to ban the casting of "statues that are to be used for worship purposes," or to prohibit bowing down before a golden calf.[16]

14. Opinion No. 2009-073, Opinion No. 2009-073, at *5 (Ops.Ark.Atty.Gen. June 30, 2009).

15. "But the First Amendment embraces two concepts, freedom to believe and freedom to act. On one hand, it prevents compulsion by law of the acceptance of any creed or the practice of any form of worship. On the other hand, it safeguards the free exercise of the chosen form of religion. Freedom to believe is absolute, but freedom to act is not. Conduct is subject to regulation for the protection of society. While the power to regulate must be so exercised in every case as not to infringe the protected freedom, the State, by general and nondiscriminatory legislation, may safeguard the peace, good order and comfort of the community without unconstitutionally invading the liberties protected by the Fourteenth Amendment," Hopkins v. State, 193 Md. 489, 496 (1949)

16. Employment Div. v. Smith, 494 U.S. 872, 877–78 (1990).

The Shikh adherents of the martial fraternity of Khalsa are to wear a sword as part of their religious practice. While I am unaware of there being any rash outbreaks of Shikhs wielding their sword in a crime spree, the government has an interest in public safety. It is not unreasonable to conclude that thousands of young men wielding swords in New York City might lead to violence. So the state of New York outlawed walking around with large knives. The Khalsaians protested that this infringed upon their religious practice. When the matter came to judgment, the court upheld the law. The court explained that the law was not instituted to cause grief to the martial order of Khalsa, but rather the purpose was to protect public safety. Its explanation said, "While freedom to believe and worship as one chooses must remain absolute and unfettered, the State may restrict acts and conduct if the intrusion is justified by a compelling State interest to protect the health and safety of its citizens."[17]

When it comes to providing biblical counsel, we are counseling in religious belief. There is also practice, but our practice—while it concerns the conduct of our own behavior—does not constitute a matter of public safety. When biblical counselors tell a man to love his wife or tell another to refrain from certain sexual behaviors, we do not endanger public safety.[18] It should not be seen as a danger

17. People v. Singh, 135 Misc. 2d 701, 705–6 (N.Y. Crim. Ct. 1987).

18. But again, I must raise a caveat at this place. There is a concerted press among some governments to begin to recast orthodox Christian belief as a danger to public health. California Assembly Resolution 99, in the words of the California Legislative Digest, calls "upon all Californians to embrace the individual and social benefits of family and community acceptance, upon religious leaders to counsel on LGBTQ matters from a place of love, compassion, and knowledge of the psychological and other harms of conversion therapy, and upon the people of California and the institutions of California with great moral influence to model equitable treatment of all people of the state." The resolution finds that, "The stigma associated with being LGBTQ often created by groups in society, including therapists and religious groups, has caused disproportionately high rates of suicide, attempted suicide, depression, rejection, and isolation amongst LGBTQ and questioning individuals." While constitutional jurisprudence at present still limits governmental agents from restricting the content of instruction, we must realize that there will be a continual press to interfere with our instruction on the grounds of police power. Should the state's omnivorous desire seek to restrict the content of our counsel, we will have to face that trouble at that time. We need to realize that the content of our counsel is not yet under state jurisdiction. A copy of the

to give biblical instruction. Moreover, a counselee who hears such instruction and goes out to lead a sober-minded life of kindness and generosity is not endangering public safety. If we were to counsel someone to perform some action which arguably could injure another, we would have trouble. But our counsel universally seeks the protection, the dignity, and the life of human beings.

So it seems odd that our counsel could possibly be deemed something injurious to public order or safety (either in the act of giving it or when a counselee acts in accordance with it). However, due to the change in society and the belief in "erotic liberty," we have come to the place where the government deems it dangerous and contrary to public safety to tell another that it would be unwise and sinful to pursue a same-sex relationship. Moreover, expecting a counselee to abstain from desired sexual conduct is likely to be dangerous to the person so abstaining.

Since the state deems a biblical sexual ethic to be dangerous, what is our way forward? We need to make plain that our counsel is instruction in the practice of the Christian religion and the counsel is given to those who wish to practice the religion. Making this point clear in our practice should provide protection for biblical counselors.

At least for present, we can counsel freely *as religious counselors providing religious instruction. Therefore, we must make plain that our counsel is religious instruction.* Fortunately for us, our work in providing counsel as a matter of religious instruction is precisely what our Lord has laid out as the central mission of the church: "And Jesus came and said to them, 'All authority in heaven and on earth has been given to me. Go therefore and make disciples of all nations, baptizing them in the name of the Father and of the Son and of the Holy Spirit, teaching them to observe all that I have commanded you. And behold, I am with you always, to the end of the age'" (Matthew 28:18–20).

---

entire resolution may be found at https://leginfo.legislature.ca.gov/faces/billTextClient.xhtml?bill_id=201920200ACR99.

Jesus commands us to make disciples. As Jay Adams writes, "Discipleship isn't one option; it is an imperative—it is the only option." Creating disciples is central to our faith, and, as Tim Pasma will explain further in chapter 7, counseling is a form of discipling. Therefore, the means of creating the best possible legal space for our work is acting in strict conformity to the command.

To understand what this means as a practical matter, I will provide an example that focuses on the question of Christian teaching on human sexuality as opposed to the requirements of therapy. This example will necessarily be narrow, but the principle it illustrates is applicable to any number of counseling circumstances: we give the counsel we give for the reason that God commands this counsel to be given. "Therapy," by contrast, entails the counselee defining the goal and content of counsel. This will often entail a counselee who seeks help becoming reconciled to beliefs or practices that are inconsistent with Christian practice.

The Practice of Human Sexuality as Religious Observance

Despite the fact that even purportedly orthodox evangelical churches have defected from classical Christian positions on human sexuality,[19] Scripture has been universally clear on the scope of permissible human sexual behavior: within the context of a monogamous,

19. See as example the March 13, 2015 letter from the elders of City Church in San Francisco: "1. As a church within the Reformed Tradition we go directly to Scripture to find counsel and to reengage the verses that talk about same sex- activity. For so long this has been a 'case closed' kind of issue for evangelicals. But in recent years, multiple respected evangelical scholars and theologians have begun to wrestle with this and a healthy debate is underway. Asking questions about *what* the Scriptures say on this issue must always be coupled with asking *why* the Scriptures say what they do and what kind of same-sex activity is being addressed. Scholars and leaders who have previously been united in their interpretations are coming to different conclusions. This does *not* mean that your view must change, but it does counsel humility with how we each hold our views. Given the status and variety of these opinions, what has become clear to us is that there is no longer clear consensus on this issue within the evangelical community." "A Letter from the Elder Board – March 13, 2015," City Church San Francisco, accessed September 7, 2020, https://us8.campaign-archive.com/?u=ba28ce8fcce6d7773f83e3a4d&id=813cfb2f88&e=c112ec2066.

lifelong commitment (marriage) between a man and a woman, alone. We must teach this, not because it is for the good of the "mental health" of a client, nor because it helps a client conform to any conflict he may feel between his desires and conscience. We must teach this because it is a necessary part of Christian faith and practice: it is a religious, not a therapeutic, command.[20]

A rhetorical tactic that has been used by some professing Christians as a work-around for clear biblical commands concerning human sexuality has been to break the command down into parts: "What" is the command? "Why" was the command given? The "why" then is used as a means to avoid the "what." The "why" for these commands is said to be something unique and time bound to the context in which the command was given. Since the "why" no longer applies, we can happily avoid the "what."

I would like to take that strategy and demonstrate that the "why" given by Scripture prohibits us from simply ignoring the "what." We will look at five specific points in the argument.

20. This does not mean that keeping God's law is a matter of indifference to practical human flourishing. Due to the distortion that sin has wrought on the human mind, we cannot reliably choose what is best for us. Like toddlers who insist on playing with knives and desire to drink bleach, we of our own volition will choose poorly. Hence, a therapy which supports bad decisions is both a support to sin and destructive of the human being. Therefore, in counseling one to obey God's law, we do not promise any immediate ease or instantaneous entertainment, but we are pointing toward what is objectively good. For instance, a monogamous marriage is of demonstrable good for human beings. E.g., John Witte, Jr., "The Goods and Goals of Marriage," *Notre Dame Law Review* 76, 1019 (2000–2001). It is interesting to see that much contemporary so-called critical writing seeks to undermine the basic structures that have made human society functional, such as marriage. If you are interested in an example of such argumentation, you can look to something like "A Critical Examination of Popular Assumptions About the Benefits and Outcomes of Monogamous Relationships" in *Personality and Social Psychology Review* (Conley, Terri, Ziegler, Ali, Moors, Amy C., et al., November 21, 2012, https://doi.org/10.1177/1088868312467087). The authors conclude, "We suggest that because the bias in favor of monogamy is pervasive, the assumption of monogamy's superiority as a lifestyle is largely unexamined in empirical psychological literature." This tells you three things. First, contemporary academic work has been infected with advocacy over objective research. Second, sin corrupts everything, even perception of reality. Third, this is why we must rely upon the Lord—and not ourselves—to determine what is best for us.

First, biblical commandments—including those pertaining to human sexuality—are absolute requirements because the commandment comes from God: "And you shall observe all my statutes and all my rules, and do them: I am the LORD" (Leviticus 19:37). Jesus gives the same basis for his instruction to create disciples by teaching them to observe all that he has commanded because he is the possessor of all authority in heaven and on earth (Matthew 28:18).

Second, conforming to the commands respecting sexual behavior is a matter of nonnegotiable holiness before God. "Strive for … holiness without which no one will see the Lord" (Hebrews 12:14). Or as Peter writes, quoting Leviticus, "but as he who called you is holy, you also be holy in all your conduct, since it is written, 'You shall be holy, for I am holy'" (1 Peter 1:15–16). When it comes to matters of sexuality, it is God who defines the nature of conduct. As Daniel R. Heimbach writes, "The holiness of sex is not about what pleases you or me, it is about what pleases God. Because sexual holiness is about keeping sex in line with God, aligning sex in any other way is unholy."[21]

Third, we see in Romans 1:18–28 that a defection from this standard is a mark of God's judgment. As John Murray explains, "This [passage] advises us of a principle which is invariable, namely that retribution is never in operation except a judgment of God upon sin. . . . The retribution consists in giving them up (cf. vss. 26, 28) to uncleanness."[22]

Fourth, the commandments respecting sexual morality lie at the absolute core of the Christian religion. Our sexual behavior is an area of our lives in which we are to bring glory to God. As Paul writes in 1 Corinthians 6:20b, "So glorify God in your body." This is no minor element of the Christian religion. Thomas Schreiner writes of Romans 1, "We need to reflect further on the main thesis that

21. Daniel R. Heimbach, *True Sexual Morality: Recovering Biblical Standards for a Culture in Crisis* (Wheaton, IL: Crossway, 2004), 144.
22. John Murray, *The Epistle to the Romans* (Grand Rapids, MI: Wm. B. Eerdmans Publishing Company, 1965), 43.

Paul advances. Failing to glorify God is the root of sin."[23] As we have seen, the Westminster Larger Catechism lays out an unmistakable teleology for human life. Our purpose does not lie in our immediate happiness (defined in terms of our personal understanding of good), but rather lies in exaltation of God: "Question 1: What is the chief and highest end of man? Answer: Man's chief and highest end is to glorify God, and fully to enjoy him forever."[24]

Fifth, the commands of God are premised upon the nature of our relationship to God. We are not in a position to negotiate or vary the commands given. Paul drives this home with the bald statement concerning the basis for his command respecting sexual behavior: "Or do you not know that your body is a temple of the Holy Spirit within you, whom you have from God? You are not your own, for you were bought with a price. So glorify God in your body" (1 Corinthians 6:19–20). As William F. Orr and James Arthur Walther write of this passage, "This places a boundary to their freedom. They are not free to do as they please because of the relationship between them and God."[25]

We have seen that the teaching and practice of appropriate sexual behavior is an integral part of the Christian faith. Because that is so, it is not subject to regulation by the state. What is true in this specific matter of sexuality is true of many other issues addressed in biblical counseling.

Here is the way in which this information (which admittedly is not exhaustive on the question of why we must counsel as we do on sexual behavior or any other aspect of life) comes to bear on the matter of religious freedom and state licensing: We must be abundantly clear not merely as to the content of counseling, but as to the basis and purpose of our counseling.

---

23. Thomas R. Schreiner, *Romans*, vol. 6, Baker Exegetical Commentary on the New Testament (Grand Rapids, MI: Baker Books, 1998), 88.
24. Westminster Larger Catechism, Question 1.
25. William F. Orr and James Arthur Walther, *The Anchor Bible: 1 Corinthians* (Garden City, NY: Doubleday & Company, Inc., 1982), 203.

When biblical counselors counsel, we are not necessarily seeking the *immediate* happiness (as subjectively defined) of anyone.[26] Therapy is designed to help someone feel better on their own terms. There is a proposition underlying much of therapy which holds that the disquiet one feels when experiencing a conflict between conscience and desire must be resolved not by giving way to conscience but by ignoring conscience. The world of therapy is not one of conviction, repentance, and grace, which impels us to live in accordance with the instruction of God. Rather, it is one of medication to alleviate anxiety, to ignore guilt as a neurosis, and to become "authentic."

However, we are not seeking some sort of reconciliation between a client's conscience, external constraints, and desires so that the client will come to a happy balance between desire and practice. The command of Colossians 3:5—"Put to death therefore what is earthly in you"—cannot be reconciled with any licensable psychotherapy. The words of William Gurnall, which express the truth of Colossians 3:5, cannot be squared with the presupposition and goal of so much therapy: "The Christian is to proclaim and prosecute an irreconcilable war against his bosom sins; those sins which have lain nearest his heart must now be trampled under his feet."[27]

This is hard work. Paul tells us to "put to death the deeds of the body" (Romans 8:13). We do not begin with the premise that our desires and "authentic" self must be made comfortable. So in one fundamental manner, biblical counseling is antithetical to psychotherapy.

This does not mean that we truly discount happiness. Our position is that therapy promises too little happiness; not that happiness is

26. This does not mean that we ignore the need for immediate human safety. Protecting life is a command of God. As the Westminster Larger Catechism explains of the sixth commandment (Question 135), "The duties required in the sixth commandment are, all careful studies, and lawful endeavors, to preserve the life of ourselves and others . . . comforting and succoring the distressed and protecting and defending the innocent." How can we tell someone in distress that God values their life and then we ourselves fail to take even rudimentary efforts to save that life?

27. William Gurnall and John Campbell, *The Christian in Complete Armour* (London: Thomas Tegg, 1845), 3.

wrong. We contend *the ultimate happiness* of the human being will consist in the fulfillment of the promise, "They shall see God" (Matthew 5:8b). This is a promise made to the "pure in heart" (Matthew 5:8a). But we make no promise of happiness based upon one's own design.[28]

The vague promise of much of American Christianity that God loves you and has a wonderful plan for your life—which is the promise of therapy[29]—is not consistent with the course of discipleship that is premised upon the command of Jesus in Matthew 16:24: "If anyone would come after me, let him deny himself and take up his cross and follow me."

When someone comes to counseling, we must be plain on the matter: we are here to teach you how to conform to the commands of Jesus, not to make you "happy." We will teach you to deny yourself, not be true to yourself. We will convey to you the requirements of holiness, not help you to fulfill the desires of your heart.

As will be discussed in chapter 9, we must make our position very clear to the counselee. We do this by explaining what we do and by providing the counselee written forms that clearly explain our aim. This is both good counseling practice and good legal practice.

Conclusion

The best way for a biblical counselor to be free to practice ministry with the least degree of state interference will be truth in advertising. We may be tempted to be less than truthful. Our desire to make our counsel palatable and to make ourselves agreeable can make it easy

28. "Man would fain work out his happiness like a spider, climb up by a thread of his own spinning. But alas! all our devices and fine contrivances are gone with the turn of a besom. He that will be his own carver, seldom carveth out a good portion to himself. They intrench upon God's prerogative, and take the work out of his hands; and therefore no wonder if their wisdom be turned into folly." Thomas Manton, *The Complete Works of Thomas Manton*, vol. 2 (London: James Nisbet & Co., 1871), 170.

29. The degree to which a licensed counselor is expected to "affirm" sexual behavior that is utterly contrary to biblical Christianity can be seen by reading through the ACA "competency" standard, "ALGBTIC Competencies for Counseling LGBQIQA." This document can be found at https://www.counseling.org/docs/default-source/competencies/algbtic-competencies-for-counseling-lgbqiqa.pdf?sfvrsn=1c9c89e_14.

for us to present our work as a means of achieving happiness: we can promise better marriages, relief from depression and anxiety, etc. But we must be very clear that such outcomes are the side effects of our counsel. We believe that human misery is the result of sin, and, therefore, the only true way to happiness is holiness.

We must also be abundantly clear that the happiness we hold out to our counselees is not the happiness promised by therapy. Our Lord was "a man of sorrows, and acquainted with grief" (Isaiah 53:3). He describes his disciple as one who "loses his life" for Christ's sake (Luke 9:24). We are told to put to death our "earthly" inclination (Colossians 3:5). These are rigorous religious practices, life-altering demands of disciples.

But this does not mean we reject joy or happiness. Rather, we embrace and seek both. It is by seeking to be the one who determines our own course and chooses our own way that we as a people and we as individuals have wrought so much unhappiness upon ourselves and others. This is the point of Psalm 1. To walk in the counsel of the ungodly is to walk our way directly out of blessedness. The one who delights in the law of the Lord day and night is blessed. This is the way into happiness. This is why Martyn Lloyd-Jones's collection of sermons on Psalm 1 is entitled "True Happiness" (a recommended volume).[30]

To the extent we are clear that we are teaching religious discipline, the law (at present) gives us room. And it is just that room which permits us to offer true happiness to those in need. But if we

30. Martyn Lloyd-Jones, *True Happiness, Psalm 1*, (Fearn, Scotland: Christian Focus Publications, 2011). Once again we raise a subject which we cannot address with the attention it deserves. I fear that this chapter may lead some to believe that Christian discipleship ends in a dour rejection of all joy and happiness. But such is absolutely not the case. We are to "rejoice in the Lord always" (Philippians 4:4). The "joy of the Lord is your strength" (Nehemiah 8:10). I can best commend to you Sermon Seven in Jonathan Edwards's *Charity and Its Fruits*. Edwards's sermon itself deserves full consideration at this point on the question of how we seek happiness and the nature of a love for happiness. The trouble, in a nutshell, is a love for happiness built upon selfishness rather than a love for God and others. This is perhaps another way to understand the fundamental distinction between Christian discipleship and psychotherapy. But that would make an already-too-long chapter of impossible length.

seek to outdo the clinical therapist in offers of present ease and a happiness that aggrandizes the self, we are selling the stuff of therapy. If we do this, we fail our God-given mission, and because we are doing what licensed therapists do, we will find ourselves increasingly in conflict with the legal regime of the state. So perhaps we can thank the good grace of God who uses the state to warn us against causing harm to the souls of human beings by feeding their selfishness through unbiblical counsel. It turns out that our safest path is the path that God has commanded.

To-Do-List

- ❒ Take stock of the counsel which you have given. The model of therapy that seeks the immediate relief and "happiness" of a counselee is great temptation for all of us. When we face someone in distress, we naturally desire that they feel better. But by doing this, have we compromised our duty of making disciples?
- ❒ Take stock of the counsel that you have given to see whether your goal has been more to be liked by the counselee than to be faithful representative of Christ.
- ❒ Be clear in your counsel that your goal is to make Christian disciples. Be clear that you use biblical commands not merely because you think they will make for the best marriage, but even more so because the commands will honor God.
- ❒ Always be clear to explain that you are not providing therapy, but are instead seeking to make disciples.

CHAPTER 4
The Local Church and a Local Lawyer

Todd M. Sorrell

A local church is wise to seek local, legal counsel when faced with situations that potentially have legal ramifications. Indeed, it is often wise to seek that counsel before the particular need arises. But what does the relationship of the local church with a local lawyer have to do with biblical counseling? In simple terms, it is about wisdom and planning, two common issues that arise in counseling. It is about doing things right and, in so doing, caring for the church and its members. While some of the following discussion may seem to relate to specific counseling needs, much of this discussion is actually counsel (or advice) to the church itself, an aspect of biblical counseling that is often overlooked.

There is no chapter or verse in the Bible that *requires* a church to establish a professional relationship with a local lawyer. But does the Bible give us *any* guidance on this topic? If so, is it a one-size-fits-all rule? For example, does a tiny rural church have the same legal needs as an urban megachurch? If not, is there any overlap whatsoever? Should a church wait until a specific legal need arises before contacting a lawyer, or should the relationship be established well before that time?

Although this is not a call for every church to run out and hire a lawyer for every issue that arises, many churches face a number of common issues that may call for a legal perspective. These include consultation regarding the nonprofit status of the church, employee handbooks, church bylaws, payment for counseling services, and important contracts with vendors. But are there other issues that might highlight the importance of access to legal counsel? Let's take a look at a handful of hypothetical scenarios to assist us in evaluating how a church should decide whether or not to have a relationship with a local lawyer.

Ways That Legal Issues Can Surface for a Counselor

Scenarios like the following play out in different ways on different days all over the country. They often generate an immediate reaction and "solution" by those in leadership without thinking through the legal ramifications of those solutions. Once the discussion slows down, however, someone inevitably raises the "can we?" or "what about?" questions that tend to lace these scenarios. Let's look at a few of these hypothetical situations.

Scenario 1: She is almost eighteen years old and has worked part-time as an assistant to the children's director (a forty-year-old male) for about a year. For the first few months of her employment, she was a model employee, but since that time her attitude and work ethic have changed. She recently sought counsel from the senior pastor and confided in him that the youth director had placed his hand on her thigh in what she described as a very uncomfortable situation during a late-night talk at a staff retreat. She thinks what happened is mostly her fault, and she simply wants to know how to stop feeling angry and dirty. She does *not* want the pastor to tell anyone, nor is she asking for anything to happen to her boss. She just wants biblical counsel.

In Scenario 1 where the seventeen-year-old reported an inappropriate interaction with the children's ministry director, the initial reaction would likely be to grab the children's director and pull him into the office to grill him about what happened during the staff retreat. Logical? Yes. Effective? Sometimes. But what about the fact that the young woman reporting the incident asked the pastor to keep it confidential? Isn't there such thing as a clergy–penitent privilege that only the individual can waive? Does her conversation with the pastor fall into this category? Also, how does the fact that she is still a minor play into the discussion? Do her parents need to be involved? And because this is the children's director who is in constant contact with kids—often little ones—is there a mandatory reporting duty requiring church leadership to involve the police or social services?

~

Scenario 2: The church operates a biblical counseling ministry. Although the church does not require any specific payment for its counseling services, it does encourage counselees to pay whatever they can afford to help with costs. Someone has sent an anonymous letter to the church claiming that such payments are illegal and that they subject the counselors to government regulation and licensure.

The situation described in Scenario 2—that of payment for church counseling services—might generate a casual shrug. After all, we've been operating this way for some time, and this is part of our religious practice. If people want to give to help the counseling ministry, who are we to stop them? But one elder wonders aloud during a meeting if there is anything in the law that addresses this point. If so, he asks, should we take steps to modify our practices as long as doing so does not negatively impact the counseling but does provide some legal protection?

~

Scenario 3: The pastor served in a senior teaching role at the same church for thirty years before he recently retired. Over the course of time, the pastor has not merely preached thousands of original sermons, but he also created detailed coursework to train the congregation in biblical counseling. There are introductory courses, courses in marriage counseling, and so on. He recently noticed that the church repurposed his course work and has started an "academy."

The courses that he drafted and taught are being used for students who pay tuition to take this training. Since this was his own work, and since he never charged anyone for the training, he is concerned. He contacts the church about his counseling training materials and seeks to share in the economic return on his own work.

The retired pastor asking if he can share in the revenue generated by the use of his training materials in Scenario 3 makes everyone feel terrible. No one wants to think of the former pastor as money hungry, but he clearly thinks that he owns some or part of the materials that he created and developed over many years. He not unreasonably wants to supplement his retirement income with the money he thinks the church is generating from his thirty years of hard work. But he prepared and wrote each lesson of that material on church computers while he was working for the ministry. Who owns them, and who has a right to future revenue they might generate? Regardless of the answer, is there a way to reach a compromise with the former pastor that would make sense to everyone involved and that could be binding on future heirs? Would a confidential agreement with the pastor on this subject make sense? Does it need to be disclosed to the congregation?

~

Scenario 4: A church located in an industrial park holds Awana club meetings at the church two nights a week. One Awana parent has sent a letter to the church indicating that his child has had recent blood tests that evidence an unusually high level of dangerous toxins. He thinks it may be from pesticides used on the church property or perhaps from chemicals used on the adjacent commercial lots. The parent wants to know what the church knew and when—and how the church will care for his child. The way in which you approach the parent as a pastor offering counsel will affect the way in which the church responds to the concerns of this parent (and the other parents). An insurance company will also be involved. The insurer will not have the same pastoral concerns you will have in giving guidance and counsel.

Scenario 4 makes everyone freeze because we are talking about a child with atypical blood tests and a claim of harmful exposure to toxins while on church property. No one has any idea what to do. Some would like to ignore the letter about the toxins and claim the parent is making a big deal out of nothing—but the child's blood tests were from an actual doctor, and they do show high concentrations of some bad stuff. The janitor claims that the pesticides used on church property are purchased from the local do-it-yourself home center, and he doesn't think it's a big deal. But he admits that he doesn't keep records of what or when he sprays. Is there some sort of requirement to keep such records for a church? Does the fact that it is a religious entity make a difference? How can the church access the list of chemicals used by adjacent landowners? Once it has those records, what should it do with them? Is current environmental testing required now that the issue has been brought to the church's attention? What sort of things do you say to the fearful parent as a member of your congregation—and how does that intersect with the fact this is also a person who may be seeking money from the church?

~

Scenario 5: An individual who last worked for and attended the church over ten years ago has recently posted an online blog about her time there. She claims it is her "time to heal" and alleges that, when she was younger, she was sexually abused by her father (a church member still in good standing) and brought that fact to the attention of church leadership. She writes of the response, "They did nothing except tell me that I should say nothing because it would hurt the church and my father, whom they claim had repented and changed. When I pressed the issue, the church cut my pay and then fired me three weeks later for no reason. They also excommunicated me and said I could never set foot on church property again." In reality, she never raised any abuse allegations with anyone in church leadership, and she was fired for embezzling church funds.

The false claims published on a disgruntled employee's online blog and described in Scenario 5 prompt some angry responses by those who read the blog and the former employee's personnel files. They want to write an online response blasting the contents of the blog to let everyone know that she lied and expose the truth about this rogue employee. Just before that response is posted, someone asks, "Are we sure we can publish something about this former employee that we learned from her personnel file? Aren't employment records confidential? And if we call her a liar, could she sue us for defamation? What if a church member reads the blog and inquires? Can we respond? And what if her father comes to us asking what this is all about and whether she made such accusations in the past to the church? Just how free are we to respond?"

Each of these scenarios should give you pause. Numerous questions should be running through your head as you contemplate what you would do in such situations. Now consider what the conversation may sound like during an elder meeting and multiply the questions that you have by the number of elders in the room. The conversation and confusion can quickly become overwhelming to even the most reasonable believers.

The Church Operates in Two Worlds

The problem is that despite church leadership and members being Christians, they operate in a secular world. This is not theocratic Israel (and it is not even early America when people and the government tended toward a Christian worldview). We live in a fallen, secular, truth-suppressing world. And those in the church are not immune from pursuing selfish endeavors, making false accusations, or simply misinterpreting events. Further, even when the issue is not one of conflict but instead relates to government bureaucracy and complex rules governing churches, corporations, and nonprofits, the layers of statutes one must wade through come from the minds of fallen men and women, many of whom do not know what it is like to operate an organization in the real world.

Trying to operate a local church in this world leads us to seek God's guidance. Perhaps the best place to find an answer to our question about the relationship between the church and a local lawyer can be found in the book of Proverbs. Proverbs 12:15 tells us, "The way of a fool is right in his own eyes, but a wise man listens to advice." Proverbs 11:14 states, "Where there is no guidance, a people falls, but in an abundance of counselors there is safety." And the well-known truth in Proverbs 15:22 advises, "Without counsel plans fail, but with many advisers they succeed."

When the Law Is at Issue, Ask a Lawyer

While there are many different applications to the general truth that believers would do well to seek good counsel before making important decisions, it can safely be said that a local church would be wise to seek good legal counsel when faced with situations that potentially have legal ramifications. Also, keep in mind that establishing a relationship with a lawyer does not mean handing over decision-making to an outsider. An experienced lawyer simply brings one perspective that should be considered along with many others.

Some may argue that establishing a relationship with a local lawyer is simply lacking trust in God. This sort of argument may sound "godly" but is in fact foolish. When a Christian landlord gets a call from a tenant in the middle of the night telling him that the sink pipe burst and water is flooding the apartment, the landlord doesn't just go back to bed and pray for God's healing hand on the pipe. He calls a plumber. If the landlord has any sense about him, he has that plumber's name already plugged into his phone for exactly this type of emergency. He has planned ahead, vetted a number of different plumbers, and has one or two on his list of trusted tradesmen. Or he has hired a management company so that he doesn't even get the call in the middle of the night. Does the landlord pray? Of course. But he also acts with wisdom and practicality.

In numerous Bible passages, God instructs wise people to plan ahead. He points to the ant that stores up in the summer to have food for the winter (Proverbs 6:6–8). He advises those who would follow him to consider how a builder first plans for a project and counts the cost before deciding to take action (Luke 14:28–30). He instructs individuals to first "prepare" before building a house (Proverbs 24:27). In short, it is profitable to plan ahead (Proverbs 21:5).

Even a bird doesn't just sit around with its beak open hoping that a worm will drop in; it gets up early to look for food. *Planning ahead is God's plan for his children.* The only warning the Bible gives about such planning is that we must not assume God is not in control or that there is any way for us to thwart his purposes (Job 42:2; Proverbs 16:9). Likewise, we must not assume what tomorrow will bring, as that is for the Lord to know (James 4:13–15). But for his glory we are to trust him and prayerfully plan. As my pastor once said when talking about trusting God during the global COVID-19 pandemic, "Trust God, but wash your hands."

A well-known instance of wise planning is found in the life of David, a man after God's own heart (1 Samuel 13:14). In 1 Samuel 17:40, David takes the time to choose five stones to carry with him to his fight with Goliath. He plans ahead for the battle, knowing that God is in control but also recognizing that God requires prudent action. Note that David does not simply close his eyes and grab the first rocks his hands touched. He makes sure that they are "smooth" before he affirmatively "chooses" them. Also note that David "put[s] them in his shepherd's pouch" (1 Samuel 17:40). He figures he will need them, but he saves them for the right time. Only when Goliath "arose and came and drew near" did David reach into his bag for a stone (1 Samuel 17:48–49). David trusted in the Lord, which led to his wise planning and gave him the victory.

Forging a relationship with a local lawyer is also a way to trust in God's provision while wisely planning ahead. Church leaders would do well to recognize that there are likely thousands of laws that impact their operations. There are legal issues that impact business operations, laws concerning insurance, business formation, and employment, and even local laws relating to licensing. There are also legal issues that may be unique to the counseling ministry of a church, such as laws concerning the way private information learned from a counselee is handled, laws impacting how to communicate sin to a spouse, an employer, or a congregation, laws concerning licensing and what may be said in counseling, and laws that seek to restrict what is taught concerning human sexuality.

Even if church leaders or counselors are not aware of every law out there, they do exist. Are some of those laws difficult to read? Do some seem like they have been written in an unknown language? Do they sometimes present a complicated maze that seems to require mental gymnastics to land on the right answer? Yes to all of the above. That is precisely why it is prudent for a church to establish a relationship with a local lawyer.

Find a Lawyer Who Knows the "Right" Law

At this point, you might be wondering why I keep using the term *local lawyer* instead of just *lawyer*. That's because each state has different laws, and although there is quite a bit of overlap, no two states are identical. For example, I live in California and the laws currently on the books fill volumes and volumes. I'll never forget a conversation I had with a colleague who had just transferred to California from Texas to practice law. He held up a tiny book in one hand (the Texas code) and a massive book in the other (the California code) and shook his head in disbelief.

There are so many laws that I often tell even my most prudent and well-financed corporate clients that they are probably (and unknowingly) in violation of a handful of laws at any given point in time. There are simply too many for most organizations to keep up with, and they are constantly being modified. That's why you need a local lawyer.

Still don't get it? Think about a situation where you might have an electrical problem at home. Unless you are trained, it's dangerous to approach that problem on your own. You're going to call a local electrician. That local electrician will not only know how to fix the problem, but he will know the local rules regarding home improvements, permits, and fees. Reduce the risk. Get it done right.

Use a Lawyer Before Problems Arise

Once you've decided that your church needs to establish a relationship with a lawyer, what does this relationship between a local church and a local lawyer look like? Again, there is no specific answer that is equally applicable or "correct" for every church, but these are some guidelines for your church to consider.

It is my strong belief that if finances and circumstances allow it, a church should establish a relationship with a lawyer *prior* to problems arising. Do not think of a lawyer as someone who only can help with legal disputes. An experienced lawyer can be instrumental on a variety of issues. In other words, even when things seem to be running fine, it is a good idea to seek legal counsel. It's like David putting the stones into his shepherd's bag for use when needed. (As many moms have said when overpacking for their children, "Better to have it and not need it than need it and not have it!") He chose five smooth stones in advance, even though God decided that he needed to use only one to kill Goliath.

Likewise, the smartest way to spend legal fees is often for prevention. I have handled numerous trials, arbitrations, and mediations, and I can tell you that addressing potential issues *before* they turn into major problems is a far less expensive way to handle things than simply waiting until a lawsuit is filed or the government issues a notice of violation.

Litigation, the whole process of being sued and going to court, is expensive. While the expense will vary from circumstance to circumstance, it will be far more than you anticipate. Every time you pay a legal bill, it will feel like you are pouring money down the drain. The goal of the defendant in a lawsuit is to stop paying money—and you are the "defendant" if you are being sued. If you win, the only thing you typically "win" is the right to stop paying money. And since most church money comes from God's faithful people seeking to rightly steward their finances and support the church, Christian leaders would do well to plan ahead so as to avoid wasting precious resources that God has entrusted to the church.

While the early and initial contact with a lawyer may be simply to establish a relationship, you may be surprised at how many of those meetings lead to discussions surrounding the organizational structure of the church, the need to update bylaws and handbooks, employee issues, insurance questions, key contracts with church vendors, and financial stewardship matters, each of which has legal implications. In other words, be proactive. Seek a lawyer.

How to Find the "Right" Lawyer

But how do you go about choosing a lawyer? Just like David "chose" certain stones among many, it is important for a church to carefully select legal counsel. You may have heard the old joke: "What do you call a thousand lawyers on the bottom of the ocean? A good start!" While it's funny and tongue-in-cheek, there is a nugget of truth in the joke. There are literally thousands of lawyers to choose from, and many of them would be a terrible fit. Just like David didn't simply pick up any stone, the local church should not assume that any lawyer will do.

To begin, keep in mind that not all lawyers do the same thing. There are lawyers who handle disputes, and there are lawyers who handle transactional matters. There are lawyers who counsel employers, and there are lawyers who work only on the side of disgruntled employees. There are lawyers who are well-versed in nonprofit law, and there are lawyers who specialize in cybersecurity issues.

That being the case, the first thing a church must do when considering a relationship with one or more lawyers is to determine what the church needs. The answer to that question is simple. The local church needs an experienced, trusted legal advisor who can guide them through basic legal issues but who also knows when the issue falls outside of his particular area of expertise. Obviously, if the church is already facing a specific legal issue, leaders need to look for someone specializing in that area.

To find such a lawyer, the first place a church can look is inside its own walls. Committed Christian lawyers are seeking to serve God through their jobs (1 Corinthians 10:31). So long as they can avoid conflicts (such as significant relationships with opposing parties, having an interest in a vendor the church is using on a matter requiring legal counsel, or being a witness to the situation at issue), lawyers with a vested interest in the church and the advancement of the gospel may be well-suited to help.[1] Also, their commitment to the church will often result in lower legal bills than others who treat the church as just another client. However, care should be taken when looking for a lawyer inside the church. You may indeed have a church member who happens to be a lawyer, but he might not be a very good one. Or he may be the type who will be offended if not called upon for assistance in every matter. He also may not understand the difference between helping a church and helping a private, secular organization with a large legal budget. Unmet expectations are often highlighted when it comes to legal bills, which is why they

1. In addition to these hypothetical conflict scenarios, when a new client forms a relationship with a law firm, the first thing the law firm will do is run a "conflicts check." The name of the new client and the opposing party in the litigation will be compared to a list of all the parties that the law firm has ever previously represented. A lawyer often cannot take the side opposite a previous client. If the party suing you was previously a client of the law firm, the law firm may have a conflict of interest.

should be addressed up front to avoid misunderstandings. (Do not assume a discount without first addressing it.) Choosing a Christian lawyer from within the local church is a decision that must be made on a church-by-church, lawyer-by-lawyer basis.

If you do not have any "in-house" lawyers whom you can call upon, look outside the church walls. Seek referrals. Look up evaluations. Speak to former clients if possible. As a general rule, it is prudent for a church to know at least two good lawyers, one who specializes in transactional and regulatory issues (corporate governance) and one who specializes in dispute resolution (a litigator). If that is not feasible, simply look for one experienced, trustworthy lawyer who knows when and how to make referrals when needed. Keep in mind that this doesn't mean the church has to retain the lawyers. The idea is to simply establish a relationship so that they can be called upon when the need arises. Just like a good plumber.

"That's all well and good," you might say, "but how are we supposed to evaluate lawyers?" The same way you evaluate any other tradesman or professional—you meet them, ask questions, speak to others who have used them, and pray about it. You want to be comfortable with the lawyers you choose, and you need to understand them when they speak. Avoid lawyers who speak too much "legalese" or who do not seem to have a knack for explaining things well. If the client does not understand the lawyer's strategy, the client needs a new lawyer.

For the church, at least two other aspects must be taken into consideration when making such a selection. The first is that the lawyer must understand who his client is—and the church leaders need to respect that relationship. There are too many church leaders who think of themselves as the client when, in reality, the organization is the client. Such confusion and overlap can lead to uncomfortable conflicts and hurt feelings. A good lawyer will always establish proper boundaries up front, letting everyone know that he will act in the best interest of the church (as opposed to trying to please everyone involved or protecting the individual interests of specific members).

The second thing a church should consider is whether it would be well-served by a Christian lawyer. Although many Christian lawyers may be unsuitable choices because they are incompetent or have no experience in the particular area at issue, there are times when having sound theology consistent with that of the church allows the lawyer to better advance church positions. In other words, sometimes it takes a Christian lawyer to understand the spiritual and theological reasoning behind certain decisions.

I have handled numerous matters for Christian organizations that have been sued by former employees who also claim to be Christians. Some of these situations required insurance to kick in to provide a lawyer for the organization. While some insurance policies allow for clients to select their own counsel, others are unclear. In those situations, I have sometimes been engaged on the side to confer with lawyers for the insurance company. I can tell you from experience that it is puzzling to non-Christian lawyers why, for example, the church or Christian organization would decide initially to take a less-than-aggressive approach in litigation with a plaintiff (the person suing) who claims to be a Christian. Or, if the purported Christian is suing the church and not acting like a Christian, a non-Christian attorney may not understand why an initial letter back to the plaintiff may call for repentance and reconciliation as opposed to coming out with legal guns blazing. The point is that God calls for Christians to act in certain ways in their dealings with Christians and non-Christians, whether in the legal arena or not. Having a believing lawyer can sometimes keep things on God's track.

More Questions to Consider

The whole point of this book is to provide counseling for you to be wise about ministry and about your church. And while our focus is primarily upon the work of the biblical counselor, we also know that much biblical counseling is done by church leaders. Additionally, some churches and individuals operate biblical counseling ministries as separate organizations. If you are still not convinced that a lawyer can help your church, perhaps the following questions will cause you to reconsider.

- Are you unsure how your church is set up in terms of governing documents or as a religious nonprofit? Does your church have bylaws that need updating?
- Does your church have employees? Are they classified as exempt or nonexempt, or do you know the difference? Are they paid hourly or by salary? Are time records kept? Do you provide the required meal and rest breaks and time off? Do staff members go on retreats? Are they paid for that time?
- Does your church have an employee manual? When was the last time it was updated?
- If you do have governing documents and/or an employee manual, does your church leadership know what those documents contain? Are they following those policies (or do they even understand them)?
- Does your church run a school of any sort during the week? Is the school affiliated with the church in any way? Are there clear legal separations between the two entities and, if not, is there a good reason why not? If someone were to sue the school and then claim that the church is also responsible, what would be your response?
- Does the church run a coffee shop or bookstore that is open to the public? Are they operated in a way that might jeopardize the church's nonprofit status?
- Does the church own or lease land? Does the church allow a pastor to live on church-owned property? Is the church contemplating building projects, fundraisers, or additional real estate investments? Does the church allow third parties to use its facilities? Does the church allow the public on its property? Does the church have single-gender bathrooms?

- As part of its fundraising, does the church ever offer prizes, raffles, or giveaways? Does the church donate money it receives from parishioners to other Christian organizations or missionaries? Does the church understand the potential tax implications of such activities?
- Have any sexual assault or sexual misconduct allegations been raised against the church or its leaders—or that supposedly took place on church property or during church activities? Has any allegation of elder abuse or domestic violence been raised?
- Is the church considering changes to employee benefits or compensation packages? Does the church have a standard separation agreement for departing employees? Is the church planning to fire someone who has been a problem employee?
- Has any allegation of embezzlement of church funds been raised? Are you wondering whether certain expenditures are appropriate or legal?
- Does the church have problematic neighbors? Are they businesses or individuals? Do those individuals have the propensity to complain to the local government about church activities or zoning issues?
- Has anyone contacted the church through an attorney? Has anyone recommended an independent investigation stemming from accusations against church employees?
- Has the church been shut down by the government? Are you not convinced that the government has that authority? Are you wondering what the consequences might be if you refuse to follow orders?
- Does your church offer biblical counseling? Does the church require consent/waiver forms for counseling? (See chapter 9 for a sample consent form.) Is it clear that the counselors are operating under the supervision of church leadership as part of the practice of religion? Are your

counselors certified or trained properly? What would your response be if someone were to claim that your counselors must be licensed by the state?

Now that you've read this, you may feel worse than when you started. Your mind has been filled with lots of new, dangerous, and scary situations that probably had never crossed your mind before. But do not be paralyzed with fear. Take heart. You know that our Lord is sovereign (Colossians 1:16–17). He is good (Psalm 34:8). His good purpose will be accomplished (Romans 8:28). And that purpose just might include having a lawyer assist the church. A good relationship with the right lawyer can help you avoid conflicts and difficulties, which can make it so much easier to do justice, to act in kindness, and to walk humbly before God (Micah 6:8).

To-Do List

- ❐ Find out whether your church has a relationship with a local lawyer.
- ❐ If you are in church leadership and your church already has a relationship with a lawyer,
  - ❐ check the status of the lawyer's law license. (This is typically a quick Internet search or inquiry with the state bar organization.)
  - ❐ inquire to be sure this lawyer is able to help your church in all the areas where it may need help. (If there are pending or anticipated issues, they would be good areas for inquiry.)
  - ❐ make sure that the relationship between the lawyer and the church (and its leaders) is clear to all parties.
- ❐ If you are not in church leadership and your church already has a relationship with a lawyer, encourage the leaders to take the above steps.
- ❐ If your church does not yet have a lawyer, begin the process of finding one (or encourage church leadership to do so).

- ❒ If it seems wise, first consider lawyers within your congregation.
- ❒ If you decide not to work with a lawyer from your church, research to find suitable lawyers from outside the congregation.
- ❒ Carefully evaluate the lawyers whose names you have collected. Pray and then select one or more lawyers for your church.

❒ Have a local lawyer draft or review a consent to counsel form that can be used in biblical counseling (see p. 250 for an example).

❒ Ask a local lawyer what he would advise in terms of an initial document review, such as employment agreements, bylaws, and organizational documents. Determine the cost for such a review.

CHAPTER 5
Business Formation and Insurance of Your Counseling Ministry

Edward Charles Wilde

In this chapter we are going to discuss three issues. The first is the types of business structures you may wish to consider in structuring your counseling ministry. We will provide a brief explanation as to how these business structures work and what advantages and disadvantages these structures could provide. Secondly, we will review the general sorts of exposure (liability) which you will face in a counseling ministry. We will provide some insight as to how the business structures might provide a level of protection when faced with such exposure. Thirdly, we will consider how insurance might provide financial assistance when you are faced with exposure.

You might think that you do not need to consider protecting yourself from a lawsuit because you won't do anything "wrong." While there are many things you can do to avoid exposure, no matter how careful you may be, being careful is not a perfect strategy. As one lawyer I used to work with was fond of saying, "Anyone who can afford the filing fee can ruin your day." And, of course, there are many lawyers who would be happy to take a case.

For another thing, biblical counseling frequently involves difficult and deeply personal matters. A counselee may not like what we say to them. We have all seen anger, deceit, and threats when we explain that Christ insists that they end an adulterous relationship, return something they stole, or forgive an injury. Or a counselee may feel embarrassed or become threatening if a counseling matter turns into a public call for repentance. A counselee who feels they have been treated badly may then initiate a lawsuit. Thus, while we earnestly wish to avoid a lawsuit, we cannot prevent one. And if one arises, we can't guarantee that you will prevail in court.

All of this could lead you to fear that you are beginning the counseling relationship with one foot in the courthouse. But you should put that fear aside. To begin, rest in the knowledge that God is sovereign and good. Next, be reassured that there are wise measures you can take to protect yourself and your ministry from legal trouble. In chapter 9, we will discuss means to avoid the basis for a lawsuit. In this chapter, we will look at methods to protect the resources of your ministry if you are in fact made a defendant in a lawsuit.

With few exceptions, civil lawsuits (that is, noncriminal cases) involve only an order to pay money. If you are sued, you will be sued on a claim to pay someone else money. Thus, the question is, How do I best protect my assets and those of my ministry? And please do not think of this as some sinful concern. People provide you assets so that you can perform ministry. If those assets are spent on litigation, the money will not go toward your ministry. Protecting those assets is a means to protect the continued existence of the ministry.

Part 1: How Choosing the Correct Business Form Can Help Protect Assets

You are faced with a number of choices when it comes to business formation. A counseling ministry can be part of a local church. It can be a wholly separate entity. It can be a separate entity controlled by a local church. How you structure the ministry should be a matter of deliberate decision. Most likely, you simply never thought about the issue. In that case, the general laws of your state have already made the decision for you. That default decision may not be a good fit for your aims or circumstance. So understand this: you are always making a decision about the form of the business. You can make this decision after careful consideration, or you can make this decision by letting the default law decide for you.

It is our counsel that you make this decision after careful consideration of your options. As we explained in chapter 4, you should make these decisions in consultation with a local lawyer. This discussion is to explain to why business formation is important and what sort of questions you should consider.

Options for Setting Up a Business

We will demonstrate the difference between a general partnership and a limited liability company and give you some examples of how business formation works and how it functions to protect assets.

Assume you own a restaurant. In a restaurant, there are activities which have the potential for injury: You have servers walking about carrying heavy trays filled with thick glass and knives and hot food on ceramic plates. There can easily be food or fluid on the ground. There are people who are not paying attention as they go here and there. And you are giving everyone food—food which is capable of passing on a life-threatening illness. One night of undercooked pork and you could be facing millions of dollars in liability. Business can be dangerous.

If you just open up your restaurant and don't take any special steps, you are running a "sole proprietorship." If you open it with a partner and you have no special documents, you are running the restaurant as a general partnership. Let's say your sole proprietorship is sued and you lose. All of your assets are on the line. If you lose, everything you own—your house, your car, your retirement account—is exposed to judgment.

Now let's consider an alternative scenario. Rather than just settle for a partnership, you decide to create a corporation. The owners of a "for-profit" corporation would be anyone who owns the stock. If you owned a restaurant, you would almost certainly have a "for-profit" corporation. Corporate ownership allows many owners to pool their money so that the business could expand beyond the resources of any one person. It also makes it possible to split ownership and control. If you are a partner in a business, you own it, and you are also responsible for controlling it. But if you buy stock in Apple, you have no duty to make decisions about technical designs or hiring programmers.

A nonprofit corporation, as we will explain, does not have stock ownership. Instead, money is pooled not to make money but to pursue some important interest (like running a church). The corporation can pay an employee a salary, but the purpose of the business is not to make money for stockholders.

In addition to pooling resources, a corporation also has the significant advantage of creating a difference between your personal assets and the assets of your business. So let's say that you have formed a corporation with other owners and have started that restaurant. You do all of the things necessary to maintain your corporation. Your corporation owns and runs your restaurant. If your business is sued and you lose in this circumstance, the corporation can lose everything, but your personal assets—your own house, car, and such—cannot be touched. You lose the restaurant, but you can still go home.

Usually. But we will get back to that in a moment.

Kinds of Entities

A corporation is a mechanism to share ownership of a business among multiple people. The ownership is divided among "shares" in the corporation. A share grants an ownership in the business, but it does not give you possession of anything in that business. You may be permitted to vote on certain decisions or to share in the profits.

The law treats a corporation as a "person." The corporation can sue and be sued. The corporation can hold property, enter into contracts, and pay taxes. Corporations cannot vote, but corporations can have a kind of birth or death.

If you're running a small business, it is often unnecessary to form a full-blown corporation. There are variants on the corporate form that could be a good fit for a counseling ministry, including the Limited Liability Company (LLC), which is the type you are most likely to use, and the religious nonprofit corporation. We will look at these two types of entities below, and then we'll note the kinds of protection these business structures provide as we consider the various forms of liability you and your ministry could face.

An LLC is like a simplified version of a corporation. It acts like a corporation by creating another "legal person" that can be sued separately from the employees. You could be a "member" of the LLC and also be an employee. The word *member* refers to ownership in an LLC. Instead of issuing shares, ownership of the LLC is divided into percentages, which are divided among members. An LLC also offers tax advantages.

Depending upon your circumstance, some or all of the people on the counseling staff could be members. It is not necessary to be a member of the LLC to be an employee of the LLC. So the LLC could have two members and ten employees. The decision as to whether to make someone a member or an employee depends upon what sort of control that person is to have over the organization. Members control the organization; employees only work in the organization.

An LLC provides some protection against liability—hence the name, limited liability company. Thus, if you run a food truck and someone eats a bad taco, you might lose the taco truck, but you won't lose your home. LLCs are relatively easy to form and maintain, and they are the choice of most small business owners.

Alternatively, a religious nonprofit corporation is a corporation that doesn't issue stock, is not really owned, exists for a religious purpose, and does not pay taxes. In very narrow circumstances, it provides liability protection for negligent actions of directors while they perform work within the scope of the corporation's stated purpose.

The directors of the nonprofit corporation direct the decisions. You may decide, for instance, to have the leaders in the local church be the directors of the counseling corporation. You could have the counselors all be merely employees.

It is important to understand that one group of people will control the business and another group of people will work for the business. It is possible for a person to control the business and work for the business. It is also possible for one person to control and another person to be an employee. These decisions will depend upon your particular circumstance and who will be involved. There is no "right answer" for this division; it depends upon your people and your circumstance.

Which should you choose? In all but the most remarkable circumstances, a normal corporation is unnecessary for your concern. Thus, the choice is between an LLC and a religious nonprofit corporation. These decisions will help control the exposure of your ministry: exposure to tax liability, governmental control, lawsuits from third parties (including counselees), etc.

Question: How would the LLC/nonprofit relate to a local church?

Someone is wondering, *Where does the local church come into this decision?* The answer to that question depends. First, the local church is almost certainly a nonprofit religious corporation itself. Most churches are nonprofit corporations. The counseling ministry could just be something the church does, like Sunday morning service.

Let us assume that there is good reason to form a separate entity to undertake the counseling. That new entity Biblical Counselors, LLC (or religious nonprofit corporation—it does not make a difference for this illustration) could be a completely stand-alone entity. It may have no relationship with any church or other ministry. As we'll see in other places in this book, the protections afforded to a religious organization will be easiest to claim if the counseling ministry is connected to a local church. But we understand that sometimes such a connection is not possible.

You will need to make a decision as to whether the new Biblical Counselors, LLC, has a direct connection to a local church or is a completely stand-alone entity. The question is not one of business entity formation but rather of wisdom and spiritual leadership.

The law permits a few different ways in which there could be a connection between Biblical Counselors, LLC, and the local church. For instance, a pastor from a local church could also be a member of the LLC or a director of the nonprofit. You could even create a sort of "subsidiary" relationship to the local church. A subsidiary corporation is sort of like a child.

When you make these decisions, you must answer a few questions: What sort of legal relationship (if any) do you want between the counseling ministry and the local church? What sort of spiritual oversight do you want for the counseling ministry? What sort of leadership do you want in the counseling ministry (will the ministry be managed by everyone involved or only a few people)?

After you have an idea of what sort of relationship you desire between the counseling ministry and a local church (from complete control by a local church to only a relationship where the church refers people to the ministry), an attorney can help you create the legal structures which will fulfill your aim. This is where your local lawyer will help. In your discussions with the lawyer, explain what sort of oversight you want for ministry. You can say we want this local church or these people from that church to direct the ministry. A good lawyer will ask the right questions to help you think through these questions.

The lawyer should ask you a number of questions, such as what concerns you have about exposure to lawsuits from counselees or other people. The lawyer will ask you questions about taxes. This entails questions about income and expenses. Like any operation, a biblical counseling ministry must think through its finances, and tax exposure is a significant financial consideration for the ministry as a whole and for those running the ministry and working in the ministry.

This is an unavoidable aspect of human relationships. As soon as you enter into any interaction with any other human being, you are becoming exposed to some level of danger.[1] You might hurt someone, you might disappoint someone, and you may also fail to do or not do something which the government has determined you must do or not do. You might find yourself sued by a counselee, or you might find yourself defending a criminal charge brought by the state. You can get in trouble for talking, for not talking, for taking money, for paying money, for investigating, and for not investigating.

Part 2: Types of Threats to Which Your Ministry Is Exposed

In choosing between various business structures, you must consider how that structure will protect against various threats to which your ministry will be exposed. In this section, we will briefly consider types of exposure.

Exposure to the State

In the end, all of your exposure is exposure to the state. The state can take your money and put you in jail—or do both at the same time. Sometimes the state's prosecution is a criminal action; sometimes it is deemed a civil action (because they are seeking money rather than punishment for a crime). The state can also issue an order

1. A lawsuit results from personal or business conflicts. Most lawsuits arise from an unmet expectation and a sense of injustice: The person bringing the lawsuit feels they have been treated unjustly. Thus, relationships which present a possibility of conflict also present the possibility of litigation. And so, you are exposed to the possibility of litigation as soon as you enter into an interaction with another human being. This does not mean that a lawsuit is likely, but it does mean that a lawsuit is possible.

commanding you to do or not do something. Even if you are in a lawsuit between two private individuals, the exposure is ultimately to the state because the state will be the party who enforces the judgment. If you lose a lawsuit and are ordered to pay a judgment, the state can send a sheriff to your business or your bank to take the money. Here we will consider the most common issues when it comes to business—entity structure.

Taxes

A government charges money from people within its jurisdiction, which is called "taxation." Governments are very touchy about taxes. You can be imprisoned for erring when it comes to taxes. (Think of Al Capone.) You can be fined when it comes to taxes. Often both things will happen.

On the subject of taxes, the LLC has advantages and disadvantages compared to the religious nonprofit corporation. One significant advantage of an LLC is that it allows you to "pass through" the taxes and deductions of the business. That means when you have a full-fledged corporation, that corporation is treated like a separate "person" with its own tax issues. As a result, money is effectively taxed twice, once while it is in the corporation's hands and then again when it is paid to shareholders and employees. An LLC basically takes away that first level of taxation so that taxes are paid only once, when money is paid to the "members."

A disadvantage of the LLC is that donations made to your business cannot be treated as tax deductible. In contrast, the creation of a proper religious nonprofit corporation allows those persons who make donations to later treat those donations as deductions on their tax returns.

A religious nonprofit corporation offers a different sort of general tax benefit from the LLC. It does not pay taxes on the income to the corporation when it is received for the particular nonprofit purpose. However, according to the IRS code, "it still may be liable for tax on its unrelated business income. For most organizations, unrelated business income is income from a trade or business, regularly carried on, that is not substantially related to the charitable, educational, or other purpose that is the basis of the organization's exemption."[2] Business income for a counseling ministry could be fees collected from counselees, referral fees paid by a church, fees received for providing training, and so forth.

In addition, there are unique limitations on what you are permitted to do with the money you receive as a nonprofit corporation. A regular corporation, including an LLC, has the freedom to spend its money as the directors see fit. But a nonprofit must pay particular care to how the money is paid out. If a nonprofit errs when it comes to money, it can lose its nonprofit status (and then be forced to pay back taxes, which will come with penalties and fines added).

Other tax considerations have to do with the people you pay to work for your ministry. These people may be determined to be employees or independent contractors. In some jurisdictions (such as California), there are serious restrictions on your ability to classify a particular person as an independent contractor. The designation typically depends upon the nature of the control an employer exercises over the worker. The designation of a person as an employee or an independent contractor has serious implications for tax law.

Whether an LLC or a religious nonprofit corporation is the better option for your ministry will probably depend upon the employees' personal relationship to their work. If the counseling ministry is their primary source of income, and if the ministry will employ just one or two people, then the LLC makes sense because it is better set up for individual taxes. However, if the ministry will employ more people, or if it has a broader mission than just providing one-on-one counseling (and will thus be looking for general donations, as opposed to the "suggested donation" for a particular act of counseling), a nonprofit religious corporation may make more sense.

2. "Unrelated Business Income Tax," IRS, accessed October 24, 2020, https://www.irs.gov/charities-non-profits/unrelated-business-income-tax.

There is not one answer for all circumstances. For instance, being part of a local church provides the greatest degree of protection for counselors if they are faced with a claim for "hate speech" (such as providing counsel respecting sexual behaviors). A local church has the greatest degree of freedom to exercise its religious freedom. But being directly part of a local church also exposes the entire church to the greatest degree of potential liability from a lawsuit. The entire church is exposed when one of its pastors is sued for giving counsel.

You might ask, "How can the same situation provide the most protection and at the same time cause the most exposure?" The protection comes from the constitutional protection for religious practice. This protection is not absolute. And in many lawsuits, the protection for religious practice is being whittled away. The exposure has to do with the church's assets. When the church is sued, everything the church owns is risked in the lawsuit. If the church loses, the church could lose everything it owns.

Let's say you have a separate biblical counselor's LLC. In that case, a court might grant less protection for religious freedom than it would to a local church (if that seems strange, it is because courts can make strange decisions). But the only assets that could be lost would be the assets of the LLC.

Balancing these competing considerations is not easy. Leaders will need to discuss these matters with an accountant and an attorney in light of your ministry's particular needs. And, as explained above, there are related questions concerning the relationship between a counseling ministry and a particular church. The various options, considering taxes, asset protection, and spiritual oversight will need to be weighed.[3]

3. We discuss business structure briefly in chapter 10, in the sections on implementing legal protections with structure and governing documents. One point requires some clarification. There are two related but separate considerations. First, there is the question of business structure: a religious nonprofit or an LLC. Second, there is the question of the relationship between the counseling ministry and a local church. A counseling ministry can be under the umbrella of a local church, or it can be a stand-alone entity. If it is a stand-alone entity, it must be either an LLC or a religious nonprofit corporation. If it is under the umbrella of a local church, there are three

Mandatory Reporting

No form of business entity can protect you from covering up or failing to report known or suspected abuse. We will discuss the question of liability protection below in connection with civil liability, but at this point, realize that a failure to report criminal activity can be a crime—particularly when it comes to child abuse. It is never the work of the church to protect the person who is using ministry as a cloak for preying upon the vulnerable.

Civil Liability

Individuals can also bring an action for liability. Liability asks a simple question: will a court make you give money to someone else? Before we say anything else, let's remember that sometimes courts get things wrong. Sometimes good people lose and bad people win. You need to know this. You can't expect to be free from liability just because you know you will never do anything wrong.

While we hope and pray it never happens, the job of a lawyer *before the lawsuit* is to assume that it will happen. So for the remainder of this chapter, we will assume that you are going to be sued someday by someone.

Liability can become very complex: the topics we are going to cover below in brief are matters which would take years of law school and then years of actual legal practice to understand thoroughly. Rather than try and teach all of the details, we hope to alert you to the sort of problems that can arise. First, we will define some common terms.

Intentional Conduct: There are two basic types of civil (as opposed to criminal) wrongs for which you may be accused—intentional actions and negligent actions. The basic difference is whether you intended to cause an injury. If you intend to cause injury, you have

possibilities: (1) The ministry is simply the function of the local church and has no separate business structure. (2) The ministry is a religious nonprofit, and the local church runs the religious nonprofit. (3) The ministry is an LLC, and the local church is a/the managing member of the LLC.

engaged in an intentional tort. Intentional torts mean something like intentional fraud or purposefully attacking someone else. Notice that the question is not intentional behavior, per se, but intent to cause injury. For example, if you are speeding on the freeway, you are intentionally driving over the speed limit. But if you get into an accident, you are only negligent because you were not intending to cause an injury; you were not intending the outcome. You were only intending the behavior.

There is really no good protection for intentional conduct. If a corporation purposefully commits a bad act, it may even be prosecuted for a crime. Insurance will not protect it from the cost of intentional acts.[4]

Negligent Conduct: We will assume that you will not intentionally hurt anyone, so we will confine our actions to negligence. Think of negligence sort of like an accident. You didn't mean to hurt anyone, but someone was hurt anyway. You had a duty to do something: give good advice, drive your car safely, or keep the floors of your market clean so people don't slip. But, rather than using reasonable effort, you slack off; you're lazy or unconcerned. If you have a duty and you don't use a reasonable effort to perform that duty, you are negligent.

Those running a counseling center, will most likely face accusations for three forms of negligence: (1) You will personally give counsel that is considered negligent; (2) you will fail to properly supervise a counselor who works in the ministry; or (3) you fail to report abuse, and someone will be hurt as the result of not being protected.[5]

What would be negligent advice? The most famous case on that issue is *Nally v. Grace Community Church*. In a nutshell, the argument was that the church was negligent in the counsel it gave to a

4. Like everything in the law, this one is complicated. An insurance policy may pay for the cost of the lawyer who defends you against the allegation of intentional wrong but not pay for the damages awarded by the court.

5. Lee v. Detroit Medical Center, 285 Mich. App. 51, 70 (2009). "As with all other mandated reports, the failure to report when required to do so would be judged under an ordinary negligence standard."

man who was suicidal and then killed himself. The man's family argued that he should have been turned over to a licensed psychologist or psychiatrist. In *Nally*, the California Supreme Court rejected the theory of holding a pastor negligent for giving religious advice. On the other hand, a separate action that involved a minister who "practiced psychotherapy" resulted in a settlement and presumably the payment of money to the plaintiff.[6]

Were a pastor found to be negligent in giving advice, the individual pastor could be held liable for the negligence. If the pastor were working for a nonprofit corporation, the corporation's assets would also be exposed in the lawsuit. This might be a reason that a church would have some separation between the counseling ministry and the church's assets.

Here is a not-impossible scenario that could come up in your counseling ministry:

A couple in an unhappy marriage comes to you. There has been no violence, but there are serious problems. The wife wants to leave because she no longer loves her husband. You tell her that she has no biblical grounds for divorce. The marriage continues, and the husband uses violence. She leaves the church and sues you, claiming that you provided negligent counsel and that she was hurt because of your negligence. Negligent counsel means counsel no reasonable person would give. A good counselor, a "reasonable" (that is, not negligent counselor) would have encouraged her to get a divorce.

In the law, the exact same event might result in several different legal claims. In civil court, the types of claims are called "contract" or "tort." Intentional wrongs and negligent wrongs are "tort" claims. A contract claim differs from tort claims in certain particulars. A contract claim can only arise from an agreement. By way of contrast, torts are rules which apply to all relationships. If a house painter does a bad job, you could sue him for breach of contract. But if a random person vandalizes your house with paint, you could sue for the vandalism (which would be a tort).

6. Fritz v. Vestal, 1994 Ct. Sup. 2921 (1994).

"Breach" of a contract occurs when you have failed to perform a contract. For instance, a counselee might say you had an agreement that you would not tell anyone about his adultery. If you communicate the fact of his adultery, you have "breached" your contract to keep the information private.

Let's say that you have been accused of negligent advice or have been alleged to breach a contract to keep a secret. The lawsuit is filed, and you go to trial.

Imagine the scene: You are not in a church office or a pulpit. Your speech is not being measured by Scripture but by the opinions of twelve random citizens who make up your jury. The jury has heard how you forced this poor woman to continue in a hateful marriage. She was hurt—and you encouraged her to stay.

An Aside: One point of this book is to distinguish the work of a "therapist" from the work of biblical counseling. The biblical counselor gives instruction in Christian discipleship. The therapist has a very different goal, primarily helping the "patient" to become happy in accordance with the "patient's" own definition. Sometimes our counsel does not result in immediate happiness. "Bless those who persecute you" is not a shortcut to what is considered a happy life.

Christian marriage requires a commitment that is foreign to our culture. It requires a struggle with our own flesh to put aside our own self-interest and exhibit self-sacrificing love for another person—even when that other person does not deserve it. With certain exceptions, divorce or separation are not options for us *even when the wider culture would consider it a perfectly appropriate reason to divorce.* So when faced with an unhappy marriage where there is no danger, no adultery, just a lack of love, we will counsel repentance. But when presented to unbelievers, staying in such a marriage may sound sexist, insane, or even abusive.

As you sit in the witness stand, the jury scowls at you. The plaintiff's attorney asks you, "Why did you tell this woman to stay in the marriage?" You answer, "God hates divorce." The plaintiff's attorney says, "So I guess God hates women because my client's life has been misery because of you. Who should be forced to live with such emotional abuse?"[7]

I'm sure you see the disparity. While your advice is perfectly appropriate within the context of biblical Christianity, it is inexplicable in a culture that thinks little of marriage and a great deal of personal ease. No one thinks physical abuse is right, but our culture has very little concern for preserving marriage.

There is thus a conflict between what our culture thinks is good and what our religion requires. If we were being judged on secular standards, biblical counsel would be negligent. That means it would be unacceptable and you would be liable.

However, if the counsel is judged not as therapy but instruction in Christian discipleship, it is permissible because we have a right to give religious instruction, which is not judged on the basis of acceptable therapy. This defense was discussed in chapters 2 and 3. A court will not penalize a rabbi or an imam or a pastor for giving direction that is not the "best" direction for that particular religion.[8] If a pastor denies the Trinity, the court will not remove the heretic from the pulpit.

If we get into the business of *psychotherapy*, we will find ourselves being judged by the standards applicable to therapists. A psychotherapist can give negligent counsel. And negligent advice has consequences. You can't use an LLC or nonprofit religious

7. When we consider matters such as "emotional abuse," we come upon a phrase which is notoriously vague and difficult to define. Since the word *abuse* is used, we immediately think of grave physical injury or sexual assault. But is a neglectful husband the moral equivalent of someone who beats or rapes his wife? Certainly, people can act in ways that are emotionally abusive, and in such a situation there is sin. The biblical understanding of love in no way condones or excuses hateful speech, degrading speech, or the like. For this reason, it is wiser for us to use biblical terminology and to avoid vague phrases like "emotional abuse." Unrepentant cruelty or degradation of a spouse is a serious sin and could lead to a public call for repentance as proscribed in Matthew 18 (tell it to the church).

8. Admittedly, the legal environment is fast becoming more difficult. However, our best legal protection will remain in making plain that we are providing religious instruction.

corporation to protect you from personal negligence. (These terms will be explained below.)

So you start to see that the questions of business formation and asset protection, and even whether you can be named in a particular lawsuit, become quite complicated.

Question: Should a biblical counselor ever refer a counselee to a psychiatrist?

A psychiatrist is a medical doctor. There are serious medical conditions involving the nervous system that can present as psychological problems. Where there is a medical condition, it should be treated by a medical doctor. A trained psychologist would be one to perform tests to determine if a particular person is suffering from a disease such as Alzheimer's disease. Whether a biblical counselor has a legal "duty" to refer a particular person to a psychiatrist or a psychologist is a complicated question and would depend upon a number of factors.

A full discussion of these issues is beyond the scope of this book. If you have a question about the legal necessity of such referrals, you should ask your church's lawyer.

Negligent Supervision

Although the corporate status of your ministry will not save you from the consequences that arise from negligence, it may offer you some protection from a charge of failing to supervise another counselor. In such an action, the individual counselor and the entity will both be sued. The counselor will be sued for giving the negligent advice, and the entity will be sued for not properly supervising the one giving the negligent advice.

As a director or managing member of the entity, you may be shielded from personal liability for such negligent supervision. What this means is that the entity would have to pay money from its own resources, but that you as an individual apart from the entity would not be personally liable. You might save your house and lose the ministry.

Failing to Report

Finally, we come to the related claim of failing to report. The danger here is all too real. Many churches and church-related enterprises have failed on the matter of reporting known or suspected abuse. The most famous of these stories concerned the Roman Catholic Church, but subsequent stories have implicated a number of Protestant churches. An exposé in the *Houston Chronicle* related a horrifying number of Southern Baptist Convention congregations that had failed to report or had covered up instances of physical and sexual abuse.[9]

Such a problem will begin with a report; it might even be a mere rumor at first. You hear that a child is being or has been abused. Either you or the counselor under your direction fails to report the abuse to the authorities. If you failed to report the abuse, it would not only subject you to potential criminal penalties from the state; it will also subject you to a civil action for negligence.

Contract Claims

In addition to being sued for committing a "tort" (the sort of rules which apply to everyone), you may find yourself a party to an action for breach of contract. Let us say you contract to rent some space for your counseling center, and it becomes financially impossible to keep the space. If the lease is with the LLC (or religious nonprofit), the landlord has the right to sue the LLC. You might lose the assets of the LLC, but you will protect your personal assets.

An important caveat: When you lease a space or otherwise undertake an obligation through the entity, you may be asked to sign a "personal guaranty." It is essential that you understand the

9. Robert Downen, Lise Olsen, and John Tedesco, "Abuse of Faith," *Houston Chronicle*, February 10, 2019, https://www.houstonchronicle.com/news/investigations/article/Southern-Baptist-sexual-abuse-spreads-as-leaders-13588038.php.

risk signing such a guarantee entails. A personal guarantee is an agreement that you personally will pay the debt if the entity fails to perform the obligation. In such a case, you lose some of the benefit of having an LLC or a corporation.

Another problem with personal guarantees is the lack of certain protections—limitations on the landlord's ability to collect—that are provided to an entity. A personal guaranty may contain language that deprives you of defenses belonging to the entity. Use caution if you are ever asked to sign a personal guaranty.

Summary

When you decide the business form of your ministry, you will need to evaluate your finances, taxes, employment, and liability exposure. In a short space such as this, we can only alert you to the existence of these issues, not provide you with answers. These questions can only be answered in the context of an individual assessment made with an attorney and an accountant. Proper resolution of these issues will be important to the management of your ministry.

As we have seen, the counseling ministry is potentially exposed to claims from the government and claims from individual counselees. Your defenses to claims by the government will be your rights to free religious practice and speech under the First Amendment. Your protection for "liability" (damages paid in a lawsuit) may involve First Amendment protections, but it will also involve other considerations that have been raised in this chapter.

It is true that First Amendment protections for speech and the practice of religion are more clearly protected when a counseling ministry is operating as a ministry of a church. This does not mean that only churches have protection; rather, like all things with the law, the nature of the protection becomes complicated when a ministry is a separate entity from a church. Provided that you make plain the nature of the counseling and religious discipleship (as opposed to unlicensed "therapy"), you will have access to First Amendment arguments.

There is no "right answer" when it comes to deciding whether to have a counseling ministry exist as a separate entity or be part of a church. You will have to weigh the realistic options and considerations of your particular circumstance. In short, there is not a contradiction between saying the First Amendment provides most protection for a church and saying maybe you should form an LLC. But there are different protections and exposures with either decision.

Part 3: Insurance Protections

We've looked at the basics of business formation, the first economic defense against a lawsuit. Now we turn to the second economic defense: insurance.

We read in Exodus 18 that Jethro traveled out into the wilderness to see how things fared with his son-in-law and the great multitude he had led out of Egypt. In verse 13, we learn that "Moses sat to judge the people, and the people stood around Moses from morning till evening." Even in the wilderness, even among a population of delivered slaves who had just seen God's power in destroying Egypt and parting the sea, these people were coming to court in an unending stream. We should not be surprised that courts today are filled with an unending stream of litigants.

The federal courts in 2019 had 286,289 civil filings.[10] In my home state of California, there were 221,090 during the same time period.[11] As for the number of laws, rules, regulations, statutes, cases, and advisory opinions, the number is endless. As the Crime A Day Twitter feed explains, "In 1982, the DOJ attempted to count

10. "Federal Judicial Caseload Statistics 2019," United States Courts, accessed October 24, 2020, https://www.uscourts.gov/statistics-reports/federal-judicial-caseload-statistics-2019.

11. "Federal Judicial Caseload Statistics 2019-Introduction," California Courts, accessed October 24, 2020, https://www.courts.ca.gov/documents/2019-Court-Statistics-Report-Introduction.pdf.

the total number of federal crimes. The WSJ said, 'Since then, no one has tried anything nearly as extensive.'"[12]

A discontented people armed with endless laws will find its way to Moses and will stand about all day awaiting a decision. No corporation or LLC and no releases can keep you from being sued. The release can provide a defense, but a release does not prevent someone from actually filing the lawsuit. (We will explain the use of a release in chapter 9.) Business formation may give you some distance, and a release can provide a defense, but that still means you have to hire a lawyer and pay a lawyer and court costs. Those fees and costs will be tens if not hundreds of thousands of dollars. That means even if you "win," the win will come at a crushing cost.

This is why you need insurance, regardless of your business structure. Insurance is a contract to share risk. The basic model works like this: Suppose it costs $100 to rebuild a house after a fire and that one out of one hundred houses will burn down each year. If one hundred homeowners all paid $1.05 a year, they could pool their money so they would have $105—enough money to rebuild the house and have money for administration and profit for the work of pooling and paying. That is insurance.

Insurance can protect against any sort of loss. Lloyd's of London (which originally started as a coffee shop) has famously insured Jimmy Durante's nose, Betty Grable's legs, and America Ferrera's smile. Among the more common sorts of insurance are car insurance, fire insurance, and life insurance. Of interest to us are various types of coverage that exist to protect those who interact with people and give instruction and hear personal problems.

"Coverage" means the sort of risk the insurance company will cover. The particular coverage will vary a bit from state to state and from insurance company to insurance company. The wording of coverage will change over time. Analysis of the language used in insurance policies is so technical, the interpretation so arcane, that insurance companies actually hire attorneys to read their own

12. "A Crime A Day," accessed October 24, 2020, https://twitter.com/CrimeADay.

policies for the insurer to give advice as to whether a claim is covered or not.[13]

You don't need to know the jargon of insurance coverage. What you do need to understand is the usefulness of insurance and how to obtain the correct insurance.

What the Insurer Pays

An insurance policy consists of an insurer and an insured. You will be the insured. A policy provides two different types of protection. It pays the defense costs, including the cost of the attorney, and it pays any damages claim.

When you are sued, the first thing you need is an attorney. As I write this chapter, I am awaiting an installer to replace a wall oven. I do not doubt that someone reading this chapter will wonder why I would ask for help to install an oven, but trust me, my mechanical skills demand the assistance of another with actual knowledge and ability. Just as the best person to install a wall oven is someone with expertise in oven installation, the best person to defend you in a lawsuit is someone with expertise in the practice of law.

The law is complex and often nonintuitive. What you can learn about the law from the Internet is routinely wrong, and even when correct, the value of the knowledge is minimal. A common problem with representing a client is the client's mistaken belief that they are helping with an understanding of the law. That does not mean clients are stupid, but that bits and pieces of information do not really help. You should not represent yourself or even try to do so. Do not

---

13. An illustration may help. Insurance policies routinely contain the clause that the insurer will "pay as damages." In California, that clause means that the policy only applies to a tort loss (a car crash or slander) and not to a breach of contract. Stanford Ranch, Inc. v. Maryland Cas. Co., 89 F.3d 618, 624 (9th Cir. 1996), "The two policies at issue in the present case provide coverage only for those sums which the insured becomes 'legally obligated to pay as damages. . . . .' California courts have consistently interpreted this language to cover only tort liabilities and not those liabilities arising in contract." How could any mortal possibly know that interpretation without the magisterium of the court?

try to negotiate your own settlements. If there is a lawsuit, be wise and have someone with appropriate experience help.

Even meritless lawsuits will sometimes result in a payment being made to the plaintiff. The reason for such payments is that lawsuits are expensive. The cost of a trial can easily exceed $100,000. A completely innocent defendant might pay $40,000 to settle the lawsuit because it would be cheaper to pay $40,000 than to pay $100,000.[14] It is not unusual for legal fees to exceed the value of the underlying claim. Thus, an insurance policy that only paid the cost of a verdict but did not pay for the lawyer to defend the case would be of limited value. Therefore, to make insurance for liability protection worthwhile, insurance policies pay for the lawyer to defend the case.

The insurance company's payment for a lawyer is based on the possibility that a claim could be covered by the policy (we will discuss coverage below). It does not matter that the plaintiff's case is utterly fraudulent. What matters is whether the allegations *if true* could potentially result in a covered loss. If you could end up paying money for a loss covered by the policy, the insurer will provide an attorney.[15]

The insurance company usually hires the lawyer for you. On some occasions, you can choose your own counsel. On other occasions, you may need to hire a lawyer in addition to the insurer's chosen counsel. There are also occasions where the insurer has to pay for two different lawyers—one lawyer chosen by the company and one lawyer whom you have chosen. The attorneys' fees and the costs of the lawsuit (filing papers with the court, hiring expert witnesses, etc.) will be paid directly by the insurer (terms and conditions apply). That is coverage for the defense of the lawsuit.

---

14. Another reason to resolve a meritless claim is that juries will believe "the bad guy." I know a pair of lawyers who lost a verdict of over $10 million. The expert witness for the plaintiffs admitted on the stand that the claim was bogus and that his report (the key to the case) was fraudulent. Even knowing that the plaintiff was lying, the jury awarded damages. It happens. All the time.

15. There are many caveats and nuances. As you hear on the commercials, "terms and conditions may apply." They always do.

A second element of the coverage is indemnification for damages. This is what you usually think of when considering insurance. If you lose the lawsuit, the insurance company pays the plaintiff. Again, terms and conditions apply.

The Structure of an Insurance Policy

A policy has two basic elements: coverage grants and exclusions. A coverage grant is the portion of the policy that explains what sort of losses an insurer will cover (car crashes, fires, etc.). These coverage grants can be very precise. For example, there is insurance for business interruption. If you cannot run your business due to fire damage, the insurance would cover the loss of income.

But an issue that arose in 2020 illustrates the difficulty with such a claim. What happens when you cannot run your business due to COVID-19 restrictions? Is your restaurant closed because of the virus or because of the health regulations that shut down your business? If you are closed due to disease, it is covered, but if you are shut down due to regulations, you are not covered.

You will need insurance that covers your practice as a counselor (insurance for giving "negligent" counsel, malpractice). You need insurance to protect against allegations of sexual misconduct (I'm not saying you will engage in such things, but you may be accused). You need insurance for personal injury and insurance for invasion of privacy/slander (coverage for what you say to other people). If your ministry has employees, you will need employment practices insurance. You may need errors and omissions coverage for officers and directors of a business. These coverages will be set forth in different portions of a policy, Coverage A, Coverage B, and so on.

Like the Lord, insurance companies give and take away. For instance, your homeowner's policy may provide coverage for negligently causing injury to someone on your property or even in your truck.[16] However, if you hurt someone while running a business

16. In *Partridge*, the insured filed the trigger mechanism of his pistol at home so that the gun would have a "hair trigger action." The insured took the gun into his Bronco

from your home, the policy would most likely exclude the loss under the "business pursuits" exclusion.

How to Get the Insurance You Need

The interactions between these coverage grants and exclusions from coverage can be complex. The meaning of the provisions may be difficult to track. In addition, you will not know all of the coverage that may be available. Different insurers provide different coverage. Insurers who provide the same type of coverage may have different exclusions.

You do not just need insurance; you need the correct insurance. For this you need the help of an insurance agent, also known as an insurance broker. Not all insurance agents are made equally so you need to do research and choose carefully. You need an agent you can trust, one who will provide you good advice. Be aware that some agents may be "captive," which means they may be permitted to sell insurance only from a certain company. You could be in a circumstance where you need insurance from Company A, but your agent may only sell Company B's product. You need someone who can help you find the right coverage.

To find you the right coverage, the agent needs to understand what you need. Before you go to buy insurance, make a list of all the sorts of things that could go wrong. Ask the advice of other counselors or pastors with greater experience. What sort of problems have they seen? What sort of problems have they heard about? When might you find yourself in court?

It would also be useful to discuss your insurance needs with your attorney and perhaps even your accountant. Take that list to your insurance agent. Ask the agent to find the coverage that will

---

truck and placed it either on his lap or on top of the steering wheel. While the insured was driving, he saw a rabbit crossing the road. He drove off the road onto rough terrain to follow the rabbit. When the truck hit a bump, the gun discharged and caused injury to a passenger in the vehicle. State Farm Mut. Auto. Ins. Co. v. Partridge, 10 Cal. 3d at 97, 97–98. Interinsurance Exchange v. Flores, 45 Cal. App. 4th 661, 669–70 (1996).

protect you. Make sure that the policy does not exclude the grant of coverage you need.[17]

Reading a Policy

First, it may not be profitable to read the policy in full (even though the law presumes that you have). What you need is to talk through the policy with your agent or attorney.

Second, the portion of the policy that you must keep handy is the "declarations page." The dec page is usually a one-page document which contains your name, the name of the insurer, the dates of coverage, the policy limits (the amount of coverage offered), a list of the coverages granted by the policy, and so on. While it is good to keep the entire policy, the dec page should be complete enough that you can reconstruct the entire policy from that single page.

Conclusion

My mother, who is now with the Lord, was a very thoughtful nurse with several special qualifications. She loved medicine. She also worked in critical care and spent every day with people who were deathly ill. Her training to always spot the problem meant that she often saw a worst-case scenario when I merely had a cold. Lawyers can suffer from the same disease. When a business client brings me for advice, my job is to anticipate everything that can go wrong. Yes, 999 out of 1,000 times everything goes fine. The lawyer is there to advise against the 1 out of 1,000 event.

I have never been sued for my biblical counsel. I have had very unhappy counselees, but I have never suffered litigation. Fortunately, litigation is rare. It would be foolish to be overly concerned about litigation. However, it would be equally foolish not to take the simple steps necessary to protect yourself from the unlikely event. Your

17. I once had a case where a new insurance broker found a policy which cost tens of thousands of dollars less than the then current policy. The difference in premium payments was because the coverage and exclusions had changed. The change in coverage ended up costing the client millions of dollars in uninsured losses.

house will almost certainly never burn down, and yet you have fire insurance. This is simply prudent.

While there are no perfect defenses to all trouble, we can still take reasonable—not perfect—precautions. Our work as counselors can create conflict when we seek to increase peace. It will happen. We live on this side of Genesis 3. What we can do is be wise stewards of the resources God provides. By creating the right sorts of business structures and by obtaining necessary insurance, we can best marshal and protect what we have.

To-Do List

- ❒ Evaluate the current status of your counseling ministry: are you better off as part of a local church, or are you better off as an independent LLC? Consider your tax liability, the number and status of your employees, and your vulnerability to lawsuits.
- ❒ Evaluate your insurance needs. Is your current policy adequate, or do you need a better one?
- ❒ Interview potential lawyers and accountants to discuss your business structure issues.
- ❒ Interview and retain an insurance broker who can protect your business.

CHAPTER 6

Termination and Reporting in Church Employment

George Crawford and Edward Charles Wilde

There is no aspect of the Christian life that lies beyond the scope of the Lord's direction. In the third chapter of Colossians, Paul begins with the command to "seek the things that are above, where Christ is." (Colossians 3:1) In the same chapter, he gives instruction to those who are employers and those who are employees (Colossians 3:22–25). Since biblical counseling involves instruction in the Christian life, all of the Christian life, including the way we understand work as employers and employees, is within the scope of that biblical counsel.

Our Christian discipleship includes the way that we organize and fulfill employment relationships in our church and counseling ministry. We certainly cannot expect that we should give counsel to an employee on dealing with a difficult boss and then be that difficult boss for someone in our ministry. Getting one's responsibility as an employer straight and understanding the ways in which church order and legal responsibility interact is critical. Indeed, the scandal in Southern Baptist Churches, as reported in the *Houston Chronicle*, made plain the need to properly manage the church and dismiss dangerous employees.

While not every biblical counselor will have an employment relationship with a church or a counseling center, for some of us, our ministry work as counselors will also be our employment. So we may find ourselves involved in employment litigation if an employee who has been discharged finds a lawyer and sues his former employer.

Handling the termination of an employee—whether pastor, counselor, or receptionist—requires great wisdom and care.

Consider this scenario: the counseling pastor at a local church left under less-than-favorable circumstances, and he moved out of state. The remaining church leadership has considered whether they should post a statement on their website claiming that the pastor's ministry ended due to disqualification. Your input as a board member or your recommendation as a biblical and/or legal counselor has been requested. What should your response be? Which biblical, practical, and legal aspects should be considered?

A level of complication that does not exist for the average employer may arise following dismissal by a church. If a cashier is dismissed from the market, it is a private matter between the cashier and the manager. In contrast, when a member of the pastoral staff is dismissed, there often is a matter of sin (or at least an accusation of sin). A counselor (or pastor) who has committed some sins may be disqualified from ministry, which usually requires an announcement to the congregation that the counselor has been removed from that position.

If the counselor refuses to repent, there will likely be another level of reporting to the congregation.

In such an instance, there will not merely be the loss of employment but also the matter of "telling the church" (Matthew 18:17). For instance, let us say that a counselor has been found guilty of sexual impropriety that arose in the context of marriage counseling, and the counselor will not repent of the sin. This creates a consideration that is not present in the typical nonchurch context. The counselor is dismissed and the misconduct, which in a secular context would have been a relatively private matter, is told to the congregation. If the counselor is unrepentant, we are told to treat such a one as "a Gentile and a tax collector" (Matthew 18:17).

Making publicly disparaging comments about one's employment is a matter for litigation. But when it comes to church discipline, telling the church is required. (And while not every reason for discharge of an employee would involve a question of sin, it is certainly a possibility.) An unrepentant counselor might see trouble coming and so hire an attorney before the matter proceeds to a public report. What do you do? Managing the church is hard enough; finances are always tight, and there certainly is not enough money for lawyers. You might also fear that you personally could be responsible for paying money to the counselor who has sinned.

Due to the trouble which can flow from seeking to make some public report of sin (or even discharging an employee), some churches may keep matters quiet. But would that be biblically faithful? Another church may go beyond biblical fidelity and, in anger, make unnecessary public reports to discredit or hurt the offending counselor. This could lead to increased legal exposure. When people are put under the stress of a threatened lawsuit, they often act in ways that are unwise or sinful. Knowing this, we need to be careful in our response.

What about an employee other than a pastor? Say you let a counselor go because you learned they are advocating positions on human sexuality that are contrary to Scripture. Or perhaps you discover that a counselor whom you employ is engaged in an adulterous relationship or homosexual practice? Even aside from the Matthew 18 concerns, there is a potential question as to whether the employment practices law will apply to your church.

Do you expect the intake secretary to be able to provide spiritual counsel and prayer to someone who comes in or calls in? If you dismiss a receptionist when you learn of some moral failing, have you dismissed an employee or someone charged with religious work? If you have received a letter from a plaintiff's lawyer or from the State Department of Labor, what happens next?

After an employee has been terminated for an offense, the leaders of the organization might feel inclined to be indecisive, to fear, or even to panic as they consider what they should do next and what the legal ramifications might be if the fired employee chooses to sue. Under the best of circumstances, the question of whether you make any sort of public statement raises something of a moral quandary. Did employment end because of conduct that would pose a danger to other congregations if it occurs again? Do you have a duty to warn others, or do you have a responsibility to keep the underlying events confidential?[1] Any decision you make in situations of this sort has potential danger. In a litigious society, the specter of possible litigation is a constant. Will the separation from employment itself expose the employer or coworkers to potential legal liability? And if you do provide information to the public, will you be exposing yourself to potential legal liability for slander or something else?

Leaders facing such a quandary need to bear in mind that Scripture tells us, while we are to be prudent and take appropriate precautions (Proverbs 22:3; 27:12), "God gave us a spirit not of fear but of power and love and self-control" (2 Timothy 1:7). Martyn Lloyd-Jones has reminded us that faith is a "refusal to panic."[2] And while the specter of a lawsuit can be intimidating, it may be helpful to remember that to the extent we fear man, we are not acting in the fear of God or giving him full and proper honor.[3]

---

1. Illustrating the problem, in February 2019, a newspaper series on sexual abuse by pastors and leaders within a large Protestant denomination found that over twenty years there had been reported abuse of approximately 700 victims by 380 alleged perpetrators, with criminal convictions of 220 individuals. Of the 380 alleged perpetrators, 35 (or nearly 10 percent) had been rehired for pastoral ministry by another church. It should be noted that where the victim of sexual abuse is a minor, most states have a statutory requirement that specific individuals who learn it has occurred must notify a law enforcement or regulatory agency (e.g. California Penal Code 11166).
2. "Faith is a refusal to panic. Do you like that sort of definition of faith? Does that seem to be too earthly and not sufficiently spiritual? It is of the very essence of faith. Faith is a refusal to panic, come what may." Martyn Lloyd Jones, *Spiritual Depression* (Grand Rapids, MI: Wm. B. Eerdman's Publishing Company, 1965), 143.
3. In the words of the prophet Isaiah, "the Lord spoke thus to me with his strong hand upon me, and warned me not to walk in the way of this people, saying: 'Do not call conspiracy all that this people calls conspiracy, and do not fear what they fear, nor be in dread. But the Lord of hosts, him you shall honor as holy. Let him be your fear, and let him be your dread'" (Isaiah 8:11–13). Also from Isaiah 51:12–13, we read, "I, I am he who comforts you; who are you that you are afraid of man who dies, of the son of man who is made like grass, and have forgotten the Lord, your Maker, who stretched out the heavens and laid the foundations of the earth, and you fear continually all the day because of the wrath of the oppressor, when he sets himself to destroy?"

The question raised of a legal advisor often has biblical, practical, and legal ramifications. And often, the biblical and practical aspects will be decisive. Put another way, a good biblical and practical solution may be all that is needed.

A foundational principle is that generally speaking, the more biblical you are in your words and actions, the less likely it is that you will find yourself in legal danger. While it is continually developing, modern Western law is still shaped by biblically consistent norms[4] to the point that your trained secondary response—after fighting off the impulse to panic—should always be to consider what would be both a practical and biblical resolution. Only after that has been done should the Christian leader consider the legal issues.

Biblical and Practical Aspects

While there are legal issues pertaining to the termination of employment of those in pastoral or other positions of church leadership, it is imperative that those in authority within the church first have a thorough grasp of the underlying biblical issues. In 1 Timothy 3:15, Paul tells Timothy that he has written so that Timothy will know how to conduct himself as a leader within the church. It has been said that the Scripture should be both our "method book" as well as our "message book." With that in mind, leaders must ask two questions: (1) what guidance does the Bible give regarding the procedure the church or ministry should follow? and (2) what principles of biblical communication should be considered?

4. Of particular significance for the topic at hand, truth is required in judicial settings, and perjury is punishable as a crime (Deuteronomy 19:16–20; Isaiah 59:4, 14–15; cf. California Penal Code Sections 118, 127–29). Probably the greatest indictment in all of Scripture for a legal system is based on its systemic disregard of truth (Isaiah 59:1–15). Promises of payment or performance in some form of quid pro quo exchange should be kept or there may be potential liability under contractual or semicontractual principles. Derogatory information disseminated concerning an individual must be true and may need to be limited as to the scope of its distribution. Civil liability may be based on both negligent and intentional conduct. Individuals with supervisory or custodial responsibility may be liable for both intentional abuse and the failure to take appropriate action to preserve or protect.

To begin with the first question, is there a principle of ecclesiastical conduct, or practice within the church, that is required, suggested, or prohibited?[5] By way of example, Paul tells Timothy that a charge of malfeasance should not even be scheduled for official review and possible action against a pastor or elder without some form of corroboration in hand (1 Timothy 5:19).[6] Once scheduled, inquiry was to be both thorough and without either partiality or prejudgment (1 Timothy 5:20). Once disqualifying conduct has been established on the part of a person previously recognized as qualified for pastoral service, the "present tense" challenge to "keep yourself pure" (1 Timothy 5:22b) may require the church to make some form of public statement.

Interestingly, in addition, Paul did not hesitate to warn of potential threats to the church from unidentified individuals within particular groups of people (Acts 20:29–31; Titus 1:10–11) or from specific individuals when they could be identified. In what may well have been statement(s) of disqualification for service in the particular role of pastor, overseer, or elder,[7] Paul identified the particular individuals but only commented on the confirmed facts that led to particular disciplinary action (i.e. Hymenaeus, Alexander, and Philetus in 1 Timothy 1:3, 19–20; 2 Timothy 2:16–18; 4:14–15).[8] Finally, Paul admonishes

5. It should be noted that if there is a biblical mandate, the question is not whether a particular communication should or should not take place but how it should be prudently carried out. Careful study should be made of the legal parameters specific to each situation.

6. While the text should not preclude necessary and appropriate inquiry and investigation based on a single report of malfeasance, a formal accusation ("kategoria") against a pastor or elder is not to be "received," or scheduled before a tribunal of some sort, without two or three "witnesses." Kenneth S. Wuest, *Word Studies in the Greek New Testament*, vol. 2 (Grand Rapids, MI: Wm. B. Eerdman's Publishing Company, 2002), 86. As the emphasis is on corroboration, a document or other tangible item of demonstrative evidentiary value may be considered a "witness" (Exodus 22:12; Isaiah 59:12; Jeremiah 32:1–15; Amos 3:12).

7. Each term referring to a difference in aspect, function, or qualification of the same individuals serving within the church.

8. Interestingly, one particular commentator raises the possibility that the men identified by Paul in 1 and 2 Timothy (Hymenaeus, Alexander, and/or Philetus) may have been some of the elders in the church of Ephesus who eventually proved to be "ravenous wolves." See notes to Acts 20:30, ed. R.C. Sproul et al., *Reformation Study Bible* (Nashville, TN: Thomas Nelson, 1995).

Timothy that elders found to have engaged in disqualifying conduct should be publicly rebuked if they are unrepentant (i.e., if they "persist" [ESV] or "continue" [NASB] "in sin" [1 Timothy 5:20]).

Second, what principles of biblical communication should leaders consider as they handle such a difficult situation? Seemingly neglected at times, Scripture does teach principles of communication that should be known and applied by the adequate and equipped man of God (2 Timothy 3:16–17) and that we disregard at our peril (e.g., grieving the Holy Spirit, Ephesians 4:30; cf. Proverbs 21:23). Contrary to the natural inclination that we often have, Scripture generally teaches that our communication should usually be "less" rather than "more" (e.g., Proverbs 10:19). Someone trained in biblical communication skills knows that he or she can increase or decrease the emotional volatility of a particular dialogue (Proverbs 15:1). What we communicate, orally or in written form, should be in keeping with, and limited by, specific approved and focused goals (Ephesians 4:29–30). A skilled communicator can present even a very difficult concept in a palatable manner (Proverbs 15:2). And as noted above, any specific charges made should be true and thoroughly confirmed by corroborating evidence (Deuteronomy 19:15; Matthew 18:16; 2 Corinthians 13:1; see also Judas Iscariot in Acts 1:17–19 and Demas in 2 Timothy 4:10). Conversely, diligent effort should be made to guard against deliberate false testimony or a conclusion based on unintentionally inaccurate or incomplete testimony. In keeping with that requirement, an appropriate record should be prepared and maintained.

Finally, you must be thoughtful about the manner in which you communicate any information. Even our most private disclosures can be broadcast (Ecclesiastes 10:20). We will be judged for even our careless words (Matthew 12:36). We must not wrongfully accuse another (Deuteronomy 5:20). Who should know about the accusation? This is particularly acute in a day when a message can travel from continent to continent with the press of a button. Think. When a statement has been posted on the internet that proves to be inaccurate, it may be impossible to notify everyone in the world who has seen it and provide a correction.

Putting the above together, let us return to the scenario of the adulterous pastor. How would this best be resolved with biblical principles? While a rebuke may have to be given within the church in keeping with 1 Timothy 5:20, posting a broad, general statement on the church's website—and outside the church—concerning a former employee would be an unnecessary action; most readers who come across the site would have no need to know anything about him. And, if there is no need to convey the information, then it would be best to say nothing at all—there is no need to even "hint" at it.

Any concern as to whether the church has a responsibility to issue a warning to other like-minded churches as a "watchman" of sorts[9] could be met by simply providing an actual description of what occurred in response to any inquiries received by the church's leadership, with each church required to perform its own inquiry in keeping with 1 Timothy 5:22, 24–25. While it may not be a popular step for the church's leadership to take, limiting communication to that which is necessary may mean that some in the church will not be provided all the information known to the leadership. And in keeping with the biblical requirement for corroboration, any factual assertions would be limited to those that could be confirmed.

Legal Considerations

While you should always use the services of a lawyer when working through employment decisions that could lead to a legal conflict, you should have an understanding of four basic questions involved. Any decision you make about employment is not merely a "business" decision. Hiring and firing, reprimanding and encouraging employees is also a matter of discipleship. As we have tried to make plain elsewhere in this book, biblical counseling is not merely a conversation with a counselor in an office. Biblical counseling is training for a way of life.

9. Cf. Ezekiel 3, 33; Acts 20:26–28.

We are belaboring this point a bit because employment relationships in Christian ministries often end up being the "worst of both worlds," employment and church. While a Christian's work should always be with an eye to serving the Lord (Colossians 3:23–24), some employees behave in ways that would be unacceptable in "secular" employment. In other situations, good employees can be overworked or mistreated.

When a church or other ministry fails to abide by both biblical principles and applicable law, we are inadequately counseling those in our charge. We are misrepresenting biblical principles. We are being poor stewards of the people and resources under our care. With that in mind, we offer the following four questions to consider when overseeing employment.

1. Are there any general legal principles or issues that need to be considered?

When we have an employment problem, we can begin by asking whether there in legal principles that could apply to the employment problem. For our purposes, the legal issues could be categorized as either "contract" or "tort."

We all have experiences with a contract. A contract is an agreement that creates a private set of laws applying two parties. Both sides have certain obligations and rights. If either side fails to live up to their obligation (they "breach" the contract), the other side has the right to enforce those rights in court (sue for breach of contract). When it comes to employment relationships, you have a contract of some sort—even if you never put it in writing. If nothing else, your course of conduct will create a sort of contract.

A "tort" is a law that applies to everyone. It is "tort" for any person to strike another person. I don't need a contract with you to make it wrong for you to punch me. Torts are the sorts of thing we already know are wrong—taking someone else's property, hurting someone else's body, and so on. When it comes to employment, torts might be things like lying about a former employee ("slander").

What about the adulterous pastor we have considered as an example? One way a church could easily go wrong is by saying the wrong thing to the wrong person. If what you say turns out to be wrong, you have slandered someone.[10]

What if it is true? Truth is a defense to a charge of slander: If someone sues you for slander, and you prove the statement is true, you should win. But making a false statement of fact is not the only sort of wrong that arises. You can commit other torts even by telling the truth. You might find yourself sued for torts such as invasion of privacy[11] or intentional infliction of emotional distress.[12] Consequences can be attached to your speech if it hurts someone else.

A different hypothetical can illustrate a contract dispute. A pastor or a counselor files a lawsuit against his former church, contending breach of contract after the church's governing body voted not to pay him the funds at issue after termination for alleged malfeasance. In that situation, it would be necessary to first carefully review both the purported contract between the church and the former pastor and the church's bylaws to determine whether those documents would have supported the desired contractual relief. For example, is there a "bona fide" contract? Was there a real and binding agreement between the parties, which is known by both sides?

---

10. According to *Merriam-Webster Dictionary*, *slander* is defined as: 1. the utterance of false charges or misrepresentations which defame and damage another's reputation 2. a false and defamatory oral statement about a person. By way of biblical example, the repeated and multiple false statements orally made concerning Christ (e.g., "He casts out demons by Beelzebul, the prince of demons" in Luke 11:15) or the apostles (Diotrephes's unjust accusations of John in 3 John 10) would generally constitute "slander."

11. Invasion of privacy is defined as, "The elements of a claim of invasion of privacy based on the public disclosure of private facts are as follows: (1) public disclosure (2) of a private fact (3) which would be offensive and objectionable to the reasonable person and (4) which is not of legitimate public concern." Shulman v. Group W Productions, Inc., 18 Cal. 4th 200, 214 (1998).

12. The intentional infliction of emotional distress is defined as "the tort of intentionally or recklessly causing another person severe emotional distress through one's extreme or outrageous acts." Bryan A. Garner, ed., *Black's Law Dictionary* (Toronto: Thomson Reuters, 2000).

Or do we have a situation where one party just assumes something to be true? While written contracts are not mandatory for most circumstances, a signed, written contract is always good because it forces the parties to be explicit about their agreement. A lack of clarity and an abundance of assumptions have caused many problems.

Was any agreement entered into in full compliance with the organization's bylaws or other organizational documents? It would also be helpful to probe the reason, or reasons, in the light of pertinent Scripture (1 Timothy 5:17–18) that the church decided not to pay the pastor. Finally, it may be helpful to probe the conduct of all parties to any purported contract that may exist to confirm that they had acted honestly and in good faith at the time the agreement was reached.[13]

In yet another hypothetical, the employment of an associate pastor has been terminated following an inquiry into allegations of conduct possibly constituting "sexual harassment."[14] In addition, the church has had to consider whether disciplinary action within the church should be taken in the form of a public rebuke pursuant to 1 Timothy 5:20. While the inquiry was inconclusive as to whether there was actually harassment, the man subsequently and repeatedly failed to comply with repeated preventive instructions to discontinue certain conduct. Resolution of this matter would require both an analysis under principles of "sexual harassment" as well as an evaluation as to whether there had been insubordination within the workplace.

---

13. As demonstrated in Jonathan Edwards's removal and departure from Northampton, a dispute over compensation may coincide with, and even conceal, substantial and possibly more serious disagreements concerning theology or ecclesiastical practice. George M. Marsden, *Jonathan Edwards: A Life* (New Haven, CT: Yale University Press, 2003), 301–5; Iain Murray, *Jonathan Edwards: A New Biography* (Carlisle, PA: Banner of Truth, 1987), 277–81.

14. While it has been further clarified by numerous appellate decisions, the United States Equal Employment Opportunity Commission has defined *sexual harassment* as, "Unwelcome sexual advances, requests for sexual favors, and other verbal or physical conduct of a sexual nature when (1) submission to such conduct is either explicitly or implicitly a term or condition of an individual's employment, (2) submission to or rejection of such conduct by an individual is used as a basis for employment decisions affecting such individual, or (3) such conduct has the purpose or effect of unreasonably interfering with an individual's work performance or creating an intimidating, hostile, or offensive working environment."

Finally, consider a scenario where an employee of a church or counseling ministry undergoes biblical counseling by pastoral personnel or clergy on behalf of the ministry. In the course of that counseling, the counselee confesses to a serious moral, or even criminal, offense. Can the employer use that information for workplace disciplinary action, including the termination of employment? If the employee fails to give any indication of repentance, can the employer use the information obtained during that counseling for the purpose of formal church discipline in keeping with Matthew 18:15–18 or public rebuke as commanded in 1 Timothy 5:20? Last but definitely not least, can the employer use that information for a referral of the matter to a law enforcement agency for criminal prosecution?

Resolution of that scenario will be fact specific, requiring careful analysis under the case and statutory law of each pertinent jurisdiction. In each aspect, it will be important to demonstrate that the church or religious organization had not represented to the counselee, either by specific statement or implicitly, that the information they provided would be totally confidential.[15] This is precisely the sort of matter covered by a written consent form (and discussed in chapter 9).

If the confessed conduct is "child abuse," not only can the pastoral counselor make a referral for criminal prosecution, he may have an affirmative mandatory duty to make such a report within a specific period of time for possible temporary placement of an abused child.[16] (The precise legal requirements vary from state to state.) If the counselee, himself, is a pastor or elder, that conduct would disqualify him from further service in that capacity, as he would no longer be "above reproach" (1 Timothy 3:2; Titus 1:7).

---

15. An appropriately phrased counseling release form can deter a claim that somehow confidentiality was promised or otherwise provided. This would be particularly important where the counselee is a former Roman Catholic and culturally inclined to expect something akin to the "seal of the confessional." Cf. Todd Sorrell's discussion herein of counseling consent forms in chapter 9.

16. California Penal Code Sections 11165.9 & 11166 (the duty to report), 11165.7 (32) (33) ("clergy" as "mandated reporters"), and 11172 (no civil or criminal liability for mandatory reporters for the making of such reports).

If the conduct is embezzlement, the information obtained can be disclosed over a possible claim of "pastoral-penitent privilege."[17] In fact, disclosing for criminal prosecution the embezzlement of church funds has been upheld over claim of privilege.[18]

Barring some representation to the employee of confidentiality, the information provided during counseling can generally be used to support workplace discipline. Finally, provided that the church is otherwise in compliance with its specified disciplinary procedures,[19] and if the information provided actually proves or confirms wrongdoing, church discipline could generally be based at least in part on the information obtained during counseling.

2. Is the employee's conduct leading to termination a matter of church doctrine or organizational documents?

If the church's doctrine and organizational documents are clearly stated, and if the misconduct, position, or adjudicative procedure is covered by the doctrinal statement and organizational documents, the church will have substantially greater autonomy in developing its course of action.

17. Evidentiary privilege, i.e., the right to prevent otherwise valid evidence from being disclosed in a court proceeding, may limit the actions that could be otherwise taken simply by preventing that evidence from being available to a court. The specific requirements of "pastor-penitent privilege" are unique for each state as well as under federal law. California's "pastor–penitent privilege" is given at Evidence Code Sections 1030–1034. Cf. Penal Code Section 11166 (d) (1). As the California privilege requires that the clergy member's "church, denomination or organization" must impose "a duty to keep [penitential] communications secret" (Penal Code Section 1032), it may not be available to most Protestant clergy.

18. People v. Edwards, 203 Cal. App. 3d 1358 (1988).

19. The church's disciplinary procedures should be specifically based on Scripture, stated in the church's bylaws or other organizational documents, and should be consented to by applicants for membership. Significantly, it should be kept in mind that the second step of the classic four-step disciplinary process for "private" sin requires confrontation with at least "two or three witnesses" so that literally "every word" may be made to "stand" (Matthew 18:16). Those responsible for the implementation of church discipline should always guard against the misuse of disciplinary procedures such as that engaged in by Diotrephes in 3 John 9–10 (i.e., without biblical authority or reason, without evidentiary support and for personal agenda).

In the seminal case of *Watson v. Jones*, the Supreme Court stated the general principle, also known as the "ecclesiastical abstention" or "church autonomy" exception. This means the secular courts will defer to "ecclesiastical courts" in matters of doctrine or ecclesiastical law.[20] In other words, a civil court, charged with a review of an action taken by a church will tend to defer to the actions taken by the church if it can be demonstrated that the action taken was in compliance with the church's known procedural requirements or was controlled by a matter of church doctrine.

Consistent with *Watson*, but thirty years later, in *Saterlee v. United States Ex. Rel. Williams*, a United States District Court refused to review the decision of a church as to whether a minister should be dismissed for immoral conduct.[21] Again, illustrating the principle stated in *Watson*, a trial court's refusal to review a church disciplinary action was upheld by a California appellate court when plaintiff's counsel failed to demonstrate any violation of the church's organizational rules.[22]

Finally, in *Stewart v. McCray*, an Indiana appellate court recently applied the ecclesiastical abstention principle and found that the trial court lacked jurisdiction over the suspension of a pastor for noncompliance with the church's bylaws, as it was ultimately a matter of the church's leadership and therefore an ecclesiastical matter.[23]

3. Is it a matter of the church's message?

In one of the most controversial decisions of our time, *Obergefell v. Hodges*, the United States Supreme Court upheld the legality of

20. Watson v. Jones, 80 U.S. 679, 729–30 (1872).

21. Saterlee v. United States Ex. Rel. Williams, 20 App. D.C. 393 (D.C. 1902). Appreciation is expressed to Deborah J. Dewart J.D., Esq. Ms. Dewart's research identified both the *Saterlee* and *Walker* cases referred to herein. Commenting on *Saterlee*, Ms. Dewart noted that the "court would not review decision of ecclesiastical court to dismiss minister on charges of immorality. Minister tried to claim a property right had been violated (loss of salary)." Deborah Dewart, "Unpublished Notes on Church Discipline Cases."

22. Linke v. Church of Jesus Christ (LDS), 71 Cal. App. 2d 667 (1945); see also Providence Baptist Church v. Superior Court, 40 Cal. 2d 55 (1952).

23. Stewart v. McCray, 135 N.E. 3d 1012 (2019).

"homosexual marriage."[24] In doing so, however, Justice Anthony Kennedy, writing for the court, made an extremely significant statement:

> Finally, it must be emphasized that religions, and those who adhere to religious doctrines, may continue to advocate with utmost, sincere conviction that, by divine precepts, same-sex marriage should not be condoned. The First Amendment ensures that religious organizations are given proper protection as they seek to teach the principles that are so fulfilling and so central to their lives and faiths, and to their own deep aspirations to continue the family structure they have long revered.

While the courts appear to be possibly de-emphasizing the freedom to engage in religiously directed "practice," the quote from *Obergefell* demonstrates that there is still substantial emphasis given to the freedom of churches and religious organizations to meet, to "advocate," and to "teach." A key question then becomes whether an employee's continued employment by a religious institution is consistent with the organization's message. If the employer concludes it is not, the employer should make appropriate findings but should be free to structure its workforce accordingly.[25] Preceding *Obergefell*, but consistent with the quote listed above, an Orthodox Presbyterian church was allowed to discharge an unrepentant homosexual organist, as his continued employment was regarded as inconsistent with the church's teaching concerning homosexuality.[26]

24. Obergefell v. Hodges, 576 U.S. 644 (2015).

25. See Vigars v. Valley Christian Center, 805 F. Supp 802 (NDCA 1992). Summary judgment of dismissal denied of an action brought following the discharge of a school librarian when the court found a triable issue of fact whether the discharge was for pregnancy or for violation of the school's code of conduct. See also Arriaga v. Loma Linda University, 10 Cal. App. 4th 1556 (1992).

26. Walker v. First Presbyterian Church, 22 Fair Empl. Prac. Cas. (BNA) 762 (Cal. Super. Ct. 1980). Commenting on *Walker*, Ms. Deborah Dewart noted that a "city ordinance forbidding employers to discriminate on basis of sexual orientation violates Free Exercise Clause of First Amendment to U.S. Constitution as applied to church that discharged

In one of the most important cases in this area, the US Supreme Court upheld the right of a church to discharge an employee of a church-owned business solely because the employee was not a member in good standing.[27] Significantly, in *Corporation of Presiding Bishop of Church of Jesus Christ of Latter-Day Saints v. Amos*, the employee worked for a totally secular subsidiary owned by the church, a gymnasium.[28] The court upheld the right of the church to terminate employment under both the free exercise and establishment clauses of the First Amendment to the United States Constitution.[29]

4. Is it a matter of the church's approved messengers, i.e., the "ministerial exception"?

In 2014, the Supreme Court addressed the concept of the "ministerial exception," i.e., a legal recognition that the termination of a particular church or religious institution employee should be exempt from legal action alleging discrimination in light of the status, position, or role of that employee. In *Hosanna-Tabor Evangelical Lutheran Church and School v. Equal Employment Opportunity Commission*, the court affirmed the dismissal of an action alleging discrimination brought by a former teacher against an evangelical Lutheran church and school.[30] In doing so, the authority of religious organizations to designate their own "ministers" was upheld under the Free Exercise Clause. In determining whether a particular employee could be

---

unrepentant homosexual organist, where church regards the organist in a congregation as part of worship team, and its teachings do not permit unrepentant sinners to take special part in musical service." Dewart, "Unpublished Notes on Church Discipline Cases."

27. The plaintiff failed to qualify for a "temple recommend," i.e., a certificate that he was a member and authorized to attend the church's temples.

28. Corporation of Presiding Bishop of Church of Jesus Christ of Latter-Day Saints v. Amos, 483 U.S. 327 (1986).

29. In keeping with that authorization, a church or religious organization may want to officially require that applicants for employment be church members in good standing. At least one local church requires that employees also be "deacon qualified," pursuant to 1 Timothy 3:8–13.

30. Hosanna-Tabor Evangelical Lutheran Church and School v. Equal Employment Opportunity Commission, 565 U.S.171 (2012).

considered a "minister," the court considered the employee's duties and title and how the employee was viewed by the organization itself.

Recently, the Supreme Court again upheld the "ministerial exception." In *Our Lady of Guadalupe School v. Morrissey-Berru*, the court upheld the termination of two teachers by two separate schools, also alleging discrimination, and again under the "ministerial exception."[31] In reaching its assessment, the court rejected a specific formula but considered the presence or lack of a formal title, the use of that title by the employee, the employee's concept of his or her own employment, and most importantly, the nature and extent of the religious duties assigned to the employee.

The implications of the "ministerial exception" are still being developed. Nonetheless, while that process is ongoing, churches and religious organizations would do well to impress upon all employees that they are each part of the organization's total teaching ministry, regardless of their formal title. And where appropriate, effort should be made to structure their duties to expressly require conduct of that nature, even to the point of possibly equipping and requiring them to teach one or more classes in basic doctrine.

Above All Else, Seek the Glory and Approval of God

While preparing this chapter, I was reminded that there is a greater danger in the church or religious institution workplace than avoiding mere potential legal liability. There is a higher standard to pursue than conduct that would not expose to legal liability. Two passages of Scripture demonstrate the point.

In 1 Samuel 3–4, we read of the misconduct of two men, Hophni and Phinehas, both sons of the high priest Eli and both serving as priests themselves at the time. In modern terms, the text indicates that they misappropriated donated assets under threat of force (1 Samuel 2:12–17). In addition, the text raises a strong probability that they had engaged in conduct we would label as "sexual

31. Our Lady of Guadalupe School v. Morrissey-Berru, 591 U.S. (2020).

harassment" and possibly even "rape" (1 Samuel 2:22).[32] The text indicates that God responded with their premature death in battle on the same day, the removal of the high priesthood from Eli's family, and Israel's loss of both the ark of the covenant and the intimate presence of God (1 Samuel 2–4).

Nadab and Abihu, two sons of the high priest Aaron, and also priests in their own right, died tragically and unexpectedly when they were "consumed" by fire from the presence of the Lord (Leviticus 10:2). The text indicates that they had engaged in inappropriate and unauthorized practices of worship, most likely while under the influence of alcohol (Leviticus 10:8–9).

Commenting on what had occurred, the Lord spoke to Moses and said, "Among those who are near me I will be sanctified, and before all the people I will be glorified" (Leviticus 10:3). God then clarified to Aaron that the priests were to "distinguish between the holy and the common, and between the unclean and the clean, and you are to teach the people of Israel all the statutes that the LORD has spoken to them by Moses" (Leviticus 10:10–11; cf. Ezekiel 22:26).

The greater danger to avoid is the disapproval and chastening, even disqualification, by God himself of a ministry or an individual serving in ministry. We must never lose sight of the fact that employment in ministry is a granted "mercy" or privilege, and not a right (2 Corinthians 4:1), and that misconduct in ministry will inevitably come to light and may disqualify (Numbers 32:23; Isaiah 59:12; 1 Timothy 5:24–25).

Similarly, the standard of conduct to pursue and to encourage within a ministry management and workforce is that which recognizes that those entrusted with that privilege must continually challenge themselves to think and act in a manner consistent with Scripture—a manner that honors the holiness and character of God (Leviticus 10:3). We must always remember that the approval of God

32. The Scripture indicates that the women "served" at the tabernacle, providing some form of assistance. While not inerrant or with final authority, Josephus indicates that they obliged some of the women "to submit to their lust by force" and that they enticed "others by bribes." See Josephus, *Antiquities of the Jews*, book V, chapter X, paragraph 1.

matters far more than the approval of men (John 12:43). While there is by no means a guarantee, it can be reasonably anticipated that in doing so, churches or ministry organizations will tend to avoid conflicts requiring legal resolution and also tend to limit conflicts that do occur to situations where action has been taken against them for attempting to do what is right before God.

Conclusion

In sum, then, when an employment termination becomes necessary and a report or record has to be made, the best procedure is often to implement a biblically sound but practical approach. Legal counsel should be consulted when specific questions emerge concerning particular areas of law. Throughout every part of the process, primary importance should be given to the reputation, honor, and glory of God.

To-Do List

- ❒ One of the best ways to avoid employment problems is to have clear, communicated employment practices. With the help of an attorney, draft an employment manual that sets forth in clear terms what is expected of employees. Ask employees to acknowledge in writing that they have received the manual.
- ❒ Make sure that doctrinal statements and rules of church order—including disciplinary procedures—are clear and included in the above employment manual.
- ❒ For key employees, such as a pastor, use written contracts.
- ❒ Decide before a problem arises how you will respond to problems such as learning of adultery. Making decisions after the trouble has already taken place often results in hurried, fearful, foolish decisions.
- ❒ Require full-time employees and counselors to be familiar with the mandatory reporting requirements for your state. Some states provide online instruction and certification in mandatory reporting. Knowledge of these laws will protect the church and the vulnerable.

Part 2

How Do I Protect Myself and My Counselees?

CHAPTER 7
A Pastoral Perspective on Legal Issues

Tim Pasma

Pastor Dan sat alone in the office feeling a bit overwhelmed by anxious thoughts and an uneasy feeling in the pit of his stomach. He had just finished reading an article on his favorite news site describing the attempts of some state legislators to codify requirements for all counselors in his state, which, he presumed, included his counseling ministry as a pastor. The writer mentioned regulations for mandatory reporting, restrictions on counseling homosexual people, and even mandated requirements for anyone who would counsel children.

The uneasy feeling in his stomach turned into a knot as the day progressed, and his thoughts ran down this unwanted track. *Are we at the place where it is impossible to shepherd and counsel God's people without exposing ourselves to some kind of legal action, not to mention prosecution? How can I protect the ministry of counseling? How can I protect* myself? *What do I need to be thinking and doing in light of the events transpiring in our country? This is not what I thought ministry would be like when I started!*

Pastor Dan is not alone in this funk, is he? Many have felt and thought the same things. Is there hope for pastors? Can we protect our counseling ministries and ourselves? Yes, we can! And we can do so in a way that honors God and remains faithful to Scripture. Our Father has not left us alone to figure all this out. Surely, we need the wisdom of those who know and work within the legal system, but we have the Scripture that tells us how we need to think and act in any circumstance, including this one. What are some things that

Dan needs to avoid as he confronts this new environment, and what can he or should he do? What is his duty as a pastor? Let's consider that together.

Don't Give in to Fear

Many pastors make the choice to quit counseling altogether. After all, if you don't counsel, you don't have to worry about civil suits or prosecution. Is this a good idea? Let's consider this question.

Take, for example, the church across the street that holds a "Blessing the Animals Day" every year. Now, if the legislature determines that having animals in public buildings—including church buildings—is a health risk or dangerously increases the spread of fleas, and it passes a law restricting animals in such buildings, we probably would not go to battle over it (well, most of us wouldn't). Why not? Because that is not an essential or even biblically mandated ministry entrusted to the church.

Many pastors see counseling in that light. I have many opportunities to teach the fundamentals of counseling, and often, as I stand before a class of about fifty to a hundred people, I ask, "How many pastors do we have here today?" Almost always I will see no more than five hands go up. Why are there so few pastors in those classes? I believe it is because many pastors think, *I'd love to go to that conference, and it would be nice to add counseling to my ministerial repertoire, but my time is so limited.* To many pastors, counseling is a nice addition to pastoral ministry but not essential, helpful but not necessary. Nothing could be farther from the truth! Not only is counseling essential; it is at the very core of shepherding—the very core of pastoral ministry!

When Jesus ascended to heaven, he left his disciples with a simple command: "Go therefore and make disciples of all nations, baptizing them in the name of the Father and of the Son and of the Holy Spirit, teaching them to observe all that I have commanded you" (Matthew 28:19). What are we to "teach"? Many reply, "All that

Jesus commands us." But that's not entirely correct, for Jesus clearly says that we need to teach others "to observe" all that he commands. Counseling is just that. It is all about making disciples, teaching people to obey Jesus in the difficult places of life. One of my mentors, Pastor Bill Goode, defined disciples as "people who translate truth into life." Have you ever thought of counseling as a means of fulfilling the Great Commission? With that in mind, would you say that counseling is an essential part of the church's ministry?

Listen to the apostle Paul describe his ministry in Colossians 1:28: "Him we proclaim, warning everyone and teaching everyone with all wisdom, that we may present everyone mature in Christ." The Greek word Paul uses here for "warn," *noutheteo*, can legitimately be translated "counsel." And so Paul is asserting that he ministers God's Word both publicly and privately for the purpose of presenting mature believers to Jesus on that great Day of Judgment. Every time I preach and every time I minister the Word in counseling, I think, *I need to do this so these folks will be able to give a good account of themselves to Jesus someday.* Counseling, indeed, is a ministry worth taking pains to encourage and protect.

Consider what the prophet Ezekiel said to the shepherds of God's people in his day:

> Son of man, prophesy against the shepherds of Israel; prophesy, and say to them, even to the shepherds, Thus says the Lord God: Ah, shepherds of Israel who have been feeding yourselves! Should not shepherds feed the sheep? You eat the fat, you clothe yourselves with the wool, you slaughter the fat ones, but you do not feed the sheep. The weak you have not strengthened, the sick you have not healed, the injured you have not bound up, the strayed you have not brought back, the lost you have not sought, and with force and harshness you have ruled them. So they were scattered, because there was no shepherd, and they became food for all the wild beasts. My sheep were scattered; they

> wandered over all the mountains and on every high hill. My sheep were scattered over all the face of the earth, with none to search or seek for them. . . . Thus says the Lord God, Behold, I am against the shepherds, and I will require my sheep at their hand and put a stop to their feeding the sheep. No longer shall the shepherds feed themselves. I will rescue my sheep from their mouths, that they may not be food for them. (Ezekiel 34:2–6, 10)

Too many pastors, believing that counseling is "optional," stand condemned by the Lord's indictment. Many love to preach, but they are afraid to counsel or prefer not to do it. They find refuge from legal problems by referring Christ's sheep to the licensed counselor up the street.

While that sounds like an easy way to avoid legal danger, it would be failure in terms of being a pastor. As a general rule, we should not refer the people in our charge to a secular counselor (but please see the excursus on psychiatric referrals in chapter 5). First, that counselor cares nothing for the Shepherd of the sheep or what he thinks is best for them. Second, as we have explained in chapter 3, there is a fundamental difference between providing biblical discipleship and psychotherapy.

Third, it is dereliction of duty. Shepherding is not merely preaching to the sheep, which, frankly, is the easiest and most fun part of pastoring. It also involves strengthening the weak, healing the sick, binding up the wounds of the injured, and guiding them back to the path of righteousness when they stray because of the sin, suffering, and brokenness of this world.

Counseling clearly belongs to the church and to her shepherds. We cannot protect ourselves by abandoning it just because we fear prosecution. As those charged with "keeping watch over" the souls of the sheep and who "will have to give an account" for them, pastors do not have that option (Hebrews 13:17).

Don't Give in to Anger

Some pastors believe that protecting themselves and their counseling ministries requires all-out war with the governing authorities or, at the very least, making some kind of public fuss about any possible mandates. Years ago, when my state was talking about mandatory reporting, the libertarian in me reared up and snarled, "If Ohio thinks I'm going to become an agent of the state in my office, it had better think again!" Certainly, we have grounds to believe that religious liberty is under threat and our freedoms endangered, but the answer is not always to go to war or flagrantly disobey mandates in the name of liberty. Sadly, evangelical Christians are known more for being cranks who have a problem with just about everyone than for living quietly and minding their own affairs (cf. 1 Thessalonians 4:11).

Romans 13:1–7 and 1 Peter 2:13–17 clearly command believers to submit to the government and foster a reputation as good citizens. Many of you readers have preached on those texts. When you have preached them, what question do you first encounter? It usually is not, "Please, pastor, tell us in greater detail how we should obey," but rather, "When is it permissible to disobey the government?" In fact, how many sermons have you heard or preached on those texts that did not include caveats on when disobedience is required (even though the texts themselves give no such exceptions)? But we cannot give in to the temptation to disobey the Scripture simply to protect ourselves. We are called to submission so we cannot resort to rebellion just because it might be easier.

Look at Jesus. He lived under oppressive regimes, both religious and political, yet he did not engage in any sort of dramatic rebellion. He quietly, faithfully ministered the gospel to the multitudes that followed him, and he spoke truth to the religious and political authorities that he encountered. In fact, he epitomized one who "speaks truth to power." But he did not agitate; he did not lead marches and protests. In fact, Matthew says that Jesus fulfilled Isaiah's prophecy: "Behold, my servant whom I have chosen, my beloved with whom my soul is well pleased. I will put my Spirit upon him, and he will proclaim justice to the Gentiles. *He will not quarrel or cry aloud, nor will anyone hear his voice in the streets*" (Isaiah 42:1–2, quoted in Matthew 12:18–19, my emphasis). The Servant of the Lord would launch a revolution without clamoring in the streets and gathering about him a gang of spiritual Brownshirts to march against and topple the oppressive system bearing down on him. Shouldn't his servants operate in the same manner?

That is not to say that one must submit in violation of his conscience, for not even the state is lord of one's conscience. Nor is it to say that you should abandon any attempt to protect our liberties. But when you must protect yourself and your ministries, the Bible makes it clear that we use different weapons. Fussing and fighting may gain some protection for the time being but at what cost to the reputation of our Savior?

Sometimes we have to remind ourselves that the glory of Christ is more important than freedom and protection. That does not mean you surrender yourself to an inevitable loss of religious freedom and protection. It does mean that you work wisely in the legal system in which God has placed you.

Engage Wisely

In the present legislative and legal milieu, many pastors believe that an onslaught of civil lawsuits and criminal prosecutions is just around the corner. That may or may not be true. Jesus had something to say to his disciples who did indeed face prosecution and persecution: "Behold, I am sending you out as sheep in the midst of wolves, so be wise as serpents and innocent as doves" (Matthew 10:16). Do you feel like a sheep surrounded by wolves? Then be peaceful, harmless, and nonviolent as doves but also exercise prudence. We may be vulnerable, but we shouldn't be *stupidly* vulnerable. So how can we engage the legal system wisely in order to protect ourselves and our ministries?

First, be convinced that seeking legal protection is neither a deficiency of faith nor an insult to God. Look at the apostle Paul (Acts 16). He and Silas have come to Philippi, and their ministry of the gospel causes certain economic difficulties for some folks. Consequently, they are hauled before the magistrates, accused, beaten, and thrown in jail. The following morning, after the extraordinary events of the night, those same magistrates send a message to the newly converted warden to release them. Paul's response? "They have beaten us publicly, uncondemned, men who are Roman citizens, and have thrown us into prison; and do they now throw us out secretly? No! Let them come themselves and take us out" (v. 37). Paul and Silas are not faithless in their response, but rather they use the means God afforded them to seek lawful protection.

Recall the imprisonment Paul endures in Caesarea because of the riot in Jerusalem (Acts 21–26). After two years, the new governor, Porcius Festus, arrives, seeking to curry favor with his Jewish subjects by offering to try Paul in Jerusalem. However, Paul, aware of the plot to assassinate him, makes a lawful appeal to the court of the Caesar (Acts 25:1–12). Although willing to die for Jesus (v. 11), he nevertheless makes this legal appeal, safeguarding his life and giving him more opportunity for ministry. Again, does he exhibit a lack of faith? No. Rather, he uses the system to protect himself and his ministry. We too should know our laws and use them for our benefit.

Second, you engage the legal system wisely by understanding and seeking to prevent the kind of legal challenges you could face as a biblical counselor. Other chapters in this book will deal with those in more detail, but the following provide some examples: You could face what is called "clergy malpractice." You could be guilty of clergy malpractice if you provide "counseling that goes beyond religious advice into the realm of secular psychotherapy" and the person receiving such "psychotherapy" suffers serious harm.[1] Certainly,

1. Church Law Center, a California Based Law Firm, "Legal Considerations for Churches that Provide Counseling Services," https://www.churchlawcenter.com/church-law/church-counseling-services/.

sexual abuse of a counselee constitutes malpractice, as does breaking confidentiality or failing to report as a mandatory reporter.

Third, we engage our legal system wisely as we approach these issues pastorally and biblically. That means, first, our own counseling requirements will exceed those of our legal system. For example, you will take extraordinary measures to keep yourself above reproach as you counsel women or minors to remove any possibility for a suit or an accusation (see 1 Timothy 3:2; Titus 1:6). You will go to extraordinary personal lengths to keep things as confidential as Scripture warrants (see Matthew 18:15–20, esp. v. 15). You will faithfully report to authorities when required since they are God's servants for good and his instrument for executing wrath and justice (see Romans 13:1–7, esp. v. 4). In this vein Robert Kellemen writes,

> Practicing ethical and legal wisdom in ministry is nothing less than being Christlike in how we practice biblical counseling. It is nothing less than ensuring that every possible safeguard is in place so that hurting people we minister to are helped and not harmed. It is nothing less than overseeing that our biblical counseling ministry fulfills God's law of love. When we do that, fulfilling the law of the land, while still necessary, will be undemanding in comparison.[2]

Finally, engaging wisely means that you take appropriate legal precautions. This book contains many chapters on ways to take appropriate legal precautions. If you have a particular question, consult the table of contents. Being prudent does not mean we do not trust God. We all see trained physicians. We have all hired experienced electricians and plumbers. We should likewise make use of the proper legal means provided by God. Remember, God instituted governments for good (even if they do not always fulfill that end). The legal system is the means by which the government interacts with the population. Learn to use it wisely.

2. Robert Kellemen, *Equipping Counselors for Your Church* (Phillipsburg, NJ: P&R Publishing, 2011), 305.

Frankly, biblical counselors ought to rejoice that the governing authorities have instituted laws that require them to report child, sexual, and spousal abuse. Evangelicals often complain that the government does not fulfill its role as servants of good and instruments of justice. With many of these laws, especially those on reporting abuse, the government is promoting justice in areas that have been neglected far too long.

Some laws can provide a testing ground of true repentance. If a man who has abused his children is truly repentant, he will voluntarily confess his sin and accept whatever consequences may result, including the legal consequences for his criminal behavior. Isn't that what "godly grief" is supposed to produce (2 Corinthians 7:8–11)?

And when counselees read the statement on confidentiality, carefully composed with the law in mind, they read a defense of biblical confidentiality and get an honest explanation of what they can expect from you. In many cases, we ought to thank God for an ally that helps us counsel better.

Neither Pastor Dan nor you should despair about the realities we face as biblical counselors. We can navigate the legal waters in which we find ourselves as biblical counselors. We have sufficient Scriptures to equip us with godly attitudes and actions that will magnify our Lord Jesus—the only goal worth pursuing.

To-Do List

- ❐ Examine your own heart: are you fearful or angry about the burden and potential conflicts of ministry?
- ❐ Examine your conduct: has fear or anger caused you to avoid the duties of shepherding?
- ❐ Examine your counsel: are you preaching or teaching anything that compromises Scripture to justify your anger or fear?
- ❐ Did you find any basis to confess and repent? Did you find any basis to alter your conduct?

CHAPTER 8

The Anatomy of a Lawsuit

Edward Charles Wilde and Deborah Dewart

While the ways in which a conflict can turn into a lawsuit are almost endless, the structure of a lawsuit is very consistent. The procedure will be the same if General Motors brings suit against a manufacturer for breach of contract, if a "confused" person brings a lawsuit against the mayor for implanting alien technology in her arm, or if a neighbor brings suit to have a fence removed. The facts will be different, the torts may be different, but the procedure is same for every lawsuit. In a sense, if you've seen one lawsuit, you've seen them all.

With that in mind, we will consider a circumstance that we have seen before. Imagine that you have counseled a married couple, but since you have known the pair for years, you are informal in how you approach the situation. You have not obtained consent to counsel, you have not clearly explained what information will be private and what information may be communicated to others.

One day the wife comes to see you at the church office. She has her husband's cell phone. She opens the phone and shows you a text exchange between the husband and another woman which clearly admits to adultery. You contact the husband and confront him with the evidence.

In anger, he explains to you that you have broken some law about his privacy. He refuses to break off the affair. You present the church board with the evidence, and the husband's attorney sends a letter to the church demanding $100,000 to settle the invasion of privacy and pastoral negligence lawsuit.

The husband is angry to be exposed. Angry to have been caught. Perhaps feeling guilty over his sin and betrayal of his marriage. And you will be the recipient of his ire.

In my first year of law school, one professor gave me remarkably true and useful advice: No one sues you because he *thinks* you breached a contract. He sues because he *feels* you cheated him.

A lawsuit is trial by combat between two adversaries. Rather than using swords, we use words. Rather than using violence in our own name, we outsource the violence to the state and ask the state to force our opponent to pay us money or move a fence or turn over some property.[1] Since it is a matter of combat, not a dispassionate search for the truth; and since it is presided over by judges who are wildly overworked, and sometimes lacking the necessary skill; lawsuits often have less-than-satisfactory results. But that result is still better than violent feuds over the proper place to set a fence.

A lawsuit begins with conscious, deliberate unhappiness and a desire to be vindicated—or perhaps to seek revenge. A lawsuit ends when the money runs out, the parties get tired of fighting, or they become frightened of a worse outcome—or maybe, by the grace of God, the parties are reconciled. But civil litigation is not designed to promote biblical peacemaking or reconciliation. On the contrary, the opportunity and likelihood of reconciliation is often destroyed, short of divine intervention.

When you strip out all the paraphernalia, the specialized language, and the odd conduct, a lawsuit is simply a conflict of the human heart and is no different than family members fighting or neighbors squabbling. It is formalized, time-consuming, and expensive, but it is only conflict.

---

1. Even a civil lawsuit, which only includes an award of money, is backed by the threat of force. Let us say that you are ordered to pay $100 to your opponent. If you do not pay, the local law enforcement official can come to your place of business and take the money out of the cash register. If you continually refuse orders to pay, you can be found in "contempt," which can result in even imprisonment. Such extreme outcomes are rare, but they are rare because everyone understands the danger.

Litigation (the process of conducting a lawsuit) is at best a means of "common grace" to mitigate the worst aspects of sin. Or, as I tell my clients, a lawsuit is marginally better than shooting each other. This means, in the end, a lawsuit can only be resolved in the way any conflict is resolved. It also means the motive driving the lawsuit is in some way an effect of the fall. The procedures will be unfamiliar, but the nature of the problem will be completely understandable.

Why Should You Care?

At this point, you could think to yourself, *Why should I take the time to understand how a lawsuit unwinds? If I ever come to be on the wrong end of litigation, my lawyer will explain to me what is happening and what to expect next.*

One of the most stressful or fearful aspects of any circumstance is the unknown, the unexpected. In a monster movie, the monster is always more fearful before it is seen. Understanding the structure and potentials of a lawsuit make it easier to live with. It is part of being wise to see potential situations and to evaluate them properly.

Relying upon such knowledge does not mean that you have no faith in God. God is good, all the time. God's goodness is often provided by means of the creature. The ability to understand disease and develop remedies is a matter of God's "common grace." One way in which God is good is providing information and the ability to understand information. Moreover, by understanding the basic manner in which a lawsuit develops, you will be in a better place to assist your attorney and evaluate your situation.

But there is another reason you should concern yourself with litigation. Even if by the grace of God, having been as wise as serpents and as innocent as doves, you have personally avoided litigation, your counselees will not have been so fortunate. Often, counselees will have found themselves on one end or the other of a lawsuit. The bad acts and madness (Ecclesiastes 9:3) of sin often result in complications involving other persons or even the police. Domestic violence will bring a criminal or a civil lawsuit. Sexual improprieties, unpaid debts, and slander can all result in lawsuits. (More about what your counselees may face in the legal system and how to help them will be provided in chapter 11.)

Gathering information is a necessary aspect of counseling. We always need to first understand the nature of our counselee's position before we can provide useful advice. Too much of one's understanding of litigation comes from social media and entertainment, which are both poor sources of information when it comes to the law. Indeed, even reporters who discuss legal matters routinely make wildly inaccurate representations about a lawsuit.

Until you experience it, it is hard to comprehend the pressure of litigation. When someone finds themself pressed into a lawsuit, they find themself being controlled by a judicial process over which they have limited power to resist. A judge can force you to appear and testify. One may force you to disclose private financial information or the content of conversations you thought were private. You will be forced to appear in a courtroom under penalty of arrest. And you will be forced to spend money you cannot afford on attorneys.

While you will perhaps never experience the pressure firsthand, you should try to gain some knowledge of the process. Therefore, we hope to provide you in this chapter with a brief overview of the typical structure of a lawsuit. We pray that you will never need this information as a defendant in a lawsuit, but we can say that you are quite likely to need this information as background for your work as a counselor.

This chapter is meant to provide a general overview of the basic structure of civil litigation. Civil litigation means two parties who sue one another in civil court. "Civil" court is different than "criminal" court. The same action could result in both a civil and a criminal action. If one person punched another person, there might be a civil action for "battery" (hitting someone). This would result in an order to pay money. There could also be a criminal action for battery, which results in jail time. In chapter 11, we will consider a specific instance of sexual assault with a particular eye to criminal prosecution.

The Stages of Litigation

There are three distinct phases of litigation: pre-filing, trial court, and appellate courts. The appellate process has two different stages: the immediate appeal from the trial court and review by the state supreme court. Appellate review may also have a third stage when a case moves from a state supreme court to the United States Supreme Court.

First, at the prefiling stage is the option for pre-court resolution. This could be informal discussion, mediation, arbitration, or some combination thereof. Most problems resolve at this point. Every time you had a conflict that did not result in a lawsuit, you resolved your trouble without the court.

Second, there is the trial stage. This is where you file a lawsuit and see a judge.

Third, there is the appellate stage. If one or both parties conclude that there was an error during the trial, they have an automatic right to appeal.

Fourth, in rare instances the case may have a second appeal to the Supreme Court.

There are two, roughly parallel, court systems in the United States. In every state, there is a state court. Most cases are matters of state law and most cases go to state court. In addition to state courts there are federal courts. Some cases must go to federal court; other cases may go to federal court.

The following chart summarizes the same information. You will see that whether you are in state or federal court, the structure of the judiciary is the same: trial court for the initial trial, appellate court for the appeal, and Supreme Court for the (rare) second appeal.

State Court	Federal Court	Comment
Trial Court Names for trial courts vary by state (for example, "Superior Court" in California and "Supreme Court" in New York).	Trial Court "District Court"	When a defendant receives the "complaint," the defendant has the right to ask the court to dismiss the action. However, it is uncommon for a case to be thrown out at this stage. What generally happens in the trial court is that you have a "right" to have your case determined in trial court.
Appellate Court Name of appellate court varies by state. (in New York, "New York Supreme Court, Appellate Division")	Appellate Court "Circuit Court"	Every party has an automatic right to an appeal.
State Supreme Court (in New York this is called the "Court of Appeals")	United States Supreme Court	You have no "right" to Supreme Court review. You must petition the court and request that your case be reviewed. Very few cases are granted review.
United States Supreme Court		In very rare cases, the final decision of a state supreme court may be reviewed by the United States Supreme Court.

Notes:

- A case can be resolved by settlement at any time.
- Any higher court may send a case "back down" to a previous court for additional work to answer a question. The most common form is the first appellate court sending a case back to a trial court for a new trial.
- A case can go "up and down" on multiple occasions.
- Review by a supreme court is not for the purpose of getting the right answer in your case but rather for creating a uniform law for the state or the United States.

What Would Start a Lawsuit?

For most ministries, there will primarily be three types of cases. First, there may be lawsuits which are common to any enterprise that has employees, makes purchases, rents property, and so forth.

Second, there may be lawsuits seeking liability on the basis of something you have done in the course of ministry. For instance, you have been counseling with a member of your congregation. The counseling goes poorly—perhaps there has been a Matthew 18 interaction, or you have instructed someone to break off a sinful relationship, or something similar. The former counselee leaves your meeting and hires an attorney.

Third, a ministry may bring or defend a lawsuit to protect its rights and set precedent for others. One widely publicized example is the mandate that all health insurance plans include cost-free coverage for contraception and even abortifacient drugs. This regulation spawned a multitude of lawsuits across the country. Another is a California law that would have required nonprofit religious pregnancy ministries to provide women with information about how to obtain a state-funded abortion. First Amendment rights of both speech and religion were at stake. In this type of case, where your ministry's constitutional rights are at issue, you may be able obtain excellent representation from one of the many fine legal defense organizations across the country.

Prelitigation Settlement Discussion

A prelitigation settlement discussion is usually optional. Typically this happens when the plaintiff's lawyer sends a letter or makes a telephone call asking to resolve informally before the case goes to court. Sometimes this letter includes a copy of a complaint that will be filed if the case does not settle.

As soon as you receive this telephone call or letter, you (1) convey the information to your leadership and (2) contact your attorney. The attorney should then "tender" the action to the insurance company.

"Tendering" a lawsuit to an insurance company is a request that the insurance company get involved in the lawsuit to pay for lawyers and to pay for a settlement or pay the damages verdict.

There are no rules for how such negotiations take place, but a few basic forms are used.

Demand and Response: The plaintiff's lawyer makes a monetary demand. You may then pay the amount demanded, reject the amount demanded, or make a counteroffer for less money.

Discussions without a Mediator: The parties sit down together or communicate by phone and try to work out some sort of resolution (usually a payment of money in exchange for an agreement not to sue). Such agreements almost always include a confidentiality provision.

Formal Mediation: The parties may also choose to use a third-party mediator. The mediator does not make a decision for either party. Rather, the mediator helps explain the pros and cons to each side. For instance, the mediator tells you that you will have a hard time proving a particular claim. The mediator may explain the difficulty, expense, and risk of litigation. Also, the mediator helps you see the other side's position more clearly and see yourself more clearly.

Why Should You Ever Settle?

A lawsuit—even a lawsuit you win—is a terrible experience. It is usually one of the worst experiences a person has during their life. Litigation is an endless sink of money and concern and time. At the very least, litigation is a constant distraction from your "real" life.

Furthermore, litigation is unfair. Outcomes are often wrong. Judges make mistakes. Juries misunderstand information. People have all sorts of biases that color their thinking. An honest lawyer will always tell you that you have only a small percentage chance of winning or losing. Most cases are 50-50. A great case is 75-25. A terrible case is 25-75. This means that even if you are completely in the right, you have a one in four chance of losing.

One aspect of litigation that often surprises and upsets the parties is reading and hearing the sort of things of which they are accused. For instance, if each side has a completely different representation of the facts, that means each side is calling the other side a liar. A plaintiff will allege that the defendant "intentionally and maliciously" did some bad act. Reading and hearing your character attacked can be extremely upsetting. Parties often demand that their lawyer do something about the name-calling.

You will be tempted to respond in the same manner. This can present a quandary for the Christian caught in litigation. How do you love your enemy (so to speak) and still protect yourself and the ministry's assets? The interchanges can be very pointed, and emotions can run high. On one occasion, after I had lost my temper, I apologized to the opposing attorney for my sharp remark. I don't believe I have ever seen a lawyer quite as baffled as that lawyer who was asked to forgive my remark.

But none of this means you should be careful what you tell your lawyer, even if you have done something wrong. A lawyer surprised by facts concerning his own client is in a difficult place. If an accusation is true, let your lawyer know immediately. Obviously, you should never lie to your attorney. Neither should you withhold important information.

Excursus on Privilege

At this point you need to understand the word *privilege*. There are two sets of privileges that are important to understand. First, there is the attorney–client privilege. This privilege is the power to speak to your lawyer in perfect confidence. With very few exceptions, anything you say to your lawyer must be kept confidential by your lawyer. You alone have the right to permit the lawyer to disclose certain facts. For this reason, you can safely confide even difficult things to your lawyer.

Another kind of privilege applies in litigation: the right to say something in the course of the litigation and be free from liability for making the statement. Almost everything that is said during a lawsuit is "privileged." Here, "privileged" means that you can't sue the other side for defamation even if their court papers are filled with malicious lies. You can think of a prelitigation settlement demand as a hold up, if it helps you understand the process. The complaint may only be a ransom note.

Economics of Settlement

Often litigation settlements are a straight matter of economics, particularly as far as the insurance company is concerned. Let us assume I am suing you for $100. If I win, I get $100. If I lose, I get $0. We each have a 50-50 chance of winning. It will cost $50 to defend the lawsuit through trial (litigation is very expensive). Therefore, the case is worth $50 to settle. If you defend the case successfully, you will pay $50. If you lose, you will be paying $50 for defense and $100 for a verdict. You will spend at least $50 no matter what happens.

Timing of Settlement

Settlement is not something that happens only before a complaint is filed. Lawsuits can be settled at any time—even after appeal. One of the most common times for a lawsuit to settle is after the jury leaves to make a decision and before the jury returns with a verdict.

A Lawsuit Begins in Trial Court

A lawsuit begins with an attorney drafting a complaint and filing the complaint with the court. The court receives the complaint, opens a file, assigns the case to some judge (this process varies from court to court), and "issues a subpoena." A subpoena is an order of the court by which the court acquires jurisdiction. When the subpoena is put in your hands, the judge has "jurisdiction" over you concerning the complaint. The judge's jurisdiction remains until the case is over or the case is sent to a different court (such as on appeal).

At the moment the court acquires jurisdiction, you are in a very different world. Today, Judge X can give you all the commands the judge wants, and you can ignore them all you like. But as soon as Judge X acquires jurisdiction, the judge's word has the force of law.

As with the settlement demand, you need to immediately involve your church leadership and the church's attorney. Do not delay. Often parties sit on the complaint until the last day and then contact an attorney. Please do not do that! It makes the lawyer's life needlessly difficult, and it makes your life worse. If you do not respond to the complaint in the time required, the opposing party can obtain a "default." That means the lawsuit is over as far as your participation. You lost, and the other side now gets to tell the judge how bad you are; you cannot respond. In addition, your insurance company may not provide you any help because you have breached your agreement with the insurance company. While a default can sometimes be reversed, it is difficult, expensive, and uncertain. Do not delay when it comes to the law.

Pleading Stage

The pleading stage is the time when the parties set up the parameters of the case. The basic documents called "pleadings" are a complaint and an answer. A complaint is a statement of facts and list of legal accusations. The complaint ends with a "prayer." A prayer is a request for the payment of money (or some other remedy). The "plaintiff" begins the lawsuit with a "complaint."

The defense has two basic options: challenge the complaint and ask for an early dismissal or "answer." Let's examine each of these options in more detail.

An immediate challenge to the pleadings rarely succeeds in ending the case (although it is a possibility). The court must assume the allegations in the complaint are true, but the allegations may not have any legal importance. For example, the complaint alleges that you wore a blue shirt and the plaintiff wants money. You respond by saying, "Even if it is true that I wore a blue shirt, it does not matter." Lawyers call this a "demurrer." The court says, "You're right; blue shirts do not violate the law." The complaint is rejected. The plaintiff either quits or files a new, amended complaint that adds additional facts or law.

When the complaint meets the minimum legal requirements, the defense "answers." The answer denies the allegations in the complaint and raises defenses. For example, the answer will say, "Yes, I am not a licensed psychologist. But the plaintiff signed a waiver in which she acknowledged that I am not a psychologist. She also agreed that she would not sue me. Therefore, even though it is true that I am not a licensed psychologist, I should prevail."

Here's where your written informed consent form is vitally important. If done correctly, that form explains that you're engaged in religious ministry, not licensed psychotherapy, and the counselee, knowing that, voluntarily agreed to participate. Hopefully your consent form also contains a biblical dispute resolution policy. Before any paperwork is ever filed with a court—perhaps when a demand is made—a copy of the signed paperwork may persuade the other person (or his attorney) to enter the mediation process. If that does not happen, your attorney may respond to the complaint by filing a motion asking the court to order the mediation as you and your counselee have agreed in writing.

Discovery Stage

This is the longest part of the case. After the pleadings and before the trial, the parties receive and give information to each other. First there is written discovery, which consists of written questions or demands for particular documents. You will need to assist your lawyer in answering the questions and obtaining documents.

Always help your lawyer. I cannot stress the importance of this enough. The lawyer did not live your life and does not know what happened. Moreover, even though the facts seem very clear to you, they are hazy to the attorney. Clients often assume facts in telling a story. We leave things out, add details (not to deceive but just because we make mistakes), and so forth. As the lawyer works with the case, you may realize that certain details are unclear or certain facts will become more or less important.

In addition to written discovery, there will be "depositions." This is examination under oath. This is very much like the sort of questioning you have seen in a movie (although it is never as interesting) where a lawyer asks a witness questions. It has all the importance and formality of a trial, except it is done in a lawyer's office. Depositions can be asked of anyone who is a witness.

By the way, "cross-examination" means when one party asks questions of a witness who is testifying for the other side. Even though movie cross-examination is often dramatic and confrontational, a lot of good cross-examination is often quiet and friendly. A skillful lawyer is one who can get a difficult witness to open up and talk. It is true that sometimes this seems like prying open a clam. But the more common procedure is to coax out the reluctant witness and get them chatting.

There may also be "expert" discovery. An expert is someone who does not testify about the facts of the case but rather about what the facts mean. For example, a medical doctor may explain why a particular medicine was a good or bad decision. The expert will assume certain facts are true and then offer opinions about those assumed facts.

Pretrial

In the weeks leading up to trial, the parties need to get the case ready. This is by far the busiest and hardest part of the case. Good trial preparation requires a lawyer to script out the action line by line, anticipate every countermove by the opposition, be prepared with a response to every countermove, and so on. The trial is a drama, and a lawyer is putting on a production in front of a neutral and a hostile audience. It takes a lot of work. You will need to be available quite a bit during this time.

The Trial

Real courtrooms are rarely like those in the movies. Most of them are not the beautiful large rooms with marble and mahogany that some of you may recall from episodes of *Perry Mason* or *Law and Order*. Instead, most courtrooms are cramped, poorly decorated rooms piled high with paper and boxes and equipment. After both parties bring in their exhibits and files and books, the courtroom will look like an episode of a reality show on hoarding. It will be hard to get around. You will be stepping around and over boxes trying not to trip!

Almost all courtrooms have the same basic elements. There is a space for the jury (the box), a space for the judge, a court reporter, and a bailiff. There is a space directly in front of the judge called the "well." Never stand in the well. Sometimes judges come unglued if you walk through the well. Do not breach this custom.

The trial is boring. A lawyer asks a question. The other lawyer objects. The lawyers go "side bar" with the judge and whisper vigorously about exceptions to the hearsay rule; the judge makes a decision and sends the lawyers back. No one else in the courtroom has any idea what just happened. Many lawyers make this worse by getting confused.

Most witnesses are frightened. They forget facts. Lots of witnesses tell untruths—both by accident and on purpose. People will say terrible things about you in public, and you have been instructed by your lawyer to not respond: don't shake your head, smile, or frown. You must become a statue. But don't be too stiff because the jury will think you are a sociopath without emotions.

The jury does not want to be there. The jurors would rather do anything else in the world. If they think you're wasting their time, they will dislike you.

Lawyers do not ever get to approach the witness and ask cutting questions to watch the witness fall into a heap and admit to lying. On a rare occasion, a lawyer may be permitted to help a witness find a sentence on a page from a document that the witness is being asked about. So forget all those brilliant movie scenes.

You will find going to trial tedious, time consuming, and unsettling as you have your life held in the hands of twelve strangers and a judge. I have never known anyone to enjoy the process of being in trial—except for the lawyers. For lawyers, going to trial is like playing a sport. This is the big game. Don't hate your lawyer for treating your life like a competitive sport. That is what lawyers do, and you are paying your lawyer to have emotional detachment. If the lawyer's personal emotions become too involved, the lawyer will make a mistake.

Statements

The trial begins with an "opening statement." This is a promise to the jury about the facts of the case. The lawyer will give the jurors an overview of what will be said and done during the trial. The lawyer specifically cannot make an argument nor provide much commentary. The opening statement is just a plain version of the facts, with an emphasis here rather than there.

After the trial, the lawyers will make their "closing arguments." Here the lawyer says, in effect, "You should do this because the other side did that." This is one of the most interesting and entertaining parts of the trial. This is the only time during the trial when anything "dramatic" can take place.

The Verdict

Assuming you have a jury, following closing arguments the judge reads the jury the "instructions." These are the rules for how the jurors are to evaluate evidence and make a decision about the law. The jury will be told how to weigh evidence and what they are allowed to consider. The jury will be told the elements of various torts, what constitutes a breach, and how to determine damages (if any).

After receiving the instructions, the jury "retires," or leaves the courtroom. In the jury room, the jurors discuss the case, returning sometime later with a verdict. The jury hands the verdict to the judge. The judge reads the verdict.

Posttrial

A trial is not the end. Before the case is appealed, the parties have the right to ask the judge to throw the case out and start over or ask the judge to change some element of the verdict. If the case involves punitive damages, there will be a separate miniature trial on punitive damages. "Damages" means the amount of money the defendant has to pay. One kind of damages is called "compensatory." These are damages that compensate for what was lost—lost wages for someone who was wrongfully terminated, for instance. "Punitive" damages are damages to punish. If a defendant committed a tort and did so maliciously, purposefully seeking to harm another person, that defendant might have to pay "punitive" damages. "Punitive" damages are punishment.

You don't need to understand all these procedures but know they may come.

Appellate Court

When the parties move to the appellate court, the documents are no longer called "complaints" or "answers." In the appellate court, the parties file a "brief." Briefs are written legal arguments. The briefs are based upon the facts which set forth in the trial, but the emphasis is on the legal issues (in a trial court, the emphasis is on the facts). By means of briefs, the lawyers fill courts with mountains of paper. Briefs are anything but brief!

After the verdict is final, you are only halfway through a lawsuit. As soon as the case is final, a clock starts. There are various confusing but critical rules about what rulings may be appealed and when the clock starts running for filing an appeal. A lot of decisions will need to be made quickly. These decisions will need to be made with a lawyer, and often they are made by the insurance company.

The good news for you—to the extent there is good news—is that you will personally be far less involved with the appellate process. The lawyer may ask you to read a draft of the "brief" for your approval. Feel free to ask questions. It is completely appropriate to ask the lawyer to explain the arguments. Appellate lawyers are often more expensive than trial attorneys. You will be paying a great deal of money, and you have every right to understand what is being done. However, you can also permit the lawyer to proceed. While it is critical that you be intimately involved with the work done at trial (which primarily involves developing the facts), it is rare that you *must* be involved with the appeal. On the whole, the appellate lawyer does the work without you.

Your Lawyer

At this point, you may or may not continue with the same lawyers. There are lawyers who only take cases on appeal. There are lawyers who never take cases on appeal and will only work at the trial court. There are also lawyers who will stick with the same case from beginning to end.

It is not uncommon for a new lawyer to join the case. This new lawyer often has more appellate experience than your trial court lawyer. Or perhaps the new lawyer is brought in to help add a new perspective to the lawsuit. If an insurance company is paying the bills, the insurance company gets to make this decision on your behalf.

As a religious ministry, it's possible you'll have a case that implicates religious liberty. You may need to file a lawsuit to protect your liberty, or you might raise religious freedom as a defense.

Either way, your case could have a profound impact on the rights of other believers in the future.

While the question of religious liberty will begin at the trial stage, the question of religious liberty is more important at the appellate stage. The reason for this difference is that the decision of a trial court typically only implicates the parties to the trial. Appellate decisions are public documents that make law for other cases. For instance, a trial court must follow a decision of an appellate court.

Therefore it would be wise to contact one or more Christian legal defense organizations to see if they can take your case or provide a referral. These groups can't take every case that comes their way, but in a context like biblical counseling, where religious liberty issues are involved, it's worth asking.

The Appellate Court Process

An appeal starts with a notice of appeal. This is a simple statement that says the "Defendant [or the plaintiff] appeals the decision of the court on Day X." When that happens, the case is transferred from the trial court to the appellate court.

There is a "golden rule" in appellate law: If it isn't on the record, it didn't happen. No new facts show up on appeal. Instead, the documents and transcript of the proceedings that were used in the trial court (testimony during trial, various arguments made before a judge) are put together and delivered to the appellate court. This process of preparing a record is expensive and tedious, but it is necessary. The appellate court can only consider evidence that is found in the record. There will be no new discovery, just an evaluation of the record "from below."

A case has two elements: facts and law.

The Facts: The appellate court accepts the facts as they were "found" by the trial court.

To discover what this means, let's consider a scenario where one witness says X was true and another witness says X was false. The jury said they believe the first witness. Therefore, as far as the appellate court is concerned, "X is true." It does not matter if the first witness lied. It does not matter if you know for a moral certainty that X never came close to being true and everyone on the planet (except the jury) knows that the first witness lied and X is not true. As far as the appellate court is concerned, "X is true."

In very narrow circumstances, you might be able to get the appellate court to disregard a finding of the trial court. For instance, let us say the jury found X is true. But let us also say that no one ever even mentioned X at trial. No X ever passed anyone's lips, and X was not contained in any document. However, the jury for some inexplicable reason found X was true.

Here is the bottom line: an appellate court mostly takes the facts exactly in the manner they were determined by the trial court. Think of it like a history book that has been written and it is the only book to use for an exam.

The Law: The law is a different matter. The law books are the same for a trial court as for an appellate court. In fact, appellate courts are far better suited to deal with legal questions. A trial court judge is often a single person reading a mountain of paper after dinner and before bed. The days in the courtroom are spent making fairly quick decisions. The trial court judge doesn't have much time to spend contemplating the law.

Meanwhile, appellate judges have a staff of attorneys whose job it is to assist the judge. So appellate courts have the ability and the time to make a careful review of the law. If you overturn a case on appeal, it will be because someone made a mistake of the law during the initial trial. For instance, the judge gave the jury the wrong jury instruction. Or perhaps the judge allowed in some testimony that the rules of evidence prohibit. The appellate court needs to determine whether there actually was a mistake of law.

That does not end the process. The appellate court must also make a determination as to whether the mistake from the trial court really matters much. Let us say that the trial court improperly kept one of the witnesses from testifying on a particular point. The appellate court takes a look and decides the trial court should have let that testimony in, but it does not really change anything. And then the appellate court explains that three other witnesses said the same thing or that the case really does not concern that point.

How the Lawyers Present Their Case

The primary method of communicating with the appellate court is through the briefs: long, written arguments that are hardly "brief." But there is also oral argument. The lawyers for each side appear before the court and make their case face-to-face. The primary thing that happens during oral argument is that the appellate judges ask questions of the lawyers, trying to figure out some point that may not have been clear from the papers. You are permitted to attend these hearings.

Then What Happens?

The appellate court issues a ruling. This is most often a long statement that explains the facts and the law and comes to a decision.

This decision might say that one side or the other side has won. The decision might say that the appellant—the person who initiated the appeal—won on point A, and the respondent won on point B. The appellate court might issue an order saying the case is effectively over, or the appellate court might issue an order telling the trial court to start all over. In some cases, a law is declared unconstitutional, or the meaning of a statute is clarified.

Whatever happens, the appellate court is the end of the case for 99 percent of all cases. You have probably heard people say, "I'm going to take this to the Supreme Court!" Actually, the Supreme Court gets to decide if your case ever goes "up" from the appellate court.

A Writ of Certiorari

An application (or petition) for a writ of certiorari means in lawyer-talk, "Will you please take my case?" After your case has completed the appellate process, the court will issue a written decision. In almost every case that is the end of the case, but there is one more possible move: the supreme court of your state (or the US Supreme Court if your case started in federal court or received a final decision in your state supreme court).

The appellate court is there to determine the outcome of your personal case. A supreme court exists to set law for the entire jurisdiction. Two basic types of cases may be taken by the US Supreme Court.

One type of case is a split between the circuits. There are twelve federal circuits. If you are in California, you are in the Ninth Circuit. If you are in New York, you are in the Second Circuit. An appeal from a federal court in Los Angeles goes to the Ninth Circuit Court of Appeal. An appeal from a federal trial court in New York goes to the Second Circuit Court of Appeal. Let us say that there is a question as to whether a Muslim mosque can play the call to prayer over a public loudspeaker with enough volume to be heard by all persons in a one-mile radius. Then suppose that in the Ninth Circuit the call to prayer is allowed, but the Second Circuit does not find this to be an exercise protected by the First Amendment. You might think that such a decision would only matter to Muslims and those who live near the mosque. But such decisions might be of importance to Christian ministries. The mosque's call to pray might be analogous to a biblical counseling center's decision to offer free counseling to those entering an abortion clinic.

When a decision has the potential for affecting a great many people—especially when there are different decisions between the various circuit courts—it could be useful to have a clear rule throughout the United States. And even though decisions by the Supreme Court are far less common than decisions of trial courts, decisions by the Supreme Court are far more important to us all. These are the decisions that we hear about in the news. These are also the decisions that control the actions of all the trial courts and appellate courts in the country. In fact, certain decisions of the United States Supreme Court can be binding, not just to nearly every federal court but also to every state court.

If your case either involves a conflict between the appellate courts, or if it involves some matter of extraordinary importance, you can file a "Petition for Writ of Certiorari" with the Supreme Court and ask to have your case heard. Unfortunately, you will almost certainly be rejected. The Supreme Court is not interested in fixing your case. The Supreme Court is concerned with fixing the law for everyone (including you). Your case is accepted only if it will help clarify the law or make the law more uniform.

Sometimes the Supreme Court will "GVR" a case—grant, vacate, remand. That could happen to your case if, when your petition is filed, the court has already granted review of a petition that raises a nearly identical legal issue. After that first case is decided, the court may grant your petition, vacate the lower court's ruling, and send it back ("remand") to the lower court to reconsider. This procedure can add lots of time to your case—and provide a golden opportunity for you to grow in patience!

Here is one more twist: If your case began in state court (as most cases do), you work your way through the court system and go to the state supreme court. If your decision involves a matter of federal law (most often with the US Constitution), you can actually seek a second review by the United States Supreme Court. Having your case reviewed by both a state supreme court and the United States Supreme Court would be like winning the lottery twice in one day—especially if you prevail!

Counting the Cost

For almost every case, there are two possible steps: trial and appeal. Your case is tried by one court and reviewed by another court. That is the end of your case. Before we move onto the question of the Supreme Court, you should consider the enormous expense that goes into a single trial and appeal.

Attorneys' fees for each side of a "regular" case to be fully prepared and tried will easily exceed $100,000. If the case runs smoothly, it takes a routine case in Los Angeles County at least one year to move from initial filing to trial.

The expense to the state is enormous. A courtroom requires a court attendant, a judge, a court reporter, and additional backstage support staff of hundreds of clerks and attendants at a large court. If there is a jury, twelve people are required by law to take two weeks out of their life to listen to and pass judgment on case.

An appeal restarts the costs. Preparing the record for appeal can costs tens of thousands of dollars. The attorneys' fees on appeal, assuming your lawyers do a thorough job, can again run from $50,000 to $100,000 without it being an unusual case.

The time from start to finish for an appeal can easily take close to a year. And again, the governmental costs are enormous. An appellate panel consists of three judges, all of whom have a staff of attorneys, attendants, and so on. There is also a security staff to protect the courts.

I once worked on a case which at heart concerned an easement purchased for $13,000. The attorneys' fees for the parties involved exceeded $500,000. The case was completed in the trial court, appealed, and then returned to the trial for another round. Cases may continue beyond the point where it is economically rational because of the parties' emotions—desire for revenge, retaliation, or justice. These are issues that implicate the human heart and the problem of sin.

Conclusion

In conclusion, the legal process is slow, expensive, and often painful. Judges and juries do their best and still make profound errors. Facts come out wrong, lawyers make bad arguments, and witnesses lie.

Lawyers are paid largely because the procedure is so strange and unpleasant that no one would do their work for free.

Still, the judicial system is an aspect of God's "common grace." It is a human means of government that resolves problems that would otherwise not be resolved short of violence. Physicians make errors, and still we see doctors because our imperfect medical care is better than no medical care. Medicine is a common grace of God given to maintain life. The judicial system, with all its flaws, is better than no judicial system.

We can go further. While there are notable errors, the American judicial system does not suffer from the rampant corruption that has marked many courts throughout history. Although the highly politicized cases make the news, routine lawsuits are judged and tried with as much ability and honesty as we could hope for in a system made up of human beings trying to determine what is just.

As counselors, we are given the duty to minister the Word of God. With such a responsibility, how must we think about the law? Seek to avoid those turns in a relationship that end in litigation. A lawsuit happens because the parties could not resolve their difficulties. How many troubles could be resolved if we took to heart 1 Corinthians 6:7? Think of the instruction the Lord has given us, which if we took to heart would resolve our troubles without judges, juries, and lawyers.

Think of how we can build cultures of grace and forgiveness in our congregation. Think of how our conflicts can function as a time for witness that we suffer wrong and commit the judgment of our cause to him who judges righteously (1 Peter 2:23). And if we must resort to courts (there will be times when this cannot be avoided), think of how we maintain our witness before judges and juries and the watching world.

Do not discourage members of your congregation who are considering a career in the law. There are many who have a blanket distain for the legal system and think that sneering and complaining will somehow make things better. Much of the trouble in the system stems from a conscious decision of many interest groups—whose interests are quite contrary to the interest of the church—to create lawyers and judges who are biased against the interest of the church or religious convictions. We should encourage—not discourage—Christian men and women to actively seek to be involved with the judicial system at all levels. It is demanding but necessary work. If the system is too often wicked and not merely wrong, then the fault may lie with us for not participating in that system.

To-Do List

- ❒ Realize that the litigation involving the church across the country, or the Christian photographer in the tenth circuit, could affect the biblical counseling ministry in your local congregation. Pray for the parties and attorneys involved in this work. Consider supporting legal societies that defend religious liberty.
- ❒ As we have counseled elsewhere in this book, establish a relationship with an attorney before you "need" an attorney.
- ❒ Take the steps set forth in other chapters in this book to avoid unnecessary exposure to litigation.
- ❒ If you find yourself in litigation, do not be consumed with fear. The heart of the king and the judge is in the hand of the Lord, and the Lord "turns it wherever he will" (Proverbs 21:1f).

CHAPTER 9

How to Avoid a Lawsuit

Todd M. Sorrell

You open the door and are greeted by a man with a thick envelope. "Are you Tripp MacArthur Adams?" he asks with a smile. Thinking that your online order of a leather-bound copy of Calvin's *Institutes* had just arrived, you confirm with a nod and a hearty, "Yes." The man's smile fades as he hands you the package. Then he says those three words that you never wanted to hear: "You've been served."

Your heart sinks. Unlike Christmas where you grew up enjoying surprises and opening gifts, you aren't enjoying this. You slowly peel open the envelope and pull out the papers inside. They are in a format you don't recognize, but your eyes are drawn toward the middle of the page where your name is listed as a defendant. You then scan up and see the name of the person who has filed a lawsuit against you. Memory after memory of your biblical counseling sessions with this person invades your mind.

As you try to read, you are also processing and analyzing your past counseling sessions with this individual, wondering what went wrong. The legalese is gobbledygook to your eyes and seems designed to hide the actual meaning of the claims. But you slowly get the gist of what your counselee is complaining about and why he included it in a publicly filed lawsuit. Your anxiety is now laced with anger that is poised to overwhelm you. You think, *Lies! This is full of lies! I was helping this guy. I took time out of my life, didn't charge him a dime, and provided solid biblical counsel. He just terminated the sessions and left.* Your thoughts are set to high speed, and you are wondering what to do. As you slow down to think about who to call (a lawyer, for example), you wonder if there is anything you could have done to avoid this entire situation. Put another way, if you could rewind that portion of your life, you wonder if anyone could have given you advice on the topic of how to avoid a lawsuit.

Perhaps the above has not happened to you—yet. But you are still looking for someone to tell you how to avoid a lawsuit, so allow me to burst your bubble: No one can give you that advice. No one can guarantee that you will never be sued. People get sued all the time, sometimes for ridiculous reasons. So don't be lulled into thinking there is some secret to employ that will insulate you from lawsuits. It doesn't exist. But there *is* good news. There is a lot that can be done to greatly reduce your chances of being on the receiving end of a lawsuit. Indeed, this section should have been entitled "How to Minimize Your Chances of Getting Sued."

With that qualification in mind, let's begin with the basics. What is a lawsuit, and why does it matter? A lawsuit is a proceeding initiated by one or more persons or organizations against another in a civil court of law. The person filing the lawsuit is called a plaintiff, and the person on the other side is called a defendant. The plaintiff claims to have suffered loss or damage as a result of action or inaction by the defendant, and he seeks money and/or an injunction. (An injunction is an order that requires the defendant to do or not do something.) In addition to being compelled to pay money damages or attorneys' fees or being subjected to an injunction, lawsuits are time-consuming and can create significant stress for participants. You do not want to be a defendant in a lawsuit.

While there are many ways to minimize the risk of being sued, perhaps the easiest insurance to have in place in the biblical counseling setting is the first document that should trade hands between a biblical counselor and counselee—the Consent to Counsel form. A Consent to Counsel form is exactly what it sounds like. It is a written document where the terms of the engagement are agreed upon, like a sort of permission slip for the counselor to begin work. Some are quite brief and simply identify the counselor and counselee and give a vague description of the counseling, while others are longer and quite detailed. The longer one is better—far better. Why? Because it discloses in more detail what can be expected, the basis for the counseling, the mechanisms for resolving conflict, and various limitations on both parties. It provides information to the counselee and may qualify as informed consent, thus making it more difficult for him to later claim he was unaware of certain information. After all, he must read and sign it.

I have heard counselors and church leaders say that such forms are unnecessary, and, in fact, that they serve to chill the organic relationship among potential counselees and counselors. Nonsense. First, if someone desires counseling, one document at the beginning of the relationship will do nothing to chill it. Second, if someone refuses a simple request to read and sign this form, what are the odds that the person will actually end up doing the homework and showing up for counseling on a consistent basis? Third, the more you counsel, the more you will realize that there are many people in need. If one person refuses to participate, there are many others who will gladly enter into this discipleship relationship as they seek to deepen their walks with our Lord.

In addition to providing information, a Consent to Counsel form provides some protection in case a counselee or third party gets the bright idea someday to consider legal action against you (or your church or counseling center). In exchange for counseling, the counselee agrees to waive certain potential claims. While there are many unscrupulous people (and lawyers) out there, most would prefer *not* to litigate in the presence of a signed document that clearly acknowledges the risks and limitations of the counseling. Consider a few potential scenarios.

Scenario 1: A depressed counselee has had suicidal thoughts. You work through those issues, and you incorrectly decide that the risk has passed or he isn't serious. He takes his own life. His family looks to hold someone accountable. Since you were his counselor, they think you should have recommended medication. At that point, would you like to have a document in your file that expressly states that you are *not* a doctor and you will not be providing medical advice?

Scenario 2: You counsel through your church, but you are not licensed by the state. The government decides that what you are doing is similar enough to family and marriage therapy that it contends you have committed some sort of legal violation by "practicing without a license." Would you like to have a document in your file that clearly states the biblical and ministerial basis for your counseling as part of your practice of religion in order to potentially remove it from the purview of state regulation?

Scenario 3: A counselee brings a crime to your attention. You are not sure what to do, but he shared the information in confidence. You plan on getting advice from church leadership. Would you like to have a document in your file that explicitly states that there are situations where absolute confidentiality will not be honored?

Scenario 4: Your counselee informs you that he is engaged in a serious pattern of sin. He refuses to repent. Instead, he terminates counseling and moves to another church. You contact the new church to advise the leaders. The counselee accuses you of divulging confidential information. Would you like to have a document in your file that specifically allows for such a disclosure?

Scenario 5: You go through eight weeks of counseling, during which the counselee repents of his unrighteous anger and starts to implement good habits. You are later informed that his wife is threatening to sue you and the church because he recently flew into a rage and hurt their young child. The wife thinks you should have referred him to anger management classes or a licensed psychologist. At that point, wouldn't you like to have a document in your file that indicates that all counseling will be governed by the Bible (and not secular psychology), that there shall be no liability arising from the alleged failure of the counselor to interpret or apply the Bible in any particular way, and that the church will not be liable for any claims raised against the counselor?

The point of considering the scenarios above is not to scare you. The point is to help you be wise and prepared (Proverbs 6:6–8; 22:3). In the discussion that follows, we will walk through a sample Consent to Counsel form. We will look at each paragraph so that you understand why it is included. At this point, however, three things must be stated.

First, while the focus of this discussion is to provide one legal perspective on counseling and how to do it in a wise way, it is important for readers to understand that the absence of a discussion on the pain and scars that sin can create is not evidence that counselors don't care about those things. They do. Deeply. In fact, the first reaction of many counselors to a threat of a lawsuit in light of something bad happening may be to agonize over the struggle now facing the former counselee or his loved ones. However, that is not the focus of this discussion. Instead, we are looking for tips on how counselors can implement best practices to reduce the chances of something bad happening (and being sued for it).

Second, the best preventive action a counselor can take to avoid being accused of misconduct is to hone his craft in a professional and diligent manner. This is biblical counseling, so be diligent to present yourself before God as one who rightly handles his Word (2 Timothy 2:15). Do not approach counseling in a lazy or haphazard way. You are an instrument used by God to mold hearts and souls. Do not take that lightly.

Third, these materials are prepared for informational purposes only and should not be construed as legal advice or a legal opinion on any specific facts. In addition, they may not reflect the most current legal developments, and each jurisdiction may have different laws, so it is advised that you not rely upon this information without seeking independent legal advice. Further, nothing in this chapter should be construed as creating an attorney–client relationship between the reader and the author. These ideas are simply shared to get you thinking about how you might want to run your counseling ministry. With that in mind, let's walk through a sample Consent to Counsel form. Bold words are highlighted for emphasis only.

Consent to Counsel Form

Paragraph 1: **Read this form carefully.** You will be signing at the end to confirm that you understand and agree to it. If you want or need separate counsel (legal or otherwise), you may obtain it prior to signing this document and participating in counseling.

Comment: This is the first thing a counselee will read. The idea is to obtain informed consent. Asking a counselee to read, understand, and agree with its contents is key. It is a lot more difficult for someone who reads this to say that you never explained the goal and limitations of biblical counseling or the rules by which you will operate.

Caveat: If possible, provide this form to the counselee before your first meeting to give him time to read and sign it. He must be informed.

Paragraph 2: Biblical Counseling: This is a **ministry of the Gospel of Jesus Christ and is part of our practice of religion**. You have indicated that you are a Christian and you are **voluntarily seeking religious guidance** (biblical counseling) from one or more other Christians. The **goal of biblical counseling is to help Christians become more and more like Jesus Christ** in attitude, thought, and action. With that in mind, **biblical counseling is the same as discipleship**. As Christians, we are called to make disciples, teaching them to observe all that Jesus commanded (Matthew 28:16–20). Our goal in providing Christian counseling is to help you live your entire life in a God-pleasing/God-honoring way. This includes, but is not limited to, providing biblical counsel to assist you in meeting the challenges of your life; shedding sin that so easily entangles; learning to develop, cultivate, and live in relationships that please God; giving thanks to God in all circumstances; living in a community of other believers **as you participate in your local church**, and learning to rely on the Holy Spirit for direction as you seek to know God through his Word (the Bible). Although the biblical advice we provide is intended to be practical, it is entirely **your decision how to (and whether to) implement** that advice. We want to help you love God and love others as we walk with you through this process. During the course of the counseling relationship, we may counsel you from the Bible that **certain conduct is sinful and must be stopped** in order to please God, and we may counsel you in **how Scripture directs Christians** to put off that sin and, instead, to live a life characterized by self-control and godliness. By signing below, you are specifically **agreeing to such counsel and are affirmatively asking** that we provide it. As stated above, we will counsel you from our **deeply held Christian, religious beliefs, and this counseling is part of our practice of religion**. Biblical counseling **is disciple-making**, and it in no way shall be construed as a sale of services. We do not charge for this counseling.

Comment: This paragraph begins and ends by placing biblical counseling squarely within the practice of religion. It's telling the government to keep its hand out of this ministry. The voluntary, ministry-based nature of such counseling is clear. Most importantly, it identifies the goal, which is to help actual believers become more like Jesus Christ, our Savior. The call to discipleship and obedience to the Word is front and center, making it wholly distinct from secular counseling or family therapy. This discusses counseling in the context of living in a community of believers and places the burden on the counselee to decide whether to take the advice or not. Unlike secular counseling, this makes it clear that the counselee will be told to put off (stop) sinful behaviors, whether the world approves of those behaviors or not.

Caveat: This paragraph concludes with two sentences that may not apply to your situation. If you do charge for biblical counseling, remove or modify these sentences.

Paragraph 3: Biblical Basis: We believe that the Holy Scriptures (the Bible) provide sufficient guidance and instruction for faith and life. Therefore, our **counseling is based on scriptural (biblical) principles** rather than those of secular psychology or psychiatry. **We are not licensed** or certified as psychotherapists, psychologists, psychiatrists, mental health professionals, marriage and family therapists, or social workers, nor are we acting in such capacities. **If you are unwilling to use the Bible as the final authority in counseling or are unwilling to do the homework assigned, you should not proceed with this counseling**. However, we do want to help, and we pray that you will decide to look to God's Word for guidance as we follow the loving example of Jesus Christ. Through the power of the Holy Spirit, we believe that your life can be transformed.

Comment: This makes it clear that the counselor is *not* relying on secular practices or theories, discloses that the counselor is not licensed in secular therapy, and indicates that the Bible is the ultimate authority for the counseling. The idea is to provide sufficient information for the counselee to understand that this counseling is part of the Christian faith, which looks to God's Word for transformative heart change.

Caveat: If you happen to be licensed in one of these areas, revise this paragraph but also make clear that biblical counseling is different from and not governed by secular practices. For example, let us say that you are a licensed social worker who provides services for the county government. You have a license from the state, and you help homeless women find shelter and training. In the evening and on the weekends, you work as a biblical counselor. The release form could say that even though you have a license from the state to be a social worker, you are not acting as a social worker when providing biblical counseling.

Paragraphs 4–5: Professional Advice, Etc.: **We do not provide legal, tax, medical, financial, or other technical or professional (nonpsychological) advice** (although we advise that you handle all matters in a Christlike and ethical way). Even though you are agreeing to participate in biblical counseling, there may be times when you need such professional advice. Although we undertake no duty to recognize when or if such advice is actually needed, if we opine that such professional counsel would be helpful, we may encourage you to seek it. Further, we are happy to cooperate with such advisors and help you to consider their counsel in the light of relevant scriptural principles. Further, **we are not responsible for nor shall we be liable for any physical, mental, or medical condition of any counselee**, whether or not such condition is affected in any way by the counseling process or counsel provided.

No professional–client or fiduciary relationship is created between any counselee and counselor. The parties recognize that the counselor may have training in matters and/or employment beyond the scope of biblical counseling. However, the **counselor is not acting in that other capacity on behalf of the counselee**. Further, it is agreed that **no church or school or any third party will incur any liability for counsel provided by us, even if such an institution is providing supervision**, generally or specifically, over this counseling and/or this ministry. Although we may take into consideration any applicable laws that you bring to our attention, it is intended that the **Holy Scriptures (the Bible) shall be the supreme authority** governing every aspect of the counseling process and that God's glory is the ultimate goal. However, **failure of the counselor to interpret or apply the Bible in any particular way shall not subject the counselor to liability or give rise to complaint** by any party. There shall be **no legal or other liability** that attaches to any counselor or institution for any advice, methods, conduct, or any act or omission related in any way to the service that is provided, and you acknowledge that you are voluntarily seeking this counsel (free from coercion, duress, or pressure).

Comment: This makes it clear that biblical counsel is the sole focus, and no other professional advice is being offered. It also specifies that the counselor has no obligation to recognize when professional advice may be needed and indicates that no professional relationship exists, even if the counselor happens to have such training. This seeks to remove responsibility for any physical, mental, or medical condition that the counselee may experience. It further seeks to insulate any church or school from potential liability, even if providing supervision.

Caveat: If you do decide to interact with a third-party professional at the request of the counselee, have the counselee sign something that expressly grants you permission to do so.

Paragraph 6: Confidentiality: Although confidentiality is often one aspect of the counseling process and we intend to guard the information you entrust to us, **absolute confidentiality is not scriptural in all circumstances**. There are a number of situations when **it may be necessary (as determined by us in our sole discretion) for us to share information with others** and/or to take protective measures. These may include situations (1) When we are uncertain how to address a particular problem and **need to seek advice from another** pastor, educator, counselor, professional, or Christian; (2) when a **counselee attends (or attended) another church**, and we believe it is important to talk with his or her pastor, elders, or others at that church and/or in leadership; (3) when there is a clear indication that **someone may be harmed** unless others intervene or are consulted; (4) when a person **refuses to renounce a particular sin** and confess it to those impacted and it becomes necessary to seek the assistance of others in the church to encourage repentance, confession, and reconciliation (see Proverbs 15:22; 24:11; Matthew 18:15–20); (5) when **criminal activity** has occurred and the counselee refuses to bring it to the attention of the authorities; and/or (6) if we believe that a person is in need of **protective services** or that a person of **familial authority** needs to be informed (e.g., wife/husband, or child/parent). Information also may be shared for **education/training** purposes (see below). Nothing shall impose any obligation or legal duty on a counselor to disclose or maintain confidential any particular information.

Comment: Biblical counseling does *not* afford absolute confidentiality, and this needs to be made clear. Scripture teaches that sin often must be addressed in the open. This paragraph provides for that possibility and also specifies a number of situations where disclosures to third parties may occur. Furthermore, it is impossible to know at the beginning of the counseling relationship what information might arise, and the counselor should advise the counselee that Scripture, practical wisdom, and the law might require disclosure of what the counselee thinks is confidential or sensitive information.

Caveat: There are times when you may be unsure if you should disclose information from the counselee to third parties. The consent provided by the counselee affords you some flexibility to seek input from others, such as church leadership or lawyers. Be discerning in such disclosures.

Paragraph 7: Attendance/Training/Education: Please make every effort to **attend every scheduled session**. Further, please encourage your pastor from your local church or one of those in its leadership to accompany you in counseling sessions. In fact, depending on the situation, we may require such attendance as **we recognize and respect the authority and the discipline of the local church in your spiritual life**. In addition, this makes transfer back to the pastoral care of your church much easier to implement. If you are not attending a church, we expect you to **attend a Bible-preaching and believing church** weekly for your own benefit and for the benefit of the Body of Christ.

Comment: Requiring the counselee to attend sessions, attend church, and involve the counselee's church leadership in this discipleship process establishes expectations. It provides no excuse or ability to take a lackadaisical approach toward counseling. It also places the counseling relationship within the context of living for Christ within the local church.

Caveat: A rare situation might call for counseling someone who attends a different church. If so, it is wise to include a pastor or elder from the counselee's church, not only so that they are aware of the situation but also so that they learn from the counseling process and are able to step in and shepherd their own local flock.

Paragraph 8: We believe that all believers should strive to make disciples for the Lord Jesus Christ. With that in mind, we not only seek additional training and/or education for ourselves, but we seek to train and educate others in the biblical counseling arena. To accomplish both counseling and training, **we may have others assist us in counseling sessions (and/or preparation) who will have access to your personal information**. Further, there may be times when we deem it appropriate to use what is learned in counseling sessions to seek input from educators and/or students or to convey what is learned to educate others, either in person, online, in print, or through other means. If this happens, **care will be taken to protect your identity**.

> **Comment:** Disciple-making not only involves the counselee but also those who are called to learn how to counsel biblically. This provides permission for others to learn from this counseling.
>
> **Caveat:** If there is no specific need to identify the counselee in this context, take care to protect the identity of the person receiving the counsel when the situation is merely used for educational and training purposes.

Paragraph 9: Termination/Records: At any time and for any reason, the counselor (as well as the counselee) **may terminate** *counseling. However,* **termination of counseling will not preclude the counselor from making the disclosures** set forth above (in the paragraph entitled, "Confidentiality") if deemed appropriate by the counselor or if compelled by other legal means. It is agreed that counseling sessions, in whole or in part, **may be recorded** by the counselor by writings, video, audio, or other nonelectronic or electronic means, and consent is hereby given by the counselee for such recordings. Although it is understood that we may (but are not required to) **keep records** of sessions and their subject matter, it is expressly agreed that we **may destroy** any and all such records of any counseling sessions or issues at any time that we deem appropriate, without incurring any liability.

> **Comment:** Although either side may terminate counseling, it should not give the counselee an easy way to avoid his sin being addressed.

Consider a situation where a married youth leader comes to you due to his adulterous relationship with a woman in the church. If he then terminates counseling without true repentance, renounces his church membership, and then goes to another church to get a job, this provision may be helpful.

Caveat: It may be difficult to maintain confidentiality of counseling records if subpoenaed by the legal process. Biblical counselors are not doctors or psychotherapists, so legal privileges of nondisclosure do not apply (although a clergy–penitent privilege may). So, for example, if a counselee's spouse hires a lawyer in a divorce proceeding who sends a subpoena for your records, you may have to produce them—if they exist. For that reason, you may want to decide whether and to what extent you keep records and for how long.

Paragraph 10: Resolution of Conflicts: On rare occasions, a conflict may develop between a counselor and a counselee. In order to make sure that any such conflicts will be resolved in a biblically faithful manner (**the Bible prohibits lawsuits in court among believers**; 1 Corinthians 6:1–8), we require all of our counselees to agree that any dispute that arises with a counselor or with any person or entity associated with the counselor and related in any way to his/her biblical counsel will be settled in the following manner: First, the parties agree to participate in **biblical mediation** to be conducted by an individual (or individuals) agreed upon by the parties or, if no agreement is reached, by a member of the biblical counseling faculty at ______________ [example: The Master's University and/or Seminary, Southern Baptist Theological Seminary, Reformed Theological Seminary] or, if one is not available, by a pastor or elder from ________________ [insert church name] or, if one is not available, by a Christian, biblical mediator located in ______________ [insert city or region] who is certified by Peacemaker Ministries and/or by the Association of Certified Biblical Counselors. The parties agree to participate in and mediate in good faith. Second, if mediation is unsuccessful, the parties will submit their dispute to legally **binding arbitration** in accordance with the Rules of Procedure of the Institute for Christian Conciliation (a copy is available upon request). Initially, the parties shall split the cost of the arbitration equally between the two sides. In light of the fact that this counseling is voluntary and not for compensation, counselee waives all rights to special and consequential damages of any nature and waives all claims for negligence arising out of any act or omission of the counselor or anyone working with him/her. This agreement and the issues raised in counseling are not matters of public interest; they are private and relate to personal faith and Scripture. Judgment upon an arbitration award may be entered in any court of competent jurisdiction so long as the terms of this agreement were followed. **Each party will be responsible for his/her own attorneys' fees**, although the prevailing party in any such arbitration shall recover his/her arbitration costs (not attorneys' fees). The determination of "prevailing party" shall be made by the conciliator/arbitrator after taking the circumstances and claims into consideration. This entire agreement shall be binding upon the counselee and his/her family members, assigns, and heirs.

Comment: The idea is to agree to conflict resolution procedures that are biblically sound. (Fill in the blanks or change institution names as appropriate.) Mediation prior to formal proceedings is a good way to resolve things without having a third party decide who is "right." If mediation is unsuccessful, then private arbitration presided over by a Christian who understands biblical counseling can be preferable to submitting the matter to someone who may not see how biblical counseling is different from secular therapy.

Caveat: You can decide what to do with the attorneys' fees provision. There are times when lawsuits are filed by lawyers who think they can extract a settlement based solely on the fact that the other side may be concerned that an unfavorable judgment will require the payment of the other side's attorneys' fees. This is a classic "tail wagging the dog" situation where the merits or actual worth of a case may be overshadowed by the potential fee award that could be imposed. For example, let's say an award is entered against you for $5,000 *plus* the payment of the other side's attorneys' fees, which they contend amount to $100,000. You can see how unbalanced that scenario is and how it can lead to further disputes over the reasonableness of the bill in light of the actual award. However, if there are limitations on damages and each side (no matter who ultimately wins) has to pay their own attorneys' fees, then unscrupulous clients and lawyers may not be inclined to file a case or keep it going. Why? Because plaintiffs' lawyers often do not have clients with deep pockets who are willing to pay significant attorneys' fees. Further, for those lawyers who take matters on a contingency basis (meaning they only get paid a percentage of the ultimate recovery), the idea of a small award or settlement is a disincentive for filing or maintaining a lawsuit. For that reason (along with the fact that even if you win your case, you might not be inclined to pursue the other side for the payment of your fees), you may want to make it clear that each side is responsible for his own fees—no matter the outcome. Keep in mind, however, that arbitration costs (which the losing party pays) can sometimes be significant, depending on how much the arbitrator charges.

Paragraph 11 (and final statements): *By signing this document, you are irrevocably waiving any right that you might have to a trial by jury or judge in a judicial proceeding.* If any provision of this agreement shall be held invalid, illegal, or unenforceable, only that provision shall be stricken, and the remainder of the agreement shall be in no way affected. All of the above is understood and agreed.

Comment: Informed consent. Pretty simple. Get a signature. Store it in your files for safekeeping.

In sum, biblical counseling is discipleship and seeks to reorient sinful heart desires toward God to restore true worship. Counselors carry the burdens of their counselees (Galatians 6:1–3), and many carry a lot of stress. Don't add to it by inviting a lawsuit simply because you chose not to use a comprehensive Consent to Counsel form. Just like insurance can be a helpful shield, so can a well-crafted Consent to Counsel form that clearly establishes expectations and limitations. And it's free.

To-Do List

- ❒ If you, your church, or your organization has a Consent to Counsel form, review it (or have leadership review it) with legal counsel. Revise the form as necessary.
- ❒ If you, your church, or your organization does not have a Consent to Counsel form, create one—or have the leadership create one—with the help of an attorney. Or just start with the sample set forth in the Appendix and modify it to fit your situation, but have it reviewed by a local attorney to ensure that it comports with the governing laws in your area.
- ❒ Once you have a Consent to Counsel form prepared and ready for use, present it to each counselee for review and signature. Although there is some customization that you might do to the form (for example, see above discussion regarding paragraph 2 [fees], paragraph 3 [licenses you may hold], and paragraph 10 [dispute resolution provisions]), do not allow the counselee to make any material changes.
- ❒ If your church or organization has multiple counselors on staff, make sure each one understands the importance of getting the Consent to Counsel form signed before counseling begins. If counseling is already in progress, have ongoing counselees review and sign the form.
- ❒ If any third party enters the counseling sessions (for example, a counselee's wife), have the third party sign the Consent to Counsel form.
- ❒ If the counselee is a minor who can understand the form, have the minor sign it, but also be sure to have the parent(s) or guardian(s) sign as well to indicate that they authorize/permit the counseling to occur pursuant to the terms set forth in the Consent to Counsel form, and that they also agree to be bound by the document in their individual and representative capacities.
- ❒ Maintain each signed Consent to Counsel form in a secure location, whether electronically or in hard copy.

CHAPTER 10
RELIGIOUS LIBERTY AND THE JUDICIAL SYSTEM

Deborah Dewart

Francis Schaeffer wrote about a "Christian consensus," which used to be present in American culture. The atheist banker and the Christian might disagree about God, but they would agree on questions about basic morality, marriage, and human sexuality. That consensus no longer exists. Some involved in politics and the legal system (including government attorneys and many judges) are not just indifferent but are actively hostile to Christianity and Christian morality.

This is no reason to be fearful or troubled. The church began in an empire that was at best indifferent and often hostile to Christianity. Christian thought was considered to be something between bizarre and dangerous. We have all heard stories of how Christians at times faced terrible persecution.

In the present moment, we are not facing violent persecution. But many Christians are facing laws that could make it impossible for them to continue in their employment and live consistent with Christian convictions. These things are not pleasant. The Scripture is plain that we may face "affliction." But when we consider this affliction, we must keep in mind that—even at its worst—this affliction is "light and momentary" and "preparing for us an eternal weight of glory beyond all comparison" (2 Corinthians 4:17).

We as biblical counselors should be the most hopeful as we consider affliction. We have seen and heard the wonderful things that God has done in the midst of human suffering. We know by experience that God works in all things when he conforms us to the image of Christ (Romans 8:28–29).

So we can look without illusion on a world that we know can quickly go from "bad to worse." Without question, there is a concerted effort to limit religious liberty and Christian practice, but we still live in a nation that was founded on biblical principles and God-given rights, with religious liberty chief among them. Protecting that liberty benefits *all* Americans, including those who disagree with us about the Bible.

American Liberty Is Founded on Biblical Principles

The American legal system presupposes God, our Creator. The Declaration of Independence declares that we are "*created* equal" and "endowed by our *Creator*" with certain "inalienable rights," including life, liberty, and the pursuit of happiness. But over the past several decades, judges have manufactured "alien" rights, including abortion and a judicially imposed counterfeit definition of marriage. These "alien" rights were never granted by our Creator. They are like cancer cells. Cancer cells threaten to destroy healthy cells. In the same way, these "alien" legal rights have metastasized and threaten to swallow our genuine, inalienable, God-given rights, such as the right to life, freedom of conscience, speech, and *religious* liberty.

Consider abortion. The Constitution guarantees the right to life, but there is no constitutional right to any particular medical procedure *except* (supposedly) the one procedure that deliberately destroys life instead of preserving it. This is an "alien" right that has no basis in the Constitution and actively defies the text by denying the right of life to the tiniest, most vulnerable human beings.

How Does the Law Threaten Religious Liberty in Biblical Counseling?

How might these threats affect your church and ministry? Does the law threaten religious liberty in your counseling, and if so, how?

How can you act wisely to prevent falling into a legal land mine? How can you best steward your constitutional freedoms?

To answer these questions, it is important that you retain a qualified local attorney to help you examine relevant laws and draft documents that clearly communicate the religious nature of your ministry. After these initial documents are drafted, be certain you have an established relationship with a local lawyer, even if that person is not on a monthly retainer (the Alliance Defending Freedom Church Alliance program works on a sliding scale with churches of all sizes regarding religious liberty documents).

One common concern is whether state licensing requirements apply to biblical counseling. In chapters 2 and 3, we discussed the ways in which we can clearly distinguish a biblical counseling ministry from the sort of psychotherapy that requires a license. Your written policies and forms should describe your ministry in distinctly religious terms, showing that it falls outside the definitions for licensed counseling. Your attorney can also help you examine antidiscrimination laws and define your ministry in a way that minimizes potential risks.

The good news is that the US Supreme Court has recently affirmed the long-standing doctrine of "church autonomy." As a practical matter, this means that the courts will not consider questions involving the internal working of a church. If a congregation fires a pastor because he denies the Trinity, the pastor cannot sue the church claiming he has a right to deny the Trinity. The court will allow him to deny the Trinity but will not tell the congregation it has to keep the heretic on staff.

There are legal protections for your ministry. But to make good use of those protections, you need to know what those protections are and how to use them. That is why you need an attorney who can help you leverage that protection as you formulate policies and draft documents for your counselors and counselees. One good way to do that is to use frequent Scripture references to support your policies and practices.

Licensing of Counselors

Every state requires a license for the practice of psychological counseling. But do you need a state license to counsel from Scripture? Does the state even have the constitutional authority to require a license? State licensing schemes typically have explicit exemptions for pastoral counseling, and the government is severely limited in its ability to interfere with the internal affairs of a church. Nevertheless, it is important to have your "ducks in a row."

First, you need a clear written policy explaining that you are doing religious ministry and *not* psychotherapy. You should use biblical terminology (sin, repentance, discipleship) to describe your ministry and disclaim secular language (therapy, mental health).

Of particular importance due to the changes in the culture and the law is the need to be clear on matters of marriage and human sexuality. If your ministry is part of a local church, then the church's doctrinal statement should be clear on this point. If you are a standalone ministry, make certain that your ministry has an unambiguous doctrinal statement. You may even want to consider adding such a clause to a consent form.

Second, it is critical to have a well-drafted informed consent form for your counselees to sign. Work with your local attorney to create the form and to be sure you remove yourself from your state's definition(s) of any counseling that requires a license. Ordained clergy are usually exempt from state licensing requirements, but even biblical counselors who are not ordained can work under clergy supervision and define their ministry so that it falls outside the statutory definitions for licensed counseling.

What if you are not ordained or working directly for a church? Do not despair. Certainly, direct involvement with a local congregation can make it more obvious that you are working in Christian ministry and not psychotherapy, whether or not a local church oversees your work. However, you will need to be very clear that you are operating as a religious ministry. You must be explicit in your organizational documents, in your counseling consent, and in your advertising (if any) what you are and what you do. While we recommend a close tie to a local church (and not merely for legal reasons), we understand that such is not always possible. In those cases, take the necessary precautions.

Other matters to cover in the form include a biblical dispute resolution policy, confidentiality, church discipline, referrals to other professionals (e.g., doctors, accountants), and a records release policy. (See chapter 9 for a thorough example and explanation of a Consent to Counsel form.)

State-licensed counselors now face challenges imposed by laws that prohibit "sexual orientation change efforts" (SOCE laws)—even if the counselor, the counselee, and the counselee's parents (if dealing with a minor) are all in agreement. Ordinances are being proposed which would limit SOCE for unlicensed counselors as well. These laws not only threaten religious liberty but also free speech, association, and conscience. So far, legal challenges have not succeeded in striking down such laws. California's SOCE was challenged by an ordained minister, who was also a licensed counselor. When the Ninth Circuit upheld California's SOCE law, the court explained that the law did *not* "prevent mental health providers from referring minors to unlicensed counselors, such as religious leaders" and did *not* "prevent unlicensed providers, such as religious leaders, from administering SOCE to children or adults." The US Supreme Court has not yet weighed in, but recent precedent suggests that SOCE laws would not withstand scrutiny because the court has refused to carve out "professional speech" as a separate category entitled to less First Amendment protection.

Biblical counselors eschew state licensing for theological reasons and instead counsel with the biblical goal of helping God's people become more like Christ. Because their work is a religious ministry to disciple other believers, not a type of psychological counseling that requires a state license, biblical counselors have strong legal arguments that they are not required to be licensed and do not fall within the scope of state SOCE laws—as the Ninth Circuit affirmed when California's SOCE law was challenged. This freedom is a God-given opportunity for *you* to help people where state-licensed counselors cannot.

Antidiscrimination Laws

Does your biblical counseling ministry fall within the scope of state or federal antidiscrimination laws—particularly those that include categories like sexual orientation or gender identity?

Laws against discrimination originally served commendable purposes. We needed to address the rampant racial discrimination that existed for decades after slavery was abolished. The Civil Rights Act of 1964 subjected private businesses to antidiscrimination laws. These laws were intended to be a *shield*, protecting people from irrational discrimination based on irrelevant criteria like race. But eventually antidiscrimination became a *sword*—a powerful weapon that is now used to attack people of faith who want to live and work according to their deepest convictions. We know this sounds a bit dramatic. Unfortunately, both the government lawyers enforcing these laws and even some judges adjudicating these laws have barely veiled their animosity to religious liberty in general and Christianity in particular.

The protected categories have vastly expanded—race, color, religion, ethnicity, nationality, marital status, and now sexual orientation and gender identity. The laws originally applied to large "public accommodations" that provided essential goods and services—mass transportation, hotels, restaurants. Later, the laws expanded to encompass private membership organizations as well. This growing expansion potentially sweeps in religious organizations. Additional protected categories and places subject to the law is part of the trend to use antidiscrimination laws as a sword rather than a shield.

Legal Defense Organizations

If you are ever sued, the first steps are to call your local lawyer and your insurance agent. But you should know that if the lawsuit touches on issues of religious freedom, there may be other resources open to you as well. There are many fine organizations involved in the battle for religious liberty. Such organizations are typically funded by donations and may be able to provide pro bono services. Your local attorney won't need to be the "lone ranger" or reinvent the wheel. There are Christian organizations at both federal and state levels, including Alliance Defending Freedom, Christian Legal Society, American Center for Law and Justice, First Liberty, Christian Law Association, Center for Religious Expression, and many others. These groups employ attorneys who are experienced with constitutional litigation, and they can also assist local attorneys. In recent years, there have been some great victories for religious freedom because of the labors of these dedicated Christian lawyers.

Court Structure

Our federal and state courts operate under a three-tiered system. A case begins in the *trial* court. That's where it goes either to a jury trial or a "bench" trial (with only the judge deciding the verdict). When the verdict is rendered, the losing party may file an appeal with the *appellate* court. Most cases end in the trial or appellate court, or they are settled by the parties with a dispute. But the party who loses in the appellate court may file a *petition* for review in the state supreme court or the US Supreme Court (federal). The petition may or may not be granted. At this level, petitions usually are not granted unless there's an important issue that will impact the legal rights of others. (For more detailed information, read chapter 8, "The Anatomy of a Lawsuit.")

Pastoral Counseling Example

In chapter 8 we discussed the procedure for a lawsuit. In this section, we would like to give you a general idea of the "substantive" law that would apply. While the particular laws that apply will vary from case to case, an example of an actual lawsuit will give you a general idea of how the legal positions could be argued.

Some years ago, the Texas Supreme Court decided a case between a counselee, Peggy Lee Penley, and her pastor, "Buddy" Westbrook, who had formerly served as her psychotherapist. It took about *seven years* from the time the lawsuit was filed until the Texas Supreme Court ruled.

Penley initially consulted Westbrook in his capacity as a licensed counselor (1998–99), then became a member of the church where Westbrook began serving as a pastor in late 1999. The dispute began in late 2000 when Pastor Westbrook initiated church discipline with Penley after she confessed to an extramarital affair. Penley sued in late 2001 for defamation, negligence, breach of fiduciary duty, and intentional infliction of emotional distress, based largely on the duty of absolute confidentiality Westbrook previously owed his counselee in his role as a licensed therapist. The trial court dismissed the claims against the church and elders but allowed Penley's claim for professional negligence against Westbrook. In 2004, the state appeals court affirmed the trial court's ruling. Three years later, the Texas Supreme Court heard arguments (June 2007) and ruled in favor of Pastor Westbrook (September 2007). His pastoral duty to exercise church discipline conflicted with his previous duty of absolute confidentiality as a licensed counselor, but Penley had voluntarily joined the church and agreed to abide by its disciplinary policies. Here is what the court said:

> Any civil liability that might attach for Westbrook's violation of a secular duty of confidentiality in this context would in effect impose a fine for his decision to follow the religious disciplinary procedures that his role as pastor required and have a concomitant chilling effect on churches' autonomy to manage their own affairs.

There are several lessons from this case. First, litigation can take a very long time! Second, courts are reluctant to intervene in the internal affairs and governance of a church (the "church autonomy" doctrine). Third, clear communication with counselees is critical, particularly in a case like this one where a state-licensed counselor steps down from that role and assumes the role of pastor.

United States Supreme Court

This is the highest court in the land, and the process of winding through the courts and getting a case to the Supreme Court takes many months or even years. Unlike the lower federal appellate courts, the Supreme Court isn't required to accept a case, and only a tiny percentage of the petitions they receive are granted. In chapter 8 we explained how and why a case may make it to the Supreme Court.

When a case comes to the Supreme Court, the "stakes" are tremendous and the work is extraordinarily difficult. Drafting the petition is a daunting task that can take months. The lawyers will revise and test their arguments repeatedly. Lawyers will even undertake mock trials where other lawyers act as judges or opposing counsel.

Litigants may have to wait many more months for the Supreme Court to grant or deny review. And all of this typically happens only after a lengthy battle—several years—in lower federal or state courts.

Religious liberty is a constitutional issue that has come before the Supreme Court many times. You may have heard about Jack Phillips, owner of Masterpiece Cakeshop (Colorado), who was sued for declining to custom design a wedding cake for two men; or Barronelle Stutzman, owner of Arlene's Flowers (Washington), who was sued by a long-term customer for refusing to custom design flowers for a same-sex ceremony. These two Christians were granted review by the Supreme Court. Phillips's case was heard in December 2017, and he prevailed in a ruling issued the following June. He faced yet another lawsuit—this time for declining to create a cake celebrating a gender transition—and his Supreme Court case was heard only after several years of litigation that brought death threats and shut down a huge chunk of his business. After Phillips prevailed,

Stutzman's petition—which had been on hold for over a year—was granted. The court wiped out the state court's opinion and sent the case back to them to "think again" after Phillips's win. But the state court refused to budge, so Stutzman had to file yet another petition with the Supreme Court. The court ultimately denied her petition, but the case was settled for a small amount, and she was able to retire in peace. Phillips and Stutzman stood strong for their faith in the face of incredible legal battles that threatened to shut down their businesses and wipe out their savings.

The Law Protects Religious Liberty with Constitutions

The first line of legal defense is the United States Constitution. The First Amendment protects freedom of religion, speech, and association. The two Religion Clauses—Establishment and Free Exercise—are two sides of the same coin, guarding against government interference with religion. The government can neither mandate nor prohibit religious exercise. The government cannot define religious orthodoxy or become entangled in redefining it.

State constitutions also protect religious liberty, often defining it in terms of liberty of conscience. Many states limit religious freedom only if it threatens public peace or safety.

The Law Protects Religious Liberty with Legislation

Federal and state laws, passed by Congress and/or state legislatures, also protect religious liberty. Sometimes there are religious exemptions from specific laws. For example, employment law (Title VII) allows religious organizations to "discriminate" on the basis of religion, even though religious discrimination is otherwise unlawful. In 1993, Congress passed the Religious Freedom Restoration Act (RFRA) restoring the standards courts had used prior to a particular Supreme Court case decided in 1990. Under RFRA, if a law substantially burdens a sincerely held religious belief, the government must demonstrate a "compelling interest" that cannot be accomplished by less restrictive means. RFRA only applies to federal laws, but many states have enacted their own version of RFRA. I would encourage any church to draft employment and hiring documents that clearly state they hire based upon religious distinction according to the provisions allowed for religious organizations in Title VII and RFRA.

In addition to religious exemptions, some laws protect conscience, a concept closely related to religious liberty but even broader in scope. For example, after the Supreme Court declared abortion a constitutional right, Congress acted swiftly to preserve the conscience rights of professionals who object to participating in it. Then in 2017, after nearly a decade of legal battles over the contraception mandate generated by the Affordable Care Act, the Trump administration wrote new exemptions for employers who hold religious or moral objections to providing contraceptive (or abortifacient) drugs in the health insurance plans offered to employees. Changes in administration need to be carefully monitored. Protections enacted by one administration may be swept away by the next. Internal documents should be reviewed and updated as the legal landscape changes.

The Law Protects Religious Liberty with Church Autonomy

Court decisions have shaped and affirmed the doctrine of "church autonomy" over many decades. Based on the First Amendment Free Exercise Clause, the church autonomy doctrine builds a legal "wall" around churches, protecting matters of internal church governance, doctrine, and employment from government interference. In 2012, the Supreme Court unanimously affirmed this long-standing doctrine in the *Hosanna Tabor-Lutheran* case. The court is rarely ever unanimous about anything and certainly not religious questions. So when the entire court agrees on a matter of religious liberty it is probably safe to call it a "miracle."

One key protection is the ministerial exception, which pertains to who a religious organization employs to preach and teach the faith—its "ministerial employees." It would be a serious intrusion on religious liberty for the state to mandate that a church retain an unwanted minister or pay crippling amounts in damages. The *Hosanna* case was about a teacher, Cheryl Perich, employed by a church-operated school. Perich was a "commissioned" minister who had to undergo training in theology and was "called" by the church congregation to her ministry position. Perich developed narcolepsy and took disability leave. When she and her doctor decided she was well enough to return to work, the school had already hired a teacher to complete the term and did not want to disrupt the school year for the children. But Perich insisted on being rehired and refused to participate in the school's biblical dispute resolution policy—something she had agreed to do when she was hired. The school terminated her employment, and she filed a lawsuit under the Americans with Disabilities Act. The Supreme Court ruled in favor of the school, holding that as a "ministerial employee," the teacher had no right to sue for discrimination.

The ministerial exception is a wonderful provision by the grace of God that enhances legal protection, but churches must have proper documents to clearly indicate their intent. The ministerial exception is broader than merely the person who preaches from the pulpit. It includes others who are essential to fulfilling the *mission* of the church or other religious organization. Clear documentation provides an extra layer of legal protection if the church ever enters litigation. Key documents include employment policies and agreements with detailed job descriptions and titles showing how each employee fulfills the church's religious mission by performing religiously based duties. For example, in a religious school, teachers are employed to teach the faith to the next generation. They are the "lifeblood" of the school because their services are essential to achieving the school's religious mission. Biblical counselors are the "lifeblood" of a biblical counseling ministry.

In 2020, the Supreme Court decided two consolidated cases to further consider the "ministerial exception" in *Our Lady of Guadalupe*. Like *Hosanna*, these cases involved teachers employed by religious elementary schools. The Supreme Court strongly affirmed the broad doctrine of "church autonomy," and that's good news for biblical counseling ministries—*especially those that operate under church authority.* The court clarified that, in the earlier *Hosanna* case, it did not intend to create a rigid test to define "ministerial employee." A "ministerial employee" is one who carries out the mission of the school, church, or other religious organization. The term isn't limited to those who preach from the pulpit. Biblical counselors, who may be employees or volunteers, carry out the church's religious mission to shepherd God's people, and they naturally fall within the broad scope of "ministerial employees." The Supreme Court's decisions confirm your freedom to choose *who* you select and retain as biblical counselors. This is why it is so important for churches to have a means by which they designate those recognized to counsel biblically under the church's authority. Proper identification by the church adds protection for the practice of biblical counseling as a ministry of the autonomous church.

The Law Protects Religious Liberty with Qualified Privilege

Another important protection is the "qualified privilege" available for communications within a church (or other organization) about its internal business. This is particularly important in connection with church discipline. The qualified privilege protects communications among the church leaders and members about internal church matters—such as the discipline of a member—that could otherwise be considered defamatory or an invasion of privacy. It is important to be sure that such communications are properly restricted to persons who have an interest in the matter. For example, an announcement about church discipline could be made in a restricted "members only" meeting that excludes visitors. This is why it is also important to have the church discipline policy clearly explained in your church documentation so that the practice is clear to all members who join fellowship.

Implement Legal Protections with Structure

Because of the "church autonomy" doctrine, First Amendment protection is at its peak inside the sanctuary of a church. If possible, it is wise to place your counseling ministry under the legal umbrella of the church and its ordained leadership, rather than a separately organized corporation or LLC. This provides the strongest possible legal protection for purposes of the First Amendment because of the doctrine of "church autonomy." (See chapters 2 and 3 for strategies to distinguish your ministry from secular counseling and chapter 5 for more information on business formation for your counseling ministry.) If it is not feasible for you to counsel under church authority, religious protection can be enhanced through well-drafted documents that spell out the religious nature of your counseling activities. Your decisions about legal structure should be made in consultation with a qualified attorney. Another way to strengthen your status as a religious ministry is to ask counselees for voluntary donations, rather than charging them mandatory fees.

Implement Legal Protections with Governing Documents

Written documents governing your church in general, or your counseling ministry specifically, should be carefully drafted with assistance from your local attorney. Below I will describe several important written documents. Be sure to define marriage and sexuality (male/female) in all of them. It is wise to include scriptural references throughout your documents—not only to root your policies in God's Word but also because courts do not want to become entangled in religious doctrine.

Articles of Incorporation

This is the document filed with your state's Secretary of State to create a new corporation. This document is created by the "promoter," that is the person who forms the corporation. It should be drafted by a licensed attorney. It is like a "birth certificate" for the corporation. Your legal name will be stated, along with other requirements that may vary from one state to another. There is typically a brief statement of purpose, which should be stated in distinctly religious terms. If you're incorporating a church, the Articles should state that the corporation is a church. The Articles are a public document that will be accessible to anyone who wants to see them.

Some states have specific provisions for religious corporations. California, for example, has three types of nonprofit corporations with three corresponding sets of applicable statutes—public benefit, mutual benefit, and religious.

Bylaws

This is a lengthy document that covers internal governing matters, such as election of officers and directors and annual meetings. Again, it should be drafted by a licensed attorney in your state. Your bylaws should provide a more detailed statement of your religious purposes, including a definition of marriage and a statement that God created the human race male and female. It would be wise to incorporate by reference a set of denominational standards, the organization's Statement of Faith, and applicable church or other membership requirements. This document will be created and signed by the person who formed the corporation. Bylaws may be modified throughout the life of the organization.

Church Membership Requirements

This will vary depending on the denomination and the way the church is governed. One major item to facilitate biblical counseling is a clear policy about the practice of church discipline that a person must agree to as a requirement for membership. The requirements should be made part of the bylaws and should be clearly communicated to all persons who become members.

Statement of Faith

The Statement covers basic doctrines (e.g., Trinity, Incarnation, Scripture, creation, sin, salvation, local church, baptism, Lord's Supper, resurrection, return of Christ, missions). It is important to include a definition of marriage and a statement that God created the human race male and female. Should you be challenged on documents concerning human nature and sexuality, it is useful to be able to show that your positions are cardinal positions of the church and not ad hoc bias against some particular person.

Policies and Procedures

The policies and procedures of your counseling ministry should be clearly laid out. Provide information on who will conduct counseling, where counseling will take place, when counseling will occur, and what will be the content of counseling. You should also have policies on the creation and retention of records. These policies need not be made part of the bylaws.

Written Informed Consent for Counselees

This form provides information so that counselees voluntarily consent to the type of counseling offered. Key sections include the biblical basis for counseling, as clearly distinguished from the psychological approach; marriage and sexuality (male–female); confidentiality and church discipline; referrals to other professionals (e.g., doctors, accountants); biblical dispute resolution; and records release policy. (See chapter 9 for a thorough example and explanation of a Consent to Counsel form.)

Biblical Dispute Resolution Policy

The best way to avoid the time and expense of a lawsuit is to require counselees to agree—*in writing*—to resolve disputes through biblical mediation or arbitration. Courts do not want to become involved in religious doctrinal disputes. Much like binding arbitration provisions used in other contexts, private dispute resolution keeps the court dockets clear for other matters. It will be well worth the cost of retaining a competent local attorney to be sure your policy is drafted according to your state's law. This is a key item to include in your informed consent form. It is similar to a "binding arbitration" clause designed to stand in place of civil litigation if a conflict arises. It is wise to include a similar policy in your employment manual.

Tax Exemption Status

Tax exempt status is an important issue to consider. Churches are not required to file an application with the IRS in order to acquire tax-exempt status, although some churches do so voluntarily. Other nonprofit organizations (including those established for religious purposes) must file an application (IRS Form 1023) with detailed information and budgets. The IRS also requires an annual "Information Return" (Form 990) from exempt organizations *except* churches. The 990 asks questions about changes to governing documents (Articles, Bylaws) and requires copies of such changes. Organizations with "average gross receipts" (based on the most recent three years) under $50,000 only file an "electronic postcard" with minimal information. You should consult with your attorney and possibly an accountant on the question of whether to specifically request a determination of tax-exempt status.

Questions have arisen as to whether the IRS might deny tax-exempt status to organizations that "discriminate" on the basis of sexual orientation or gender identity. Justice Alito raised the issue at oral argument in *Obergefell* in 2015 (the case that redefined marriage). In 1983, the US Supreme Court held that the IRS could deny tax-exempt status to a school (Bob Jones University) that prohibited interracial dating among its students. That ruling was based on the compelling interest in eliminating *racial* discrimination in *education*. This rationale has not been extended to other types of discrimination or contexts other than education. But the danger is there. This is one of the reasons I am so strongly in favor of maintaining biblical counseling ministries under the umbrella of a *church* rather than some other legal entity. Churches do not file the Form 1023 (Application for Recognition of Exemption) or the annual Form 990, so their documents are not subject to government scrutiny. They do have to file employment forms, such as W-2s and quarterly reports, but these contain only the necessary financial data and nothing about the church's doctrine.

Definitions and Distinctions

The following definitions and distinctions are important to include in your church documentation. These things should be consistent threads throughout your documents in order to ensure that the church's religious doctrine and views are rooted in Scripture and clear to all who participate in the church's ministries.

- Distinguish religious discipleship ministry from psychological counseling, and more specifically, distinguish ministry from state-licensed counseling as defined by your state's statutes.
- Distinguish your religious counseling ministry from your state's applicable legal definitions for licensed counselors and use biblical definitions and terms; look for clergy exemptions.
- These distinctions reduce or eliminate applicability of SOCE and similar laws.
- Use distinctive biblical terminology (e.g., "life-dominating sin" versus "addiction" and "discipleship" versus "counseling") to distance your ministry from the psychological mindset.
- Distinguish the goals of biblical counseling (e.g., becoming more like Christ versus using techniques to change same-sex attraction to opposite-sex attraction. We must be careful to distinguish our goals from very flawed "therapies" such as

"conversion therapy." This is particularly important because someone outside the biblical counseling community may, through either malice or negligence, seek to describe biblical counsel as being comparable to such things). We cannot be too clear.

Informal Ministry

Encourage person-to-person ministry within the body of Christ without relying heavily on a formalized counselor–counselee relationship. Distance yourself from the professional in-office-only relationships established in psychotherapy; instead, *minister* to one another in the body of Christ.

To-Do List

- ❐ Always be explicit that you are practicing a religious discipline.
- ❐ Always communicate that we are providing biblical counseling, which is Christian discipleship in all areas of life.
- ❐ Support the efforts of other Christians who are involved in litigation concerning religious liberty.
- ❐ When a case is at the appellate level (before an appellate court or the Supreme Court) it is permissible for nonparties to file a "friend of the court" brief. These "amicus" (Latin for "friend") briefs can be very useful. Be willing to put your name on such a brief when the opportunity arises. In this book we have identified a number of Christian legal associations that litigate religious liberty issues. Contact one of these associations and express your willingness to file such a brief.

CHAPTER 11
What Your Counselee Faces in the Legal System

Edward Charles Wilde and Tonya Braun

Should you come within the scope of the legal system, whether as a result of crime or civil dispute, you will quickly find that you have very little say over your own life. Whether victim or offender, plaintiff or defendant, the legal system exercises such enormous power over the individual that the most wealthy and powerful person may soon find himself the equal of a "common" criminal as they both share the same cell. The most wealthy and powerful person may find that the state can strip him of fortune and destroy his reputation by a single verdict.

And if the most powerful can be caught up, then members of our congregations will certainly find themselves in this net. In this chapter, we have the hope of simply alerting you to what it is like for your counselees who fall into the hands of the legal system. What we hope is that this introduction will help you to know how to ask the right sort of questions to understand the nature of your counselee's life under the law and, thus, be able to provide them with the wisdom and counsel they need.

To be a victim is to create a kind of vulnerability that is difficult to understand when you have not experienced the same thing. And every criminal complaint will involve at least one victim. It may be the person who claims injury. Unfortunately, some people lie about being injured by another. The accused in this circumstance is the victim. You may not know whether you are counseling a victim or a perpetrator.

The criminal justice system will prove to be overwhelming for the victim and the accused. For the victim, the system can seem uncaring and even abusive. Information that is gravely personal and painful will be examined clinically and "objectively." Strangers will pry into the life of the victim to help. Often victims consider themselves victimized by the system.

For the accused (even if not guilty), the system will strip away all agency. Their life will come under the control of another. The accused will be forcibly housed with violent criminals. To be imprisoned is not merely degrading, it is dangerous.

If you have no idea of the overwhelming fear and pain the system can inflict on even the victim or the innocent, you will be unable to respond with wisdom to those involved. In addition, due to the complexities of the system, well-meaning counselors can inadvertently violate the law or compromise the legal rights of the parties. The information in this chapter can only familiarize you with the outlines of what takes place. It would be wise to speak with people who have experience in dealing with victims and the criminal justice system (such as an attorney who defends or prosecutes criminal cases). Assuming you have insight and knowledge into these areas when you actually lack experience is dangerous for you and could easily be harmful to those whom you wish to help.

Criminal Justice

Today, women and men are subjected to horrific sexual violence. Today, women and men may commit barbaric acts of sexual violence upon others. These people will come to you for biblical help. If you counsel long enough, you will counsel Tamar—and you will counsel Amnon.

Every story in the Scripture that includes multiple wives ends with significant sorrow for the family. Sometimes the sorrow was a matter of vicious mocking, such as Peninnah who mocked Hannah for having no children. And as painful as that must have been, it pales before the trouble which befell King David.

Having many wives led to many children from different mothers. It happened that among these half-siblings, Amnon became infatuated with Tamar. Through a ruse, Amnon managed to get Tamar alone, at which time "he violated her and lay with her" (2 Samuel 13:14).

Scripture makes plain that our sympathy should lie with Tamar. Amnon's lust was thwarted by Tamar's virtue. As the text reads, "for she was a virgin."[1] Thwarted to the point of illness, Amnon went to his friend Jonadab, who was "a very crafty man" (2 Samuel 13:3). He was excellent in being evil. The scheme worked as planned, and Tamar was ravaged. The resulting pain she suffered is heartbreaking.

As for Amnon, we are to see him as a wicked man, one outside the scope of Israel's covenant:

> In his readiness to compromise Tamar's virtue, however, Amnon was implicitly pagan. To emphasize the point, the biblical narrator deliberately patterns the portrayal of Amnon's actions and emotions after Shechem, an immoral Canaanite in the Torah. Shechem, like Amnon, was the first-born son of a ruler who also raped the daughter of an Israelite leader and ended up dead (cf. Gen 34:2–3, 26). Amnon is portrayed as one who chose the way of the Canaanite; thus, readers are prepared to accept the fact that he will suffer the fate of the Canaanite.[2]

David, as king, held the final say in criminal matters. Apparently, he was unwilling to vindicate his daughter by judging his son, and so Amnon remained unpunished. Since David would not punish his wicked son, Absalom (Tamar's full brother), took the law into his own hands and killed Amnon. This led to a series of events that

1. Her virtue may not have been the only brook to his desire, "Amnon's plans were thwarted because Tamar, being an unmarried girl or virgin (see Wenham, VT 22 [1972] 342–43), may have been confined to women's quarters and carefully guarded (see Ackroyd, 121). He was hardly suffering from genuine love-sickness but rather from frustration that he could not do what he wanted with Tamar (cf. Gen 22:12)." David A. Hubbard et al., "Editorial Preface," in *2 Samuel*, vol. 11, Word Biblical Commentary (Dallas: Word, Incorporated, 1989), 174.

2. Robert D. Bergen, *1, 2 Samuel*, vol. 7, The New American Commentary (Nashville: Broadman & Holman Publishers, 1996), 380.

culminated in David being thrust from his throne and Israel thrown into civil war. We see that one sin (Amnon's lust) led to a second sin (Amnon's deception and rape of Tamar), which led to a cry for justice on behalf of Tamar, which led to David's injustice in not vindicating his daughter and punishing his wicked son, which led to another killing, which led to a civil war and the death of many.

Sin has consequences. Sin calls out for the need of some judicial resolution. And God, in his goodness, has instituted government for the purpose of carrying out "God's wrath on the wrongdoer" (Romans 13:4). When God's wrath is not carried out, sin multiplies. "Because the sentence against an evil deed is not executed speedily, the heart of the children of man is fully set to do evil" (Ecclesiastes 8:11).

But such crimes are not a thing of the ancient world alone.

How Life Appears for a Modern-Day Tamar

What should you do when you meet a modern-day Tamar? Let's call her Kate. And to make this easier, we will call Amnon Mike.

The criminal process for Kate may be a long and arduous one filled with confusion. Her experience will depend on many variables, one of the greatest being the individuals she comes in contact with and how each person treats her. This may begin with you. If you, as the counselor, are the first person that she discloses to, your response will be important. The incident itself may be very confusing for her, and she may blame herself. Encourage her to report it to the police and offer to be there with her when she does (Romans 13:1–5; 1 Peter 2:13–15). Additionally, be familiar with your state's mandatory reporting laws, and if you are required to report, let her know and ask if she would like to make the report with you. Not only might it be comforting for her to have someone with her whom she knows and trusts; it can be helpful to have a second set of ears because her thoughts may resemble a tornado. It may be difficult for her to process and remember all that she says.

Kate may have had previous contact with the police, and if that interaction was difficult or even victimizing (this may occur with former prostitutes who were sexually abused by police officers), she may be resistant to report. If she shows resistance, ask her what her concerns are, if she has ever reported anything to the police in the past, and what that experience looked like.

There is another reason Kate might be hesitant. Just as David did not hold Amnon accountable, so it often happens that the victim's own family pressures him or her not to report the crime or to drop the charges—especially if it is a matter of sexual assault or domestic violence.[3] It is common for a family to be aware of previous abuse and to continue to protect the offender rather than the victim. Sometimes in a case of sexual assault, the offender's family pressures the victim not to report. And sometimes the pressure from either family takes the form of threats.

Contrary to popular belief, once a crime has been reported, in most jurisdictions the victim in the case does not have the authority or power to drop the charges. When the case is referred to the prosecutor's office from the police department, it is the prosecutor who decides to file charges. The criminal justice system is set up for the due process of defendants. This means that victims are only considered as witnesses in the case. Not until the 1980s did victims receive rights within the criminal justice system through the Victims' Bill of Rights.[4] These bills vary from state to state so familiarize yourself with your local law. It would be helpful for you as a counselor to know the provisions of your state's Victims' Bill of Rights and to provide a copy to the victim if needed.

---

3. The authors were involved with a recent incident in which a member of a church was pressured to go easy on the adult son of a prominent member of the congregation who had sexually abused multiple children, including the member's son. When the parents provided statements concerning the damage done, they were attacked by other church members as being "unloving."

4. "Crime Victims' Rights in America: A Historical Overview," Office for Victims of Crime, last modified April 2005, accessed September 4, 2020, https://www.ncjrs.gov/ovc_archives/ncvrw/2005/pg4b.html.

In addition to helping Kate understand her legal rights, as a counselor you should also be aware of and responsive to the physical, emotional, and spiritual trauma she has suffered. Sin brings with it shame, fear, and sorrow, even when one is the victim rather than the offender. This is one place where a thoroughly biblical understanding will be far more profitable than that offered by commonplace psychological and psychiatric treatments.

Consider how deeply Kate has been sinned against. The wrong calls out for justice. But no earthly justice can ever bring about full satisfaction for the wrong committed. A biblical understanding can let her know that a just God will always bring complete and true justice. The Psalmist's cries for justice and deliverance will provide a comfort that no court could ever deliver.

To counter the overwhelming sense of shame she feels, we can show her the promises of "praise and glory and honor at the revelation of Jesus Christ" (1 Peter 1:7). The vile abuse of the sinner is not the last word. The vindication of Jesus Christ will be the final say.

This is plainly not a comprehensive explanation of the counseling that should be offered at this time. At this point merely understand how much good we have to offer: the Scriptures offer true comfort, justice, mercy, and honor in the place of fear, shame, and sorrow. The Scripture provides hope.

One source of fear for Kate is Mike himself. Once she has reported the assault, and he has been arrested, a judge will set bail, which is a deposit made with the court to guarantee that you will return to court on a designated day. If Mike or his family pays the amount set by the judge, he will be released from jail. Kate may have the right to address the court in order to tell the judge why she is afraid and to ask that he not be released, but the decision is up to the judge alone. If Mike is released, this time will be particularly difficult for Kate; as he will know that she has reported, and she may fear retaliation. The criminal justice system is unable to protect her if he is released; it will be up to Kate to create a safety plan. The church can help her with this in practical ways, such as giving her a place to stay for the first couple of days after he is released to see what his reaction may be. Even if Mike doesn't seek to harm her again physically, he may begin spreading rumors among their family and community, slandering her character.

After the report and arrest, the case is sent to the prosecutor, who will make a decision to file charges or not. If the prosecutor chooses to not file charges, this may be difficult for Kate as she may not feel believed. There are a variety of reasons why charges may not be filed, and it can be helpful to reach out to the prosecutor's office to understand their reasoning. For other victims, not having charges filed may be a relief. If charges are filed, then there will be an arraignment hearing. The arraignment is the first occasion on which the accused is brought before a judge. The judge informs the accused of the charges made against him, tells the accused of his constitutional rights, and then asks for a "plea." The plea is whether the accused admits or denies doing the action of which they are accused. If Mike pleads "guilty," he is admitting he did the act. If he pleads "not guilty," he is denying he did the act. There is also a less-common plea where the defendant does not admit or deny but agrees not to fight the charges. At the arraignment, the judge determines whether the accused will be released (usually with conditions, such as bail) pending the trial of the action.

At this hearing it is routine that the offender pleads "not guilty" in order to negotiate and resolve the case later.[5] Kate may feel astounded that he is saying he is not guilty because he knows what he did. Assure Kate that this is routine and that his attorney most likely advised him to plead in this way. He will have an opportunity to plead guilty later. Sometimes at this hearing the victim is blamed for the offender's actions, primarily by the defense attorney

5. A plea of not guilty has the effect of forcing the government to prove its case against the accused. For many reasons, few criminal cases ever result in a trial. What usually happens after the arraignment is that the prosecuting and defense attorneys negotiate a resolution commonly known as a "plea arraignment" or a "plea deal." The prosecutor will ask for five years, the defense attorney will offer no jail time, and they will agree on two years. This "deal" is then brought to the court, and the court enters a final judgment.

and sometimes by the defendant's family. It is helpful to prepare her for this possibility and provide Scripture for her to focus on during this time. It is also common for victims to recant their statement out of fear, shame, or love for the offender. It is important to remind her that lying is a sin against God and that she needs to place her trust in him for the outcome of this case and for working in Mike's heart.

Additionally, at this hearing the judge may impose some type of no-contact order, such as a domestic violence order, sexual assault order, or a condition of release. Some orders may have criminal consequences if they are violated, and it will be helpful to understand which order has been put in place and what it stipulates. Kate has a right to ask that the order not be imposed or that it be modified to allow for some contact but not all contact. Such accommodations can be helpful if the victim shares finances with the offender or has children in common that they need to communicate about. Once again, the decision of whether to modify or recall the order is up to the judge.

Once the initial hearing is completed, the case will be resolved in one of three ways: an agreed recommendation, a trial, or a dismissal. The most common way a case is resolved is through an agreed recommendation, more commonly known as a plea agreement. A plea agreement gives Kate the opportunity to provide her input on what she would like to see happen in the case. The prosecutor's office may ask what is important to her, such as what type of charge, jail time, and treatment she would like to see, and whether she would like Mike to register as a sex offender. The prosecutor then weighs her input while looking at other factors, such as the facts of the case, how strong the case is for trial, and Mike's criminal history. They also have to take into account various legislative restrictions. For example, only certain crimes come with a sex offender registration, and some jurisdictions have standard sentencing ranges that dictate how long someone can be incarcerated for a given crime.

It can be difficult for Kate to wrap her head around these limitations and understand the prosecutor's decision. She has a right to call the prosecution and ask questions regarding the status of the case and the process. It will be helpful if she has an advocate assigned to her case to better help her understand how the process works and why decisions are made and to have her voice heard. When a case resolves, there is often a compromise, whether that means a reduced charge, a treatment option, or less jail time. Resolving through an agreed recommendation has two benefits: it guarantees a conviction, and it saves Kate from the incredibly difficult trial process, which is the second way a case can resolve.

The trial process is grueling, especially for a victim of sexual assault. Kate will be asked to be interviewed by Mike's attorney. Not only will she have to talk about the horrific incident that happened to her, but they will be looking for ways to discredit her. The questions the attorney asks may be blaming in nature, such as whether she fought him off or screamed for help. They may also ask why she did not report right away, implying that she is either making the incident up or exaggerating. They may look for possible motives for why she would make a false report against Mike. Kate has been brutally violated, and she now has to endure accusations that it is her fault. She will need to be encouraged to stand in the truth. Encourage her to keep in mind 1 Peter 2:19–23, which reassures us that when we suffer from doing right, we please the Lord. Like Jesus, she is to place her trust in the Lord.

Kate will then be asked to testify, not only in front of a judge and twelve jurors but also in front of Mike. She may fear having to see Mike even more than she fears discussing such a humiliating experience in front of strangers. After she puts herself in such a painfully vulnerable situation, the jury may come back with a verdict of not guilty. The burden of proof is incredibly high in criminal cases, and because sexual assault and domestic violence often occur behind closed doors, proving the case can be very difficult.

This difficulty could lead to the third possible outcome of the case: a dismissal. If the prosecutor does not believe it will be possible to prove the case, he or she may choose to dismiss it. This can happen at any time prior to the final judgment.

Be aware that if Mike is acquitted or the case is dismissed, then the no-contact order will go away. Mike will be a free man. Therefore, it may be wise for Kate to seek out a civil order prior to trial if she would like one. Many advocacy programs can help Kate petition for a civil protection order, or she may get her own lawyer to assist. She would then go to a "civil" (as opposed to a criminal) court and explain the basis for her fear. Mike has a right to be present and respond to her petition. The judge would issue an order (which may also include children, if applicable) as well as modifications to allow some contact if Kate requests it (i.e., phone and/or written contact to discuss specific issues). The difference between civil and criminal orders is that Kate will have more control over her civil order, whereas the judge controls the criminal order. Additionally, the burden of proof is much lower in a civil case than a criminal case. Violating either of these orders can result in additional criminal charges.

As you can see, the criminal process is long, confusing, and complicated—and sometimes disappointing. Kate will be on an emotional roller coaster and will most likely experience a cocktail of emotions, including fear, anxiety, shame, anger, and discouragement. It is normal for victims of crime to change their wishes throughout the process because they, too, are trying to work through their interpretation of the event. It will be important for Kate to have a biblical view of her suffering and for her to work toward a heart of forgiveness toward Mike, even if he is not remorseful.

This forgiveness will take time and be difficult. The adversarial nature of the criminal justice system creates an "us versus them" mentality. Mike will be advised to not admit to what he did until he has either pled guilty or been found guilty at trial. He will have the option to speak to what he did at the sentencing hearing. When Kate is slandered by Mike's attorney, it may open old wounds or create fresh cuts that she will have to continually forgive. Kate will continue to accumulate blows that she will have to forgive, and she will have to fight the easy temptation to become bitter.

Extending forgiveness is not incompatible with seeking appropriate judicial punishment for Mike's wrongdoing. It does not mean that Kate treats the sin as if it were not sin. Rather, it means, as a practical matter, that she turns judgment over to the Lord, including the verdict of the state (Romans 12:19–13:7). A heart that trusts the Lord and forgives her enemy will help her face him at trial and be more at peace with the decision of the criminal justice system.

If the case comes to an agreement or Mike is found guilty in a trial, Kate will then have the opportunity to make a victim impact statement at the sentencing hearing if she chooses to do so. She can share with the judge (and Mike) how the crime has impacted her and what she would like to see happen as part of his sentencing. She can also extend forgiveness if she is ready to do so. This is a great opportunity for Kate to be a witness for Christ. We are so thankful that the Lord gives us a criminal justice system, but in this fallen world, it is far from perfect. Kate may not see justice through the legal process or on this side of heaven, but she can still be transformed to the likeness of Christ by learning to endure suffering as she depends on the Lord, learning to love her enemies, forgiving as God has forgiven us, and showing grace and mercy.

A Note on Forgiveness and Justice

This is an element which may be easily misunderstood. Since this matter is so difficult to understand and apply in this circumstance, we are repeating and restating our direction here. The purpose of forgiveness is not to allow sin to go unpunished. The purpose of forgiveness is to protect Kate! This concept is one of the great wonders of the gospel.

There are two seemingly incompatible lines of authority present here. First, the government has been appointed by God for the purpose of punishing wrongdoers (Romans 13:4). This is an element of common grace which we must embrace. In our example, it is morally right for Mike to be prosecuted. Moreover, all sin will be fully punished. God's elect will be vindicated. And even though we suffer *unjustly* and our faith is sorely tried, these trials will result in "praise, glory, and honor at the revelation of Jesus Christ" (1 Peter 1:7). Kate will receive honor from the Lord despite the injury of this world, and he will be glorified by her steadfast trust of him as she faces this tragedy head-on.

Second, there is the seemingly paradoxical Christian call to love one's enemies. But this is not actually inconsistent with requiring the prosecution of an offender. We have seen instances of this principle being misused and misapplied in such a manner as cause further injury to a victim. *A misuse of this principle can easily result in the counselor sinning against Kate in the name of being* "godly." The timing and manner of forgiveness will take great wisdom and care. For those with little experience in counseling the abused, it is quite possible to not realize the depth of the injury which is done by physical and sexual violence.

You must understand that perpetrators can hijack the biblical commands of forgiveness and use the Bible and forgiveness as a weapon to wield against their victim. Unwitting counselors can be brought into this misuse of good biblical injunctions, because perpetrators are often skilled manipulators who fool their counselor.

The essential characteristic of Christian forgiveness is to leave the matter of judgment to "him who judges justly" (1 Peter 2:23). Our forgiveness of those who sin against us is grounded in the recognition that justice and judgment ultimately belong to God. To withhold forgiveness from a human perspective is to put Kate in the position of demanding a judgment and seeking justice which she will not fully obtain on this earth. Having been involved with the legal system for decades, we can assure you that even a "successful" outcome will not provide that sense of relief which comes from justice.

One final point which is often lost when discussing forgiveness: leaving the matter to the judgment of God does not mean the parties are reconciled. We must be careful not to collapse the categories of forgiveness, reconciliation, and restoration.

While forgiveness is required from the Lord toward our enemies, it does not mean trust is fully restored. Do not jump from forgiving one's enemies to the conclusion that the victim must be reconciled to the perpetrator, much less restored to a prior version of the relationship. Reconciliation requires more than forgiveness from one party in a conflict; it requires genuine repentance from the other party. Yet, reconciliation does not remove all consequences of sin. Repentance from the aggressor does not nullify consequences due to their sinful actions.

What Do You Say to a Modern-Day Amnon?

Knowing what to say to Mike depends upon whether we know for certain that he has done wrong. For the sake of this example, let's assume that, as in the story of Amnon, you do know Kate is the victim. We will assume that Kate made a report and identified her attacker. In this case, the police promptly confirmed evidence of Mike's guilt and obtained the necessary permissions to arrest him. When you first learn of the problem, Mike has been arrested and processed.

Mike will either be held in jail to await his criminal trial, or he may be released on bail. If he is in jail, you need to familiarize yourself with the procedures for meeting with prisoners. There will be specific times and places for visitation. Making contact to arrange such visitations may be difficult. The jail will be unpleasant for the individual incarcerated and even for members of the public who visit. You may find yourself feeling fear even in the parking lot.

To maintain the safety of everyone, the government imposes enormous direct control over those in a lockdown facility. There are doors, bars, and armed officers everywhere. Since everything is made from concrete and steel, jails can be surprisingly loud. Little effort is made to make your visit private, and great care will be made to keep you from giving anything to the prisoner.

As for Mike, life has changed in ways he likely never contemplated. Immediately upon arrest, he will be physically restrained to prevent injury to others or himself. He will be handcuffed and put into the back seat of a car without handles on the inside of the doors. His clothing and possessions will be taken away. He will be forced to wear a uniform that proclaims his status as a prisoner. He will be kept in a box with one or more unkind men.

He will have no privacy at all. He will sleep where permitted. He will leave the box when told. He will be stripped of all apparent agency and shuttled about with the other prisoners like cattle. He will face the potential for violence at the hands of prisoners and sometimes at the hands of jailers.

As the legal proceedings continue, he will remain in a state of harrowing uncertainty. When one falls into the system, the state exercises remarkable power. The state has more money and power than any defendant. Every step of the way will be one of constant pressure. Few people can afford the best lawyers for criminal defense. So the counsel you give Mike will—among many other things—need to take into account the anxiety that will follow from such constant pressure.

The fact of a criminal proceeding puts you as a counselor in a remarkably difficult position. You may need an experienced criminal defense or prosecuting attorney to help you sort out what is permissible. Can you ask questions about whether he is guilty? You see, if he confesses to you that he is guilty, you may find yourself as a witness at trial because you heard his confession. You must consider what will happen as you speak to Mike or other witnesses to the (alleged) crime. You need to determine whether you are engaged in illegal or improper "tampering" with witnesses. Demanding a confession immediately may be problematic when it comes to negotiating a resolution of the matter.

A single event can give rise to many potential criminal charges. The distinction between the various charges may be inconsequential or invisible to you and yet have quite consequential outcomes as to the nature of the sentence. A "confession" may need to be quite precise and may require the assistance of Mike's attorney. None of this is to say that you are seeking to hide Mike's crime or injure Mike's victim once again.

What we wish to emphasize at this point is that you must be careful not to interfere with the criminal justice procedures. The rules are difficult, and the demands will not necessarily correspond to your expectation or intuitions. The consequences for failing to adhere to the correct processes in your counsel could even result in your criminal prosecution.

This does not mean that we ever act to cover sin. "Take no part in the unfruitful works of darkness, but instead expose them" (Ephesians 5:11). It Mike has sinned, it would be vicious to seek to deny justice to the woman he has injured. But we also must be careful in how we go about this work. Make sure you understand the legal complications of what is done. Also, remember that our work as counselors must put scriptural demands ahead of legal procedures.

Our position is further complicated because our goal is to bring out repentance. The criminal defense attorney is seeking to protect the judicial system, which means the defense attorney will force the government to prove its case and prove that at each step of the way it has proceeded in accordance with law. This may lead to conflict between your counsel and Mike's defense attorney. Our goal is true repentance because a right standing before the Judge of all is of far greater importance than the judgment of a mortal who can only ever render partial, imperfect justice.

There is no general advice that would apply to all situations. What you need to know is that counseling the defendant in a criminal justice system presents a number of issues. You will need the help of other believers to be careful in your counsel and the help of an attorney to navigate the pitfalls on every side. Do not take to yourself the duty to make legal decisions. Be careful to understand your legal responsibilities, but always be diligent to keep your attention fixed on your goal. You are there to make disciples after Jesus Christ. This would not be the first time that a notorious criminal came to know Christ because the government brought him to punishment.

It is far more important to save his life for eternity than it is to avoid a temporal punishment.

The Civil Suit

The criminal action may put the "bad guy" into prison, but it usually does not do anything to help the victim of the crime. Where there has been a theft, putting the thief in prison does not put money in the victim's pocket. Kate may have peace knowing that Mike is jail, but she has not received anything from Mike. The victim has the potential of bringing a civil suit to recover monetary damages from the offender. (It is true that even if the defendant is found "not guilty," Kate could bring a civil suit against Mike. However, it is less likely to take place if he prevails in criminal court.)

In addition to being sued for damages, Mike could lose his job (a criminal conviction for a violent felony will do that). Not being able to pay his debts, Mike will find himself in bankruptcy court. If Mike is married or if he has children (whether or not he is married to the mother), Mike will most likely end up in family law court.

But most of the civil suits your counselees face will not be the result of a crime. You may be asked to help counselees in the midst of divorce or bankruptcy court. Each type of court comes with its own procedures. To understand what is happening with the counselee, you need not understand the intricacies of any court, but it would be useful to have a general idea of what is taking place. So we will briefly address some common situations that may befall a counselee.

The Civil Action

The civil action will conform most closely to what you expect when you think of a lawsuit. There are two parties, each represented by attorneys: the plaintiff, who initiated the action, and the defendant. It is also possible for each side to sue the other, in which case both parties are plaintiffs and defendants. Rather than cover all of the aspects of a standard lawsuit here, we refer you to chapter 8, "The Anatomy of a Lawsuit."

Family Law Court

Family law work is usually not legally complex, but it is emotionally difficult. Moreover, the legal system is completely unable to respond in a useful manner. The legal system is designed to resolve commercial disputes and adjudicate crime. It works best with binary decisions like, Did you steal the money? It does very poorly with questions like, What would be the best way to raise these children?

The most unanswerable questions in family law court do not involve the division and payment of money (that is rather straightforward in most instances). The difficulty comes over what to do with the children. While the courts have various means to try and mediate a resolution, there is no right answer. No matter what is decided, someone will be unhappy.

To complicate matters, older children may be brought into the decision-making. While this can be helpful, it also puts enormous pressure on the children and leaves them vulnerable to manipulation by the parents. The judges in most cases do want to do what is best for the children. If a child desires to be separate from one parent or to live with one parent, that information would be useful for the court to know.

In these circumstances, one or both parents may make allegations against the other of physical and sexual abuse. These allegations must be taken seriously, but they are so common and so routinely a matter of manipulation and slander that the judges become inured to the claims of both sides. Remember here the advice we gave above: do not assume that accusations are true, and do not assume they are false. Moreover, if the judge does not immediately believe an accusation made in this context, you can understand why the court may look upon an apparently grieving parent with a jaundiced eye.

An Opportunity to Provide Biblical Instruction

We all know that times of crisis provide an opportunity for a counselee to take biblical directives to heart. We also know that those who find their lives "out of control" are often more receptive to such counsel; indeed, they often demand counsel at these times.

To be caught up in the judicial system from a divorce or a bankruptcy is quite common. Therefore, counselors should be aware generally of what these processes are like so that the counselor has some awareness of the sort of counsel that is needed. We always need good data. The understanding of the judicial system that comes from watching movies or speaking with a friend is most often wrong—often, wildly wrong. If you provide counsel based upon what you imagine is the circumstance, you may actually do harm where you meant to do good. Certainly, you do not need to understand the procedures in great detail to provide good counsel. However, you should understand the degree to which the counselee feels vulnerable to powers that are often bewildering.

What Family Law Court Does to the Counselee

Consider what takes place in a family law court: The most important things in one's life—family, home, and finances—are all put into the hands of perfect strangers. (Indeed, all of the court personnel from the judge on down must be perfect strangers to the case.) The judge has remarkably broad authority. A judge can decide, "You will not see your children again." Or, "You may only see your children on Wednesdays." A judge may decide that someone whom your counselee no longer trusts will be seeing the children or even raising the children. The former spouse may have a new spouse—someone whom the counselee may not know and has no reason to trust will be raising their children. Your counselee will be powerless to stop it. Understanding how this is affecting your counselee will be important to help them.

Bankruptcy Court

In contrast to the complexities of family law, the mechanics of bankruptcy are straightforward. Someone who cannot cover his debts comes to court and files a "petition," which is a comprehensive catalogue of debts and assets. If the petition demonstrates that the person is in fact "bankrupt," the court then creates an "estate." All of the property and all of the debts of the bankrupt are frozen in time. A "trustee" is then appointed by the court to distribute the bankrupt person's assets to the creditors. Specific rules govern the payment and priority of the creditors.

After filing the petition, the bankrupt's work will be largely done in most instances. Following the "discharge" in bankruptcy, the former bankrupt will now merely be a normal citizen without overwhelming debt but also with very bad credit.

A note about bankruptcy: Bankruptcy is a commercial transaction that has been designed to protect both the bankrupt and the creditor. It protects the bankrupt by putting a limit on the economic damage debt can do. We have made a societal decision that it is better to permit bankruptcies than to force families into penury and forcibly create homelessness. There are similar provisions in the Mosaic law for debts to be forgiven and land returned.

Bankruptcy protects creditors by preventing someone from simply refusing to pay debts. There is such a thing as "involuntary" bankruptcy where the creditors bring the petition. When a bankruptcy petition is filed, all of the available assets are distributed to the creditors. It also protects creditors by permitting them to keep their books current, rather than keeping an open book for years without any possibility of payment. A bankruptcy filing may permit bad debt to be taken as a tax deduction.

A further note applies here. Filing for bankruptcy is not necessarily an immoral act. While some people may purposefully run up their credit cards immediately before declaring bankruptcy and thus incur debt they have no intention of repaying, at other times bankruptcy is simply a function of the economy. If the factory closes or a parent dies of cancer, should we crush the children in debt?

You could think of bankruptcy as an alternative performance under a contract. If you have a job, you will pay the debt in this way. If the factory closes down in your city, you will declare bankruptcy. Indeed, the reason credit cards have very high interest rates and a mortgage has a comparatively low rate has to do with the bank factoring in the risk of bankruptcy.

The Pressure of Doing the Work of Litigation

We have mentioned the pressure people caught up in the legal system feel as a result of not having power over their own lives. We have also mentioned the pressure they feel knowing that they could lose the things most precious to them. There is another kind of pressure that may not be obvious but should not be overlooked: the overwhelming pressure that comes with participating in litigation.

For instance, bankruptcy and divorce require the parties to fill out extraordinarily invasive and complex forms. It takes hours at best to gather and fill in the information. Imagine facing one of the worst crises of your life. And then imagine being required to create detailed records and answer personal questions posed by a stranger who will then publish the information in public records.

Even though a lawyer will help with the work, there is a great deal that the lawyer cannot do. The lawyer does not know how much money you make nor how to answer the accusation that you abused your child. Moreover, the lawyer is unlikely to be a source of sympathy for your counselee. In fact, to do the work correctly, the lawyer should maintain emotional distance. The matters involved are so painful and emotional that a lawyer's seeming lack of concern is helpful for seeing issues clearly. It is similar to the rule that a surgeon should not operate on a member of the surgeon's family.

The necessary distance which a lawyer must maintain differs from the compassion which you must show as a counselor. Being aware that the lawyer will be emotionally distant should remind you of the need to fulfill the role of compassionate counselor.

The Remembrance of Things Past

There is more to keep in mind as you consider how best to help your counselee. A lawsuit is like a plow turning up one's memories. The sheer power of the lawsuit will undoubtedly cause many problems and concerns to "surface." Pressure in the areas of family and money will reawaken hard things the counselee experienced or learned about family and money throughout his or her life so that you will probably be dealing not only with present problems but also with past problems. Indeed, for the counselee, all of life will become current.

Consider the process of medical diagnosis and treatment. A physician uses a number of tools to diagnose a patient. Various tests are used to examine symptoms. X-rays provide pictures of the inside of the patient. And in surgery, the patient is opened up, and the heart and lungs can be directly seen and touched and themselves opened.

Counseling is similar. When we counsel, we usually deal with symptoms, though over time we work to see more directly. When a counselee is in litigation, we are seeing a person under the knife. All will be exposed.

When you are counseling someone who is going through bankruptcy, that person is feeling more than merely the present pressure of litigation and debt. There is the past, which usually comes with painful memories of failure, poor choices, and difficult circumstances. Then there is the future, which can be daunting at the best of times but feels especially so when the present and the past have collapsed.

What to Keep in Mind

Here is the takeaway. You will counsel people who are entangled in the legal system. They will be under extraordinary pressure—pressure that may cause them to question everything they've known and to consider things they've never thought about before. The most basic elements of their life—their liberty, their family, their home, their finances—will be endangered. They will be forced to deal with these problems in public, before strangers. The objective pressures will cause enormous subjective pressure.

Being so endangered, your counselee will be more than usually vulnerable to the words of others, just as the patient opened to the surgeon may easily find their life destroyed or saved. An open chest may be a blessing or a curse. Your duty is to understand both the objective and subjective pressure upon the counselee so that you can provide the "wisdom from above," wisdom that is "first pure, then peaceable, gentle, open to reason, full of mercy and good fruits, impartial and sincere. And a harvest of righteousness is sown in peace by those who make peace" (James 3:17–18).

You cannot solve the problems of the counselee's past, present, or future. But you do know someone who turns all things to good.

To-Do List

- ❒ When a counselee becomes involved with the legal system, make sure to understand the general nature of what your counselee is going through.
- ❒ Help your counselee to keep their eyes on God's good will. The legal system is imperfect, and it too often comes to the "wrong" decision. But God is sovereign even over difficulties and trials.
- ❒ Learn how to work with the counselee's attorneys if necessary. This might be particularly important if you are counseling someone accused of a crime.
- ❒ Familiarize yourself with your state's Victims' Bill of Rights.

CHAPTER 12
Gender, Sexuality, and Religious Liberty

Deborah Dewart

The primary conflict between Christian practice and the state has been and will likely continue to be questions of gender and human sexuality. As biblical counselors, we will necessarily be taking very clear positions on these issues. There are a number of ways in which we could find ourselves involved in legal proceedings.

The purpose of this chapter is to simply inform you by providing an outline of the law as it currently stands. The way in which these issues may arise will be shaped to some extent by the scope of your ministry. Do you offer counseling only to church members? Do you extend it a little further and serve members of other local churches or professing Christians?

If your counsel is expressly limited to either members of your congregation or at least those who are professing Christians, your legal position will be stronger. However, Christian ministry must not merely aim for what is safe. The gospel is not for the perfect but for those who need saving. "God shows his love for us in that while we were still sinners, Christ died for us" (Romans 5:8). The counselor has the message that God saves sinners—like the counselor.

So while keeping our message limited to those who already profess is "safe," it is not always what we are called to do. Many biblical counseling ministries operate as evangelistic efforts, offering counsel to the community at large—including unbelievers—as an evangelistic outreach. As Christians, we contend for the faith, but we also speak the truth in love, knowing that God's grace extends to persons who disagree with us.

Faith Church in Lafayette, Indiana, is an example of a ministry that offers counseling to the community, and—praise God—some counselees have come to saving faith through the church's counseling ministry. But that option requires careful planning and an incredible amount of prayer to address and hopefully prevent potential legal challenges.

The issues of religious liberty impact the church in multiple ways. One way is in the counseling room, where you will hear about the legal challenges your counselees face. This should not be a surprise—Jesus promised that in this world we *will* have tribulations. In fact, you may encounter a "new species" of counselee—a godly man or woman who would normally not seek counseling but who is hit by a lawsuit that forces a choice of whether to obey God or man. It could be a man like Jack Phillips, the Colorado bakeshop owner (Masterpiece Cakeshop) sued for declining to custom design a wedding cake for two men. Or it might be a kind grandmother like Barronelle Stutzman, sued by a long-term customer of her Washington floral shop for gently declining to custom design flowers for a same-sex ceremony. Believers like Jack and Barronelle need wise counsel, along with other forms of ministry from their church families, as they stand trial—literally.

Such cases raise the question, When does it become necessary to "obey God rather than men" (Acts 5:29)? You can help your counselees draw that line according to biblical principles. Barronelle Stutzman graciously served a homosexual customer for nearly ten years before "drawing the line" at his request to design flowers for a same-sex ceremony. The cake baker, Jack Phillips, gladly served all customers by selling other products that were not offensive to his faith. He "drew the line" at custom designing a wedding cake for two people of the same sex. It is not always easy to discern the line between serving others and violating conscience.

In order to meet the challenges they and their counselees may face related to gender and sexuality, biblical counselors need to know what is happening in the American government and classrooms.

What Is Happening in the Government?

When we think of the current legal environment, we must consider more than just questions of how courts are interpreting particular statutes. When we think of the law, we need to understand that the law is an extension of the political will of the majority. The majority of our fellow citizens vote for politicians. The politicians enact laws. The courts apply those laws. Often the courts develop new laws.

It is unquestionable that a marked change has taken place in both how the courts and the legislature understand marriage, sexuality, and the protections for free speech and the free exercise of religion. In 2013 the Supreme Court struck down the federal Defense of Marriage Act, which had defined "marriage" for purposes of *federal* law as a marriage between one man and one woman.

Two years later its decision in the case of *Obergefell v. Hodges* redefined marriage—with all of the accompanying legal benefits—to include two persons of the same sex. This opinion upended state marriage laws across America. The legal fallout from these rulings has been tremendous. But it doesn't end there. Since 1964 Title VII of the Civil Rights Act has prohibited employment discrimination based on certain protected characteristics such as race and sex. "Sex" has historically been understood as the biological reality that an individual is either male or female, and this is how it was understood at the time the act was passed. But in its 2020 decision in the *Bostock v. Clayton County* case, the Supreme Court redefined that word, too, so that it now includes sexual orientation and gender identity.

This is how the *Bostock* case developed: The owner of a Christian funeral home in Michigan found himself in federal court after a male employee decided he was really a woman and demanded that he be allowed to present himself at work as a female. The funeral home had a dress code, and this biological male wanted to dress according to the code's requirements for female employees. The owner declined. He was concerned about the impact on the grieving families he served. The employee was terminated and later sued the funeral home. Alliance Defending Freedom represented the employer. The trial court ruled in the employer's favor, but the appellate court reversed the decision, and eventually the Supreme Court granted review. At about the same time, two other federal appeals courts heard cases involving homosexual employees. In all three cases, employees argued that "sex" refers not only to male and female but also includes "sexual orientation" and "gender identity."

In mid-June 2020, the Supreme Court finally issued its opinion, ruling that Title VII's prohibition against discrimination "because of sex" prohibits discrimination because of "sexual orientation" or "gender identity." The opinion also contained a statement of the court's ongoing support for religious liberty, noting the First Amendment and Title VII's protection for churches and religious organizations. The court declined to rule on how its opinion will be fleshed out in other contexts—bathrooms, locker rooms, housing, athletics.

The implications of *Bostock* are wide-ranging, and they have already begun to unfold. Just two months after the Supreme Court announced its opinion in *Bostock*, a federal appeals court (the Fourth Circuit) issued a ninety-page opinion in the ongoing case of a biological high school female who decided she was a male and demanded to use the school bathrooms reserved for boys. Here is how the court summed it up: "After the Supreme Court's recent decision in *Bostock*, we have little difficulty holding that a bathroom policy precluding Grimm [the plaintiff] from using the boy's restrooms discriminated against him 'on the basis of sex.'"

Gavin Grimm is a biological female. The high school she attended allowed her to use the boys' bathrooms, but there was intense backlash against this decision from parents. The school then accommodated Grimm with a private faculty restroom and eventually built several single-stall bathrooms that were available to any student desiring more privacy. But Grimm complained about the "stigma" and avoided using the restroom altogether, resulting in urinary tract infections. Grimm developed suicidal tendencies. She had sex reassignment surgery and amended her birth certificate, but the school refused to change its records to show her sex as "male." Situations like this are tragic and devoid of biblical hope. Biblical ministry is desperately needed.

In addition to developments in the courts, the House of Representatives in 2019 passed the Equality Act that would create nationwide laws against discrimination based on sexual orientation and gender identity—with no religious exemptions. The ultimate fate of this law is uncertain, but many states have passed "SOCE" laws that prohibit sexual orientation change efforts by state-licensed counselors. While these laws are written for the purpose of stopping "conversion" therapy, the language is often much broader.

This is a place where we must be clear that we are counseling people in the matter of Christian life and practice, which entails our sexuality. Our aim is not to stop unbelievers from engaging in homosexual behavior, per se. Our goal is never merely ceasing from engaging in some sinful practice. The most "moral" person who does not know Christ will be as damned as any other. However, *as Christians* we are called upon to put sexual immorality to death (Colossians 3:5).

As we have described elsewhere, it will often be easier to explain that our ministry is directed toward Christian discipleship when that ministry takes place within the context of a church or under the oversight of a church. However, we also understand that is not always possible. Accordingly, it is important to define your counseling ministry in distinctly biblical terms so as to remove yourself from the scope of laws that regulate the work of state-licensed counselors. If we do not clearly define these terms within our biblical counseling ministry, we will be subject to court rulings. (For a more detailed discussion of the issue of state regulation and the need for a careful definition of biblical counseling, see chapters 2 and 3.)

What Is Happening in the Classroom?

Changes in the culture and the law are bringing about corresponding changes in public schools. The changes that are taking place are exemplified by a case in Wisconsin, recently filed by Alliance Defending Freedom. The case arose in response to a Madison school district policy *that is designed to keep information from a child's parents* if the student is confused about gender and expresses an interest in adopting a transgender identity. The policy requires all school employees to address the student by a new name and pronoun of the opposite sex, and even allow the student to use opposite sex facilities—*all without parental notice or consent. In fact, all school employees are instructed to further deceive parents* by reverting to using the student's normal name and pronoun when parents are around.

The school district—Madison Metropolitan School District—has adopted policies to "disrupt the gender binary," which means that they are seeking to put an end to the understanding that each person is born immutably male or female and instead promote the idea that gender is separate from biological sex and can be fluid. This case has clear implications for parents of children in public schools. Another incident occurred in Madison, Wisconsin, in 2018 when a science teacher showed elementary school children (kindergarten through fifth grade) a video about the teacher's gender transition.

It may be that you find yourself counseling a school employee who is troubled by the district's policy of deceiving parents—that person greatly needs biblical wisdom. Or perhaps you will have counselees who are parents concerned that their children's schools have policies like those above or use a sex education curriculum that conflicts with biblical teaching. These parents may be agonizing over decisions about whether to homeschool. To counsel such a family, you will need to know not only what the family is like—whether homeschooling is a good fit, whether they can afford a private school, or whether they can successfully shepherd their children through the public school—you will also need to know what is happening in your local schools and the wider community and what affordable options might be available. These families, too, stand in great need of biblical wisdom.

Parental Rights in the Constitution and the Counseling Room

The Supreme Court has repeatedly—and recently—confirmed the constitutional right of parents to direct the upbringing of their children. In 2020, the court affirmed that bedrock principle when it decided a Montana case involving state tax credits used to fund scholarships for private education. The state supreme court invalidated the program because families were permitted to use their scholarships at both secular and religious private schools, but the Supreme Court reversed the decision. A state has no obligation to finance private education, but if it does, it cannot discriminate against religious schools. This case is a great "win" for both religious liberty and parental rights. It potentially means more educational options for counselees like the parents above who are concerned that what their local public schools are teaching and advocating clashes with biblical teaching.

Free Speech

Perhaps you wonder what a parent or what you—as a pastor or other biblical counselor—may say to a child who wants to transition to the opposite gender. Does the state have any jurisdiction over what a church or pastor or parent can say about what the Bible teaches? No. That question is addressed not only by the First Amendment religion clauses—the Free Exercise Clause in particular—but also by the Free Speech Clause.

Please do not think the issues of free speech are at a distance from you or your church ministry. Ordinances are being proposed in the United States that would limit not only licensed religious counselors *but potentially even pastors* from giving biblical wisdom to consenting minors who are gender confused or engaged in sexual immorality. While we wish these were hypothetical, here are some situations that you might encounter in the counseling room:

- a parent whose child wants to transition to the opposite sex or whose child identifies as homosexual

    - How does the parent (your counselee) speak to the child? Will a social worker find the parent to be "abusive"? Will the child rely upon the parent?
    - Is the parent divorced? If so, is this the custodial parent? In cases involving conflicts between the parents over a child, courts have been favoring the parent who seeks to encourage the "nontraditional" sexual expression.
    - Is the child eighteen or over—or getting close to that landmark? If so, prayer may be that parent's only option because the parent will have no directive power over an adult child.
- a person who previously transitioned to the opposite gender through hormones and/or surgery but now regrets it and wants to follow Christ
- a person whose husband or wife (or some other family member) has come out as homosexual or transgender
- a former homosexual who has made a profession of faith and wants to follow Christ but still struggles with temptation
- a small business owner who is sued for refusing to accommodate an employee's demand to "present" as the opposite sex (dress code, bathrooms) or refusing to provide services that facilitate a same-sex relationship or ceremony
- an employee threatened with termination for not accommodating transgender or sexual orientation demands

You may also encounter the following situations. While these problems could (and probably will) arise even when your counseling work is limited to the congregation, it will be even more prevalent if you open your counseling ministry to the local community. You may be asked to counsel

- a parent who supports a child's gender transition (or homosexuality);
- a person wanting to transition to the opposite sex;

- a gender-confused adult who demands that you use his or her preferred pronouns; or
- a homosexual who seeks (or even demands) your acceptance of his or her lifestyle, refusing to accept the biblical view.

What Resources Are Available?

It is important that you keep up with what is happening in our nation and world. As biblical counselors, you have an important role in helping other believers address legal challenges in these areas with biblical truth, care, and compassion. There is help available if you need it—first to *prevent* litigation then to *prevail* if you are ever faced with it.

Both helpful legal news and legal defense are available through many fine national and local Christian legal organizations. These vary in size and services offered. They are typically nonprofit organizations supported by donations and may be able to offer help free of charge.

An excellent overall information resource for churches is the Church Law & Tax Report. They offer information about current legal developments through their newsletter and webinars. Their website also offers many written resources on specific topics, including child abuse reporting laws, employee compensation, tax laws, and risk avoidance. For local information about issues relevant to families and school children, check out the family policy council in your state.

The Christian Legal Society is a membership organization for Christian attorneys. This is a good resource for sample documents and information that may help connect you with Christian attorneys who practice in your state. The annual Christian Legal Society conference is a valuable way for Christian attorneys in your church or community to learn more about the legal challenges facing your church and counselees. Each year, there is an updated workshop about "legal hot spots" for churches. Christian Legal Society also engages in religious liberty litigation and often submits friend-of-the-court briefs in religious freedom cases.

If you need more than information, one of the best Christian legal defense organizations is Alliance Defending Freedom. This organization has represented many Christians across the nation who have faced religious liberty challenges, and their attorneys have been victorious in several landmark US Supreme Court cases. Alliance Defending Freedom recently initiated a Church Alliance membership program for churches to proactively address religious liberty concerns. There is a modest membership fee based on a sliding scale that depends on the size of the church. This program is a worthwhile investment that would be a huge help to your church and counseling ministry in drafting the documents and policies you need to protect your religious liberty and prevent litigation.

The Becket Fund for Religious Liberty conducts litigation across the country and has won significant victories in the US Supreme Court, including the well-publicized Hobby Lobby case in 2014, which upheld the religious liberty rights of a for-profit corporation that objected to including abortion-inducing drugs in its employee health insurance plan, and a victory in 2020 reaffirming church autonomy in the selection of "ministerial" employees.

These organizations are not alone. Here are several more that can serve as helpful resources for you and your church:

- Family Research Council
- Pacific Justice Institute
- Christian Law
- Center for Religious Expression
- First Liberty
- Advocates for Faith and Freedom (based in California but expanding)
- American Center for Law and Justice

For churches, counselors, and others who are concerned about legal issues they may face, it can be a great reassurance to know about these organizations that defend religious liberty.

Going Forward

The issues about sexuality and other religious liberty concerns can be addressed through well-drafted documents that spell out the religious nature of your ministry and distinguish it from the methods and theories of state-licensed counselors. Be sure you include a biblical dispute resolution policy, signed by the counselee at the beginning of the relationship, because this can deter litigation or lead to an early dismissal if a case is filed against you. Be sure you define *what it means to be a Christian* so that it necessarily includes adherence to the biblical view of marriage and sexuality. Communicate clearly that your beliefs about marriage and sexual morality are *religious* beliefs rooted in Scripture. Cite specific Scripture often in your governing and policy documents—for church membership, biblical counseling, employment, and use of your facilities by outside groups. You do not want to find yourself entangled in a lawsuit with a counselee or other person who professes to be a Christian but practices homosexuality or transgenderism with no intention or desire to change. Be consistent throughout areas of church ministry and your written documents.

To-Do List

- ❒ Don't allow the current political environment to leave you fearful. God is still sovereign.
- ❒ Be diligent to make plain why we counsel the way we do. Be ready to give a defense and explain why biblical teaching on human sexuality and marriage is a critical aspect of Christian life. We can no longer rely upon a broad belief in the culture that boys are boys and sexuality is only right within the context of a heterosexual marriage. We need to be prepared to understand the theological basis for our beliefs and counsel.

Author Biographies

Editors

T. Dale Johnson Jr. is the executive director of the Association of Certified Biblical Counselors. He served seven years as an associate pastor before completing his PhD in biblical counseling at Southwestern Baptist Theological Seminary. Dr. Johnson now serves as associate professor of biblical counseling at Midwestern Baptist Theological Seminary, where he is also the director of counseling programs.

Edward Charles Wilde is an attorney whose practice emphasizes real estate, corporate and commercial law, and trust disputes. He received his law degree from the University of San Diego, his master's degree from The Master's University, and his bachelor's from UCLA. Edward teaches biblical counseling at The Master's University in Santa Clarita and is a certified biblical counselor with the Association of Certified Biblical Counselors.

Contributors

Tonya Braun has been an advocate for domestic violence victims for more than fourteen years. Having worked in a variety of organizations such as batterer's intervention, emergency shelters, the military, and the criminal justice system, she has been blessed with a comprehensive view of domestic violence and the community's response. She has a master's degree in criminal justice with a victimology concentration from Seattle University and is currently studying to complete her master's in biblical counseling at The Master's University.

George Crawford is a graduate of Occidental College and the UCLA School of Law. He has served as a prosecuting attorney and administrative law judge for the state of California. George has also served as an adjunct faculty member at The Master's University since 1991.

Deborah Dewart is a graduate of Westminster Seminary (Escondido, CA) and an attorney admitted in North Carolina, California, the US Supreme Court, and all federal circuits. She is the author of *Death of a Christian Nation* and regularly writes briefs about First Amendment issues, as well as articles about the unbiblical nature of counseling psychology.

Tim Pasma has ministered at LaRue Baptist Church as a pastor since the spring of 1985. Tim earned a bachelor's degree from Cedarville University (1977) and a master of divinity degree from Grace Theological Seminary (1981). He is also a fellow in the Association of Certified Biblical Counselors and serves on its board of trustees. He has lectured frequently on counseling issues at counseling conferences and for a number of Christian organizations.

Todd Sorrell has been a California licensed attorney for more than twenty-five years, spending the majority of his career as an equity partner in a large international law firm where he practiced in the dispute resolution group, which included litigation, trial work, arbitrations, and mediations. He has founded a number of successful businesses, has taught at the university level, and has authored two books (*The College Choice* and *Journey to the Bending Light*). Todd has a master's degree in biblical counseling from The Master's University and is ACBC certified.

Glossary and Additional Legal Information

action: A general purpose term to describe a legal proceeding. It has no particular legal significance, but it is commonly used as a synonym for "lawsuit."

administrative law: Administrative agencies make "regulations." The legislature decides to delegate some particular area of governance to the executive branch, for instance, tax collecting (IRS), regulation of vehicles (DMV), or medical safety (FDA). The legislature passes a law, which is signed by the executive, to create the administrative agency. The legislature also votes for money to run the agency. The executive then appoints people to run the agency. The agency then begins to run itself. Within the boundaries set by the original legislation, the agency begins to make "rules" and "regulations."

allegation: A statement made in a pleading, which asserts some fact or proposition to be true or false.

answer: A pleading filed in a lawsuit that responds to a complaint. It typically entails an answer and a set of allegations that offer an excuse or explanation for the alleged wrong.

antidiscrimination laws: Any of a number of different laws that prohibit persons engaged in public commerce from refusing to serve someone on the basis of some particular characteristic. Until recently, the laws concerned only "public accommodations" (such as a restaurant or grocery store) and prohibited a public accommodation from refusing to serve someone due to the color of their skin (for instance). Recently, the scope of such laws has expanded to include businesses that were not previously considered to be "public accommodations" (such as a wedding photographer) and to prohibit discrimination even if it violates one's religious convictions or entails speech. The constitutional permissibility of such laws is in flux as of the time of this writing.

appeal: A request that a "higher" court review the conduct of a trial court's decision. Such reviews typically only concern the application of law; rarely do such reviews consider the factual determinations of a trial court.

appellant: The person initiating the appeal. The opposing party is called a "respondent." At the trial court, the party beginning the action is called a "plaintiff," while the responding party is called a "defendant."

appellate court: The court that hears an appeal, as opposed to a "trial court."

arraignment: The stage in a criminal proceeding with a judge that determines whether the state has sufficient evidence to proceed against a defendant.

bail: A deposit made with the court to guarantee that you will return to court on a designated day. A defendant in a criminal action can be released from custody pending trial if the defendant "posts bail"—an amount of money that will be forfeited if the defendant does not appear at trial.

bankruptcy: A legal proceeding by which one's debts are "discharged" or renegotiated. If for some reason a business or individual is unable to pay their debts (usually a contractual obligation), that person can file bankruptcy. The bankruptcy proceeding may result in all of the person's property being sold to pay the debts. After everything is sold, the debts no longer exist (they are discharged), and the person starts over. Alternatively, the debts are renegotiated, usually with a longer time to pay them off and/or a lesser amount to pay.

binding arbitration (including related terms, e.g., conciliator/arbitrator): An arbitration is an informal trial. If it is binding, the parties cannot also go to a state or federal court for a trial.

bona fide (as in "bona fide contract"): Literally, "good faith." In legal usage, it is used to emphasize something as being truthful or genuine. A "bona fide" contract is a good, enforceable contract.

brief: The name of the legal document containing the argument filed by a party in an appeal.

child abuse: Precise definitions vary from state to state, but in general, the physical or sexual injury of a child.

church autonomy (or ecclesiastical abstention): The legal proposition that a court will refuse to hear a dispute over the internal workings of a church. If your pastor denies the Trinity, you cannot sue him for being a heretic.

civil action: Legal actions that do not involve criminal prosecution by the state. Sometimes a wrong may be the subject of a criminal prosecution *and* a civil action. For instance, if one person physically hurt another, there could be a civil action for battery and a criminal action for battery.

clergy–penitent privilege: The legal proposition, which varies from state to state, as to whether a pastor can repeat what the pastor hears in counseling. For instance, the attorney–client privilege prohibits a lawyer from revealing what he learns from a client.

common law: The general legal system that the United States inherited from England. It was a legal system that was "common" to the entire kingdom.

complaint: The first document filed in a civil action. It consists of a statement of facts and a claim that these facts show a defendant did something in violation of law. It will also contain a "prayer" for "damages."

Consent to Counsel form: A document that you should have a counselee sign prior to instituting counseling.

coverage, coverage grant/grant of coverage: An insurance policy will cover only specific events. For example, an automobile policy will only cover matters involving an automobile. The "grant" is the scope of events covered by the insurance policy.

crime: An action that violates a law deemed to have been committed against the State. For instance, murder is a crime and is considered to be a wrong done to every person. A criminal action is prosecuted by the state. The penalty for a crime is typically a monetary fine or incarceration in a prison.

damages: The amount of money that a defendant must pay to a plaintiff in a civil action, if the plaintiff wins.

defendant: The person who responds in a lawsuit.

deposition: Examination under oath.

embezzlement: Theft of money entrusted to you.

errors and omissions coverage: A specific kind of insurance that applies to errors made by those who run a business.

establishment clause: The portion of the First Amendment to the federal Constitution that prohibits Congress from "establishing" a religion.

exclusion: A limitation on the "coverage grant." For instance, your automobile policy may say it will cover you if you get into an automobile accident, but it may "exclude" a crash that takes place when you are drunk and driving.

file a complaint: Submitting a complaint to court. This starts a lawsuit.

First Amendment: The First Amendment to the Constitution as adopted in 1789. It contains limitations on the power of the congress to make laws that restrict speech, religion, press, or petitioning the government.

free exercise clause: The portion of the First Amendment that guarantees the right to "free exercise" of religion.

hearing: Any proceeding before a judge where the judge hears the parties present an argument.

indemnification: A duty to pay another's specified debt. An insurance policy is a promise to pay (or to pay you if you pay) certain debts, such as the cost incurred from an automobile accident.

informed consent: Before you permit someone to do something (consent), you know the ramifications of your decision. For instance, a doctor will tell you the risks of a medical procedure before you consent: you must be "informed" about the risks first.

injunction: An order of a court that requires you to do some action or prohibits you from doing some action. For example, the court may order you to tear down a fence.

intentional conduct: You do something on purpose, and you intend the consequence. It is an "accident" if you intend to drive fast but lose control of your car. It is "intentional" if you deliberately drive your car into another car.

invasion of privacy: The law protects certain aspects of your privacy. If someone intentionally "invades" that protected area (for example, by stealing your mail), there has been an invasion of privacy. Additionally, if you tell someone something in confidence, and that person repeats that confidential information in public, that might be an invasion of privacy.

jurisdiction: The scope of a court's authority to act. A court in California has no jurisdication over two people from Texas who get into a car crash in Texas.

lawsuit: Typically refers to a "civil action," which is the process of one person appearing in court and seeking some redress against another person.

liability: The responsibility to pay money (it can be used in different ways, but this is the general meaning in a civil action).

licensed vs. unlicensed counselors: A license grants permission from the state to do something (a fishing license or a license to practice law). A mental health counselor is typically required to have a license from the state.

Limited Liability Company (LLC): A form of business similar to a corporation in terms of its ability to limit liability exposure (typically only assets owned by the LLC can be lost in a lawsuit). It has a simplified structure compared to a corporation and "flow through" taxes so that the individual can exercise the tax position of the company. Consult a tax accountant to fully understand the tax issues.

litigation: The name for the whole process of what takes place in a lawsuit.

mediation: An informal procedure whereby parties to a lawsuit seek to resolve their differences. The mediator cannot force the parties to settle their lawsuit, but a good mediator can often convince the parties to take a particular resolution.

ministerial exception: A general proposition of the law that certain things done by a clergy member are not subject to review by a court.

negligent conduct/negligence: A failure to use reasonable efforts to prevent injuring another person. You are negligent if you speed and cause an accident.

no-contact order: Typically used in "family law" matters. It is an order from a court telling one person they may not "contact" another person. For instance, an abusive ex-spouse may be ordered to stop texting the fleeing ex-spouse.

personal guarantee: A promise of an individual to answer to the obligations of a corporation or LLC. For instance, if you form an LLC that has never conducted business before, the landlord may require you to execute a personal guarantee that you will pay the rent if your business fails and the LLC disappears.

plaintiff: The party who starts a civil lawsuit.

pleading: Papers filed with the trial court that specify what the defendant allegedly did wrong and the defendant's response.

prayer: The remedy that a plaintiff requests in a civil action.

proceeding: Any sort of hearing involving a court or administrative agency. This is a very general term.

psychiatrist: A medical doctor who has received special training in matters involving the nervous system. Often a psychiatrist may also employ "talk therapy" where, in addition to prescribing medication or administering a medical procedure (such as electroconvulsive therapy), the doctor will give advice and direction.

psychologist: A clinical psychologist (there are many types of psychologists who have nothing to do with "therapy") is a licensed professional who typically has a master's degree in some psychological discipline and has also fulfilled the licensing requirements for a state.

punitive damages: These are damages to punish a civil defendant who loses a lawsuit. A lawsuit is meant to make you "whole." If I buy a car from you, and the car doesn't work, you need to repay my money. But if you purposefully deceived me, the court might require you to pay even more money than I lost. That extra would be "punitive damages."

regulation: A law created by an administrative agency.

release form: A contract which "releases" another person from legal duties. If you rent a bounce house, the company that rents you the house will have you sign a "release" saying you won't sue them if a kid flies through the opening and lands on his head.

Religious Freedom Restoration Act (RFRA): A law passed by Congress to define the scope of religious freedom in the United States. In certain circumstances, it provides greater protection than the First Amendment.

religious nonprofit corporation: A type of corporation that is not run for profit but is run to advance a religious purpose.

right: The power to assert some sort of claim, typically in contrast to governmental action.

rule: Sometimes a law governing procedure or a law used by an administrative agency.

served: The delivery of a legal document from either a party or a court.

sexual assault: A physical attack upon another person that includes a sexual component.

sexual orientation change efforts: A general reference to techniques designed to train a person against same-sex attraction (for instance).

slander: A false statement that injures another person's reputation.

SOCE laws: These are laws that prohibit efforts to change same-sex attraction.

statute: A law passed by the legislature and signed by the executive.

subpoena: An order from a court directing a party to appear at court for some purpose. (It can refer to events that do not actually take place before a judge.)

tender a lawsuit: When you have been sued, you can deliver a copy of the lawsuit to your insurance company with a demand that the insurance company pay for a lawyer to defend the lawsuit (assuming you have the right to some sort of insurance). When you give the lawsuit to the insurance company and ask the insurance company to defend you, you have "tendered the lawsuit."

Title VII (of the Civil Rights Act of 1964): The portion of the Civil Rights Act that prohibits discrimination on the basis of sex.

tort: A civil law that applies to all persons, whether they agree or not. These laws prohibit one person from causing injury to another, whether it is injury to their person or property. This often overlaps with crimes. If you steal your neighbor's car, you can be criminally liable for theft and civilly liable for conversion (the civil tort of stealing).

trial court: This is the court you see on TV. There is a judge and often a jury. It refers to the first court that hears the facts of a criminal or civil action.

Victims' Bill of Rights (*or* Victims' Bill of Rights): These laws (which vary from state-to-state) say that a victim has the right to know when the defendant is being tried or to be informed of the date on which a criminal has a parole hearing.

writ of certiorari: If you file a complaint, you can proceed to trial. After the trial, you can take an appeal. If your lawsuit raises issues that would affect other parties (such as a clarification of the law on some issue), the state or federal supreme court may wish to take the case. The supreme court has no obligation to take any case. Parties who would like to have their case reviewed after an appeal can write a "this is why you should take my case" document and send it to the supreme court. That document is called a "writ of certiorari."

A Brief Explanation of the Ways Laws Are Created

What you learned in civics class: The "regular" way law is made involves the legislature passing a "bill" which is then sent to the executive (the president or governor). The bill is then signed or vetoed. If the bill is signed, it becomes a "statute." If the bill is not signed, it is returned to the legislature. If the legislature votes on the bill again and a supermajority (such as two-thirds) vote for the bill, it becomes a law over the executive's veto. It is still called a "statute."

Law made by judges: A great amount of law is made by judges. There are three levels of courts: trial courts, appellate courts, and the Supreme Court. All cases begin in the trial court [there are rare exceptions involving narrow constitutional issues that don't concern us]. After the trial, the case may be appealed to an appellate court. As explained in chapter 8, some cases may end up in the Supreme Court.

This involves two similar procedures. One involves the manner in which a judge interprets an existing law, such as a statute. All laws will face some ambiguity in some circumstance. The judge must resolve the ambiguity. This resolution is written down as a "case." The judge's written opinion is now law. The decision of an appellate court is controlling for the trial court. The decision of the Supreme Court is controlling upon the appellate courts and the trial court.

Sometimes judges will develop a new legal doctrine based upon existing law or legal principles. This is a legal precedent that goes back to English law prior to the founding of the United States.

In either instance, a decision made by a judge is found in a case. A lawyer will refer to a case as "law," a "case," or "precedent." (*Precedent* merely means it is a prior case.)

Note: in most states the highest court is called the supreme court. But in New York, the supreme court is the trial court, and the highest court is called the superior court. In California, the trial court is called the superior court, and the highest court is called the supreme court. In the federal system, the trial court is called the district court, and the highest court is called the Supreme Court.

Appendix: Sample Counseling Intake Forms

Consent to Biblical Counsel/Discipleship

On the date set forth below, it is agreed that____________ ("Counselor") will provide biblical counseling services to________ ("Counselee") on the following terms and conditions:

Biblical Counseling: This is a ministry of the gospel of Jesus Christ and is part of Counselor's practice of religion. Counselee has indicated that Counselee is a Christian and/or is voluntarily seeking religious guidance (biblical counseling) from Counselor, as a part of Counselee's practice or pursuit of religion. Counselee's testimony or evangelistic precounseling will establish that the counselee is a candidate for the end goal of biblical counseling, which is to help Christians become more like Jesus Christ in attitude, thought, and action. Counselor's goals in providing counseling are to help Counselee to know the God of the Bible more fully and vitally and to live life in a God-honoring way. This includes, but is not limited to, providing biblical counsel to assist in: meeting the challenges of life; increasing in true worship; applying the gospel and God's sufficiency daily; shedding the sin that so easily entangles; learning to develop, cultivate, and live in relationships that please God; giving thanks to God in all circumstances; living in a community of other believers through participation in a local church; and learning to rely on the Holy Spirit for power and direction through prayer and Bible study. Although the biblical advice Counselor provides is intended to be practical, it is entirely Counselee's decision how to (and whether to) implement that advice. Counselor wants to help Counselee love God and love others through this process.

Biblical Basis: Counselor believes that the Bible provides sufficient guidance and instruction for faith and life. Therefore, counseling is based on biblical principles rather than those of secular psychology or psychiatry. Counselor is not licensed or certified as a psychotherapist, psychologist, psychiatrist, mental health professional, marriage and family therapist, or social worker and is not acting in such capacities. If Counselee is unwilling to use the Bible as the final authority in counseling or is unwilling to do the homework assigned, Counselee should not proceed with this counseling.

Professional Advice: Counselor is not providing legal, tax, financial, medical, or other technical or professional advice, and Counselor undertakes no duty to recognize or opine when such advice is actually needed, and the parties further agree that no fiduciary or professional client relationship is being created between Counselor and Counselee as a result of this relationship.

While the counselee may provide remuneration for the ministerial services provided pursuant to this agreement, such remuneration does not change this relationship from a religious to a "professional" or "fiduciary" relationship.

Confidentiality: Confidentiality is conditional. Although confidentiality is often one aspect of the counseling process and Counselor intends to guard the information received from Counselee, there are a number of situations when it may be necessary or prudent (as determined in Counselor's sole discretion) for Counselor to share information with others. Counselee agrees that Counselor may share information in at least the following circumstances:

- When Counselor is uncertain how to address a problem and needs to seek the advice from a pastor, supervising counselor, or educator (Proverbs 11:14; 24:6).

- When there is concern that someone is being or may be harmed unless other persons or protective services intervene (Romans 13:1–7).
- When Counselee expresses clear and specific suicidal intent, Counselor may take reasonable measures for the safety of Counselee. Reasonable measures may include notifying police if the Counselee will not cooperate to involve him or herself in a watch-care program or facility.
- If Counselor has reasonable cause to believe that an adult is in need of protective services, Counselor may take reasonable measures to prevent harm. Reasonable measures may include directly advising the potential victim of a threat or intent and/or informing the appropriate protective and/or law enforcement agencies.
- If there is a claim of, the observance of, or clear reasonable cause to suspect the physical or sexual abuse of a child with whom Counselor comes into contact or who is associated with someone to whom Counselor is in contact with, reasonable measures maybe taken to ensure the child's protection and/or to fulfill the legal mandate to report such harm to the appropriate governmental protection agencies.
- When Counselor becomes aware of any other criminal activity Counselee is engaged in and Counselee refuses to bring to the appropriate biblical and/or legal authorities.
- When counseling someone who is under familial authority (e.g., wife to husband, child to parent) and if deemed safe by Counselor, Counselor may encourage Counselee to inform Counselee's familial authority of critical issues and/or Counselor may inform the familial authority (Ephesians 5:22–6:4).
- When a person refuses to renounce a particular sin and/or refuses to confess it to those impacted, Counselor may, in Counselor's discretion, seek the assistance of a trusted

member or leader of any involved church to encourage repentance and/or reconciliation (Proverbs 15:22; 24:11; Matthew 18:15–20).

- When Counselor deems it appropriate or necessary to discuss information with a training observer or an assisting advocate who is involved or observing counseling.
- When Counselee makes a complaint against Counselor, an ACBC counselor, or a biblical counseling center or other related organization, handling it biblically may involve sharing information with an assisting local church shepherd and/or the appropriate person(s) within the ACBC organization for complaint resolution purposes.

Please be assured that our counselors strongly prefer not to disclose your personal information to others (if not needed), and they will make every effort to help you find ways to resolve a problem as privately as possible.

Liability: It is intended that the Holy Scriptures (the Bible) shall be the authority governing the counseling process, and that God's glory is the ultimate goal. However, failure of Counselor to interpret or apply the Bible in any particular way shall not subject the Counselor to liability or give rise to complaint by anyone. There shall be no legal or other liability that attaches to Counselor or any related institution or person for any advice, methods, conduct, or any act or omission *related in any way to the service that is provided*, and Counselee acknowledges that Counselee is voluntarily seeking this counsel (free from coercion, duress, or pressure) with a full understanding of the nature, purpose, and effect of this agreement.

Termination: At any time and for any reason, Counselor or Counselee may terminate counseling. However, termination will not preclude Counselor from making the disclosures set forth above if deemed appropriate by Counselor, or if compelled by other legal means. Counselor is not required to keep records, but if records are made, Counselor may destroy any such records without incurring liability.

Resolution of Conflicts: On rare occasions, a conflict may develop between a Counselor and a Counselee. In order to make sure that any such conflicts will be resolved in a biblically faithful manner (the Bible prohibits lawsuits in court among believers; 1 Corinthians 6:1–8), the parties agree that if a conflict arises, the conflict will be resolved according to the ACBC dispute resolution proceedings, which are then operative. That conflict resolution policy may be found at https://biblicalcounseling.com/acbc-member-complaint-case-policy/.

By signing this document, you are irrevocably waiving any right that you might have to a trial by jury or judge in a judicial proceeding.

If any provision of this agreement shall be held invalid, illegal, or unenforceable, only that provision shall be stricken, and the remainder of the agreement shall be in no way affected.

By signing below, the parties agree to the terms and conditions set forth in this document and acknowledge that Counselor would not enter into this counseling relationship without each term set forth above.

All of the above is understood and agreed:

[PRINT NAME] ________________________________

[SIGNATURE] ________________________________

Dated: ________________________________

Personal Data Inventory

Date: ____

Please be aware that there are no wrong or right answers to the following questions. Your honest answers will help us to know and serve you better.

Personal Info

Name: ______________________________ Sex: ❒ M ❒ F

Email: ______________________________ Age: _____

Best phone number to reach you ( ) - DOB: / /

Address: ____

Education (last year completed): _______________________

Current Occupation (or responsibility): _________________

How many hours do you work in a week at your job? ________

Who do you live with (their relationship to you)? __________

Help us get to know you. Mark on each continuum line below how you would describe yourself, generally.

More Analytical	________	More Creative	More Energetic	________	More Calm/Sedate
More Outgoing	________	More Shy	More of a Leader	________	More of a Follower
More Easygoing	________	More Serious	More of an Open Book	________	Harder to Get to Know
More Decisive	________	More Unsure	More Confident	________	More Nervous
More Introverted	________	More Extraverted	More often Happy	________	More often Sad
More Dependable	________	More Forgetful	More Sensitive	________	More Direct/Blunt

More of a Hard Worker	________	More of a Procrastinator	More Moody	________	More Even-Tempered
More Logical	________	More Feeling Led	More Others-Minded	________	More in My Own World
More of a Fixer	________	More of a Worrier	More Self-Conscious	________	More Carefree
More Organized	________	More Haphazard	More Cautious	________	More Spontaneous
More Independent	________	More Reliant	More Gracious	________	More Critical
More Slow to Act	________	More Impulsive	More Patient	________	More Impatient
More Go with the Flow	________	More Controlling	More People Oriented	________	More Project Oriented

Are you in a significant relationship other than marriage? Explain and include how long: ____

____

Marriage and Family

Marital Status: ❒ Single ❒ Engaged ❒ Married ❒ Separated ❒ Divorced ❒ Widowed ❒ Remarried

Spouse's Name: ______________________________________

Length of Marriage: ____________

Spouse's Current Occupation (or responsibility): ________________

Weekly Hours: _________

Children's Names	Age	Sex	Are They Living?	By Previous Marriage?

Have you ever been separated before? ❒ Yes ❒ No

If yes, please explain: ___________________________________

Has either of you ever considered or filed for divorce? ❒ Yes ❒ No

If yes, please explain: ___________________________________

Have you been married before? ❒ Yes ❒ No

If yes, please explain: ___________________________________

Is your spouse in favor of your coming to counseling? ❒ Yes ❒ No

Is your spouse willing to come to counseling (if needed)? ❒ Yes ❒ No

Health Info

Rate your health: ❒ Very Good ❒ Good ❒ Average ❒ Declining
❒ Other ___________________________________

Date of last medical exam: _______ Report: ___________________

Physician's name: ___________________________________

Address: ___________________________________

List all prescriptions and over-the counter medications you are currently taking (include diet pills, laxatives, birth control pills, cold and allergy medicines, aspirin, etc.). Continue on back as needed.

Med: ____________________ For What? _____________
Med: ____________________ For What? _____________
Med: ____________________ For What? _____________
Med: ____________________ For What? _____________

List all important present or past illnesses, physical difficulties, injuries, or handicaps:____
____
____
____

Do you have any chronic medical conditions?______________________

Have you used drugs for other than prescribed medical purposes?

❒ Yes (Past) ❒ Yes (Now) ❒ No

What Drug?____________________ How Long? ___________

Have you used more than the prescribed amount of any medication?

❒ Yes (Past) ❒ Yes (Now) ❒ No

What Drug?____________ Amount: ______ How Long? __________

How much of the following type of beverages do you consume daily or weekly?

Alcohol ___Coffee ___Tea ___Soft Drink ___Water ___

On a scale of 1-10, how healthy do you eat? ___ Do you smoke? __

How often do you exercise? _______ Times/Week ❒ Rarely ❒ Never

How many hours of sleep do you average each night? _________

Has there been any recent change? _________

Is this sleep uninterrupted? _______

Have you ever experienced hallucinations, seen distorted faces, or heard voices? ❒ Yes ❒ No

If yes, please explain: ______________________________________

Have you ever had a severe emotional upset? If so, please explain: ______

____

Have others noticed any significant changes in your emotional or mental state, memory, or work abilities? ______________________________

Are you willing to sign a release of information so that your counselor may write for any counseling and medical information that might be helpful? ❒ Yes ❒ No

Background Info

Please answer these background questions to the best of your ability, so we might minister to you more sensitively and wisely. These questions are *not* meant to imply: (1) that we cannot now know God as sovereign, good, and sufficient regardless of our past; (2) that God cannot use our past for good; (3) that our past is our identity; nor (4) that we will/must be determined by our past.

Were you raised by both biological parents? ❒ Yes ❒ No
If no, please explain: ______________________________________

Rate your parent's marriage:

❒ Unhappy ❒ Average ❒ Happy ❒ Very Happy

Are/were your parents divorced? ❒ Yes ❒ No
Explain briefly when and the basic circumstances: _______________

Describe your relationship with your mother: ______________________

Describe your relationship with your father: _______________________

How many older siblings do you have? Brothers ___ Sisters ___

How many younger siblings do you have? Brothers ___ Sisters ___

Describe your relationships with your siblings: _________________

Check all the following that best describe the parenting style of your childhood (M=Mother, F=Father):

Excessively authoritative/ Very high control	❒ M	❒ F	Rules/Instructions without relationship	❒ M	❒ F
Excessively permissive/ Too low control	❒ M	❒ F	Disengaged/ Excessively preoccupied	❒ M	❒ F
Generally balanced leadership/Authority	❒ M	❒ F	Caring involvement/ Instruction	❒ M	❒ F
Manipulative (selfish, angry, guilt trip)	❒ M	❒ F	Perfectionistic/Very performance driven	❒ M	❒ F
Leading by example	❒ M	❒ F		❒ M	❒ F

Check all the following that best describe the predominant atmosphere(s) in your home as a child:

❒ Happy	❒ Secure/Safe	❒ Open/Honest	❒ Truly Christian
❒ Sad/ Depressing	❒ Tumultuous/ Uncertain	❒ Closed off/ Private	❒ Outwardly Religious
❒ Calm/Relaxed	❒ Angry/Hostile	❒ Loving/ Encouraging	❒ Non-Christian

Was there any substance abuse in your family? ❒ Yes ❒ No

If yes, please explain: ______________________________

Other and later life:

Other than your parent(s), describe people who have had a significant influence in your life (positive or negative): ______________________

____

Has there been any abuse in your past?

❒ Physical ❒ Verbal/Emotional ❒ Sexual ❒ No

If yes, by whom? ______________________ What age? ___

Have you ever seen a psychologist, psychiatrist or received counseling before? ❐ Yes ❐ No

If yes, list counselor(s): ______________________________

and dates______/______/______to______/______/______

____

and dates______/______/______to______/______/______

____

and dates______/______/______to______/______/______

What were you seen for? ______________________________

What was the outcome? Was it helpful? ______________________________

____

Do you carry significant guilt? ❐ Yes ❐ No

If yes, for what? ______________________________

Any job difficulties? ❐ Yes ❐ No

If yes, please explain: ______________________________

Have you ever been arrested? ❐ Yes ❐ No When? ______________

Describe the circumstances: ______________________________

Describe any recent, significant event(s) in your life (i.e. job loss, birth, death, successes, etc.): ______________________________

____

____

Spiritual Life Info

Church/religious experience as a child (Denomination and length of time): ______________________________

Church/religious experience as an adult (Denomination and length of time): ______________________________

Do you attend a local Christian church? ❐ Yes ❐ No

Name of the church you attend: ______________________________

Are you a member? ❒ Yes ❒ No How long? ____________________

Have you been baptized? ❒ Yes ❒ No At what age? __

Church services/functions attended per month: _____________

Are you part of a small group: ❒ Yes ❒ No

Who is your small group leader: ______________________________

Do you attend church with your spouse? ❒ Yes ❒ No

If no, please explain: ______________________________________

Do you consider yourself as "saved"?

❒ Yes ❒ No ❒ Not sure what you mean

Does your spouse consider himself/herself as "saved"?

❒ Yes ❒ No ❒ Don't know

Have you come to the place in your spiritual life where you know with certainty that you would enter heaven after death? ❒ Yes ❒ No

If you were to die and stand before God, and he asked you why he should permit you to enter heaven, how might you respond? ______

____

Explain recent changes in your spiritual life, if any: _______________

____

How often do you pray to God?

❒ Never ❒ Rarely ❒ Sometimes ❒ Often

How often do you read the Bible?

❒ Never ❒ Rarely ❒ Sometimes ❒ Often

Do you regularly give financially to the church/God's work?

❒ Yes ❒ No

Do you serve at your church? How? __________________________

____

Problem Check List

Please mark 1-3 on all that apply (1=Mild, 2=Moderate, 3=Severe). Circle where there are options.

_____	Abuse at present (sexual, physical, verbal)	_____	Drugs	_____	Memory
_____	Anger	_____	Drunkenness	_____	Mental confusion
_____	Anorexia	_____	Envy or jealousy	_____	Moodiness
_____	Anxiety	_____	Fear	_____	Overwhelmed
_____	Apathy	_____	Finances	_____	Perfectionism
_____	Bitterness	_____	Gambling	_____	Poor concentration
_____	Bulimia	_____	Gluttony	_____	Pornography
_____	Children	_____	Grief	_____	Procrastination
_____	Communication	_____	Guilt	_____	Rebellion
_____	Conflict (fights)	_____	Health	_____	Same-sex attraction
_____	Deception	_____	Homosexuality	_____	Self-injury
_____	Decision-making	_____	Infidelity	_____	Sex (lust, impotence…)
_____	Depression	_____	In-laws	_____	Sleep
_____	Drastic change in life circumstances/ lifestyle	_____	Loneliness	_____	Other

Pre-Counseling

Please take some time to think through what has been happening in your life that brings you to counseling. This section will help us get to know your current situation better, in order to match you with a counselor and/or provide the best help. Use the following questions as a guide to journal about what is going on in your life and heart.

1. What has brought you here? Describe the main problem in your life as you see it. (Include when it began and any other very significant events or information.) ____________________

2. What have you done to try and resolve the problem on your own? ____________________

3. Why do you *now* want to seek help? ____________________

4. What types of thoughts come to your mind in your current situation when you feel disappointed, discouraged, angry, and/or fearful about the situation? ____________________

5. What are you hoping we can do for you? ______________________

____

____

____

____

6. Is there any other information you think we should know?______

____

____

____

____

Scheduling

Please check the time and days that you are available for counseling.

	SUN	MON	TUE	WED	THU	FRI	SAT
Early morning (6am-9am)							
Morning (9am-12pm)							
Early afternoon (12pm-3pm)							
Afternoon (3pm-6pm)							
Evening (6pm-9pm)							

Do you have flexibility with your schedule?

❒ Yes, on these days ____________________ ❒ No